INFANTILE PSYCHOSIS

and

Early Contributions

THE SELECTED PAPERS OF
MARGARET S. MAHLER, M.D.
Volume I

INFANTILE PSYCHOSIS

and

Early Contributions

JASON ARONSON INC.
Northvale, New Jersey
London

THE MASTER WORK SERIES

First softcover edition 1994

ISBN: 1-56821-421-9

Library of Congress Catalog Card Number: 79-51915

Manufactured in the United States of America. Jason Aronson Inc. offers books and cassettes. For information and catalog write to Jason Aronson Inc., 230 Livingston Street, Northvale, New Jersey 07647.

CONTENTS

PART THREE
On Child Psychosis

Contents

INTRODUCTION

The papers which fill these two volumes represent less than a quarter of Margaret Mahler's extensive analytic writings. Yet, although relatively small in bulk, they span more than three and a half decades and register both the essence and enormity of her work.

Each of us had kept abreast of Mahler's publications over the years, vicariously partaking of her process of discovery and enriching our knowledge and understanding. But when we learned it was our privilege to write this introduction, we agreed we should first peruse all of the papers in the collection. It is for the reader of these volumes to delve into the rich material of each individual paper. We, in turn, shall attempt to record the impressions made upon our minds as we reread them in succession.

Our journey from paper to paper heightened our sense of the range of Mahler's accomplishments and yet of the unity of her work. In fact, our retrospective study of her earlier papers in a number of ways was not so much a reexperience as it was a new experience. This was partly because the intervening years had developed in ourselves a keener appreciation of her profundity and clinical acumen, but primarily because we could thus glimpse with increasing clarity the evolution of those ideas which had culminated in her final stroke of creative power, that is, in her conceptualizations of the separation-individuation subphases. At the same time, we realized that for many, ourselves included, the magnitude of this most recent achievement may have temporarily dimmed those earlier contributions which, however, presaged what was yet to come.

It seems fitting that the first paper in this collection, "Pseudoimbecility: A Magic Cap of Invisibility," is also the first that Mahler presented in this country (to the New York Psychoanalytic Institute and Society, 1940). This paper, together with the second of the series, "Les Enfants Terribles," attest to Mahler's gifts as a psychoanalyst, but even more, these earliest papers provide hints and signs of her inherent interest in the preoedipal era. Further, up to this point in time, Mahler's direct contact with infants and toddlers had been as a pediatrician and director of a well-baby clinic, and she here demonstrates her ability to recast prior experience within a psychoanalytic frame of reference.

One of the links between these two papers (and between them and what is to follow) is Mahler's interest in motility. Through her discussion of lively and graphic clinical material, Mahler reveals her appreciation of the preverbal (and later nonverbal) affectoexpressive and gestural language of mother and child. In the first paper she illustrates how the perpetuation of this unconscious communication may lead to the maintenance of a "secret libidinal" interchange. On the other hand, in the second paper, she demonstrates how, with the waning of this early mother-child communication, the child may fleetingly regain access to the world of adult sexuality. In the one paper she focuses on the finer affectoexpression which makes for the mother-infant communication, an advanced inference for the early 1940s. As she puts it, this is the archaic common language of human beings which is, and remains, the language of affect. In the other paper, she emphasizes the gross body motility of the "aggressive surprise" actions of her child patient—his sudden jack-in-the-box body-phallus movements. It is noteworthy that this theme of motility not only occupies a major role in her earlier work but reemerges in her separation-individuation studies as she perceives the nuances of the to and fro movements of mother and child in body and gesture. One might add in passing that what briefly appears in these early papers, also to reappear later but with abundant amplification and elaboration, are allusions to the developmental history of omnipotence.

To return to Mahler's interest in motility, her classic papers on tics encompass consideration of the ego's success or failure to gain control over the motor apparatus. Drawing on metapsychological, neurophysiological, and constitutional factors, she delves further into mother-child interactions and presents us with outstanding genetic-dynamic formulations, clarifications, and useful classifications of tic symptomatology. Her special attention to the aggressive drive was also advanced for the time and one among many indications of her constant awareness of the scientific atmosphere of the moment which she herself helped to create. Further, her appreciation of the role of the aggressive drive in psychological development, and specifically in the interaction of the motor apparatus and the ego, contributes to her excellent description of the changing function of the growing child's motility in respect to affectomotor experience, performance, and defense. Concomitantly she shows due regard for the ego's controlling and inhibitory functions which normally are adequately developed by latency. Thus she explains the prevalence of established tics and "impulsions" at this time of life.

Mahler illustrates with convincing clinical data the different classes of tics: the predominantly psychologically-based "symptomatic tics" and the predominantly organically-based tics. In the latter, a constitutionally vulnerable ego is bombarded by the involuntary, unpredictable, and sometimes well-nigh violent tic movements. Of no small significance are her therapeutic admonitions and the therapeutic methods which she advocates in cases of these severely disturbed tiqueurs. In her discussion of treatment modalities, Mahler is again cognizant of the aggressive drive, utilizing the concept of drive neutralization to supplement psychotherapy as she recognizes that interpretation of structural conflicts is in and of itself insufficient and often hazardous if not executed with extreme caution.

As Mahler wrote in 1968, the follow-up study of former child tiqueurs "brought the disorganizing effect of generalized tics into the focus of my interest, so that my work centered thereafter on the immediate study of psychosis in children." Actually, Mahler's first paper on psychosis was published in the same year as was her definitive paper on "A Psychoanalytic Evaluation of Tic in Psychopathology of Children: Symptomatic Tics and the Tic Syndrome."

Taking her place among those few pioneers (Bender, Despert, Kanner et al.) who recognized the existence of childhood schizophrenia, Mahler, however, approaches the problem from genetic, dynamic, and structural viewpoints, demonstrating how the psychotic infant is unable to use the external maternal ego for structuralization of his rapidly maturing and concomitantly vulnerable, rudimentary ego. Thus her early interest in mother-infant interaction continues but she now penetrates further and further into the complexities of the mother's and infant's behavior vis-à-vis each other, underscoring that the main cause of the child's proclivity for alienation from reality and his ego fragmentation are rooted in disharmony within the mother-child relationship.

Among Mahler's significant contributions is her delineation of the symbiotic psychosis which is to be differentiated from the autistic psychosis. As with her tic studies, in investigating these conditions she applies ego psychology and the extended concept of drive development, including the significance both of neutralization and the lack of neutralization.

Repeatedly turning to her knowledge of normal development as a reference point for comparison and contrast of pathological phenomena, Mahler expands and refines her knowledge in both areas, thereby also expanding and refining her understanding of the autistic and symbiotic phases as she had conceptualized them. In this context, she now introduces the concept of separation-individuation in that she states that the success or failure of the symbiotic phase promotes or impedes the subsequent individuation process. Of singular importance is the distinction she makes between the mother's pathology and that of the child's innate ego deviation, observing that the psychotic child may evoke responses even in the ordinarily devoted mother that are deleterious to his separation and individuation.[1] And again she demonstrates her steadfast awareness of the central role of traditional psychoanalytic concepts when she underscores that the process of individuation is burdened not only by the widening world of reality but by the child's phase-specific psychosexual conflicts.

1. In these early papers Mahler still speaks of separation *and* individuation.

Mahler's discussions of children with excessively distorted symbiotic phases conveys how her marked empathy and intuition enabled her to grasp the intricacies of the dynamic unconscious of these very sick children and to arrive at brilliant reconstructions. The papers which deal with these extreme pathological conditions exemplify also her application of academic psychology (for example, syncretic experiencing) to analytic thinking and her skill in translating psychiatrically known behavior manifestations into dynamic terms. Finally, her keen observational skills and her enormous empathy for the inner life of such sick children resulted in her awareness of the child's need for protection within a corrective symbiotic experience. This insight, in turn, led to her tripartite treatment design which involves mother, worker, and child, with the mother and worker engaging together in the child's rehabilitation. Such a treatment plan is graphically described in the two final papers of volume 1 and bears witness to Mahler's readiness to perceive the gifts of her co-workers and to inspire understanding and devotion in them. And further, in the last of these two papers, "On Sadness and Grief in Infancy and Childhood," she elucidates how the emergence of these two affects in the psychotic child signifies a therapeutically restored symbiotic object.

In volume 1 we can clearly follow the development of Mahler's ideas toward her intensive and extensive study of separation-individuation. She conceives of the normal autistic phase.[2] The "symbiotic unity" in her tic papers evolves into the phase of symbiosis and the omnipotent dual unity. Hatching is introduced in the concept of the second birth experience. She hints at differentiation through her description of the child's increased perceptual awareness and experimentation with the mother's body. The child's "separating, uniting and exploring" foreshadows the practicing period. The psychotic child's reaction to loss of symbiotic omnipotence (already hinted at in "Pseudoimbecility: A Magic Cap of Invis-

2. In the light of more recent knowledge one might refer to this as a quasi-autistic phase. However, Mahler stresses in particular that "the main task [of this period] is that with predominantly physiological mechanisms the homeostatic equilibrium of the organism be maintained under the changed postpartum conditions " (Mahler 1974, p. 94).

ibility") and his ambitendency—fear of separation yet fear of re-engulfment—and the associated negativism (found also in tiqueurs) anticipates the later rapprochement period. The theme of development of self and identity emerges and reemerges. And last, in speaking of object representation, Mahler employs the phrase, "the way to object constancy." Hence she enables us to glide effortlessly into volume 2.

Mahler's continual comparisons and contrasts of psychotic with normal development, and her desire to pinpoint more precisely those elements which contribute to skewed development, led to her observational studies of normal infants and toddlers. In accord with Heinz Hartmann, she believed that "The study of the preverbal stage is a testing ground for many of our assumptions." More specifically, her aim was to investigate in detail the separation-individuation process which culminates in established object and self-representations and stable identity formation. In order to achieve this end, she conceived her carefully planned multipartite research design which involved analytically trained observers who with free-floating attention could apply genetic-dynamic insights to observations of collective and individual behavior in mother-infant interactions. The papers in volume 2 represent the impressive outcome of these studies.

Mahler's separation-individuation has by now attained a deservedly prominent place in psychoanalytic dialogue and discourse. Yet, and perhaps inevitably by virtue of its widespread application in a relatively short time span, the term is sometimes stretched so far as both to travesty and deform its original meaning and to obscure the scientific premises on which it rests.

From her studies of psychotic children, Mahler concluded that in average children who have experienced adequate symbiotic phases there ensue normal and ubiquitous intrapsychic separation-individuation processes which occur in conjunction with the development of autonomous ego functions. As a corollary, in its correct usage separation-individuation refers only to the first three years of life. Further, in studying these separation-individuation processes, Mahler's intent was not to add any new theory as, for example, might be erroneously inferred from the phrase "object relations theory." To the contrary, and as she, herself, reminds us, commencing with the discovery of the infantile neurosis, psychoanalytic theory has encompassed both drives and object relations. Her ultimate aim then was to integrate into our existing body of developmental knowledge detailed and systematic findings on the beginning enfoldment of object relations with their numerous variables. Her theoretical frame of reference was fundamentally and consistently psychoanalytic and, although her accent was on the genesis of the ego and of self-identity, she was ever aware of the reciprocal relationship between ego and drive development.

The interpretation of her data, albeit proceeding from the phenomenological, reflects Mahler's unusual capacity to feel her way into the *intrapsychic* life of the infant and toddler. This capacity would seem to arise from her extensive theoretical knowledge, rich clinical experience as a seasoned analyst of children and adults, familiarity with young children acquired from her earlier pediatric practice, and her deep reservoir of empathy—to all of which we have already alluded. It was doubtless the synthesis of these attributes which enabled her to fathom the child's affectomotor-gestural language in the separation-individuation subphases[3] and rendered her constructions free of adultomorphisms. As she put it, "My psychoanalytic eye let myself be led wherever phenomenological sequences would lead me" (personal communication).

The papers in volume 2 extend over a period of fourteen years. Although the symbiotic phase is now relegated more to the background, Mahler regularly refers to symbiotic phase-adequacy as the sine qua non for the child's successful passage through the separation-individuation subphases and as a determinant of mood proclivity. Even more, the interrelationships of the mother's and infant's cues in the symbiotic phase provide that basic configuration which marks a particular infant as the child of his particular mother. In her observations she both follows the variations and vicissitudes of each individual child's behavior and searches for common, age-specific behavioral sequences and affective reactions which allow her

---

3. Mahler has stressed the difficulties in deciphering observable phenomena in the pre-ego (that is, autistic and symbiotic) periods and has explained how she gleaned her knowledge of symbiosis by examining it in its later pathological and regressive manifestations.

to arrive at the special characteristics of each subphase. Motility (including in particular approach and distancing behavior) and nonverbal communication now are pivotal to her observations.

As Mahler shifts her emphases from the autistic and symbiotic phases to the mother-infant polarity, and from the mother's to the child's role in the mother-child interactions, she adds much to our knowledge of the differing leitmotifs among mothers. She further investigates the effects of each mother's leitmotif on her child from the vantages of the mother's conscious and unconscious fantasies and her changing attitudes contingent on her changing maternal tasks as the child moves from one subphase to the next. But equally impressive are her descriptions of the average (as opposed to the psychotic) child's resilience and adaptive powers which enable him to modify his behavior in accordance with the mother's selective responses to his rich repertory of cues and to elicit supplies from her, sometimes despite highly unfavorable odds; and in this connection she felicitously refers to what Ernst Kris characterized as the child's "rich flux of developmental energy." In brief, she gives due regard throughout to the child's innate endowment, to the mother-child interactions, and to the mother's emotional availability which she recognizes as the most indispensable single factor of the "average expectable environment" within which normal separation-individuation proceeds.

It will be noted that there is some redundancy among the papers in volume 2. These papers were originally published in numerous journals and anthologies so that repeated descriptions of the symbiotic and separation-individuation subphases were unavoidable if the reader was to be provided with a necessary background for the progressive and cumulative understanding of Mahler's ideas. Because she was always observing, always thinking, and because she did not make her theories fit too tightly, she was likewise often changing and developing new themes and variations. As she repeats her description of the subphases, we can view the ways in which she refines, modifies, and introduces additions to her dynamic interpretations of the observational data. The differentiation subphase is expanded to encompass early indications of adaptation and defense. The practicing subphase is divided into two periods and the rapprochement subphase is given added significance by her insight into the implications of the rapprochement crisis for future health or pathology. Separation-individuation come to be regarded as comprising two different yet indivisible tracks in that neither process can approach completion without achieving sufficient synchronization with the other. Finally, by correlating the development of self- and object representation with its inherent conflicts, and drive development with its inherent conflicts, she contributes to a developmental history of adaptation and defense, moods, narcissism including the vicissitudes of omnipotence, and ultimately, identity formation. We shall comment on some aspects of the foregoing.

Mahler traces the beginnings of the hatching process, which lead to the break-up of the mother-infant dual unity and hence to an increasing awareness of the self as distinct from the object, to the differentiation subphase. It appears to us that her searching inquiries into this subphase may generally have received less attention than they deserve. This may in part be due to the less obviously dramatic character of this subphase. Actually, through her astute observations, Mahler describes how the child awakens to the outside world and presents us with valuable data on individual variations ranging from the optimal to the less than optimal. For example, she perceives differing degrees of outward directedness concordant with the measure of the mother's availability. She discriminates between diverse stranger responses and mild stranger reactions (including curiosity) at one end of a spectrum and extreme stranger anxiety at the other end. She relates incipient defense formations to this subphase thereby again demonstrating trends toward adaptation and maladaptation. Finally, in her minute accounts of individual children's behavior, we can discern differences in the initial capacity for neutralization as evidenced in the child's curiosity and thoughful manual explorations.

Mahler's empathic perceptivity led to her constant awareness, very possibly at times initially preconscious, of phase-associated moods. We might say parenthetically that it has occurred to us that her sensitivity to mood cadences may have played a role in her detection of the behavioral clusters which led to her delineation of the subphases. In her exploration of moods, she is cognizant of and enlarges upon drive-related aspects as, for example, pleasure as opposed to unpleasure, and need-satisfaction as opposed to frustration with its resultant distress rage. Although Mahler observes a predominant mood characteristic for each subphase, she postulates that an individual's mood proclivity is solidified in the rapprochement period. She adds much to our understanding of the preponderance of depression in women when she elucidates the futher lowering of self-esteem in the girl during this subphase through recognition of the sexual differences.

As in her earlier papers, Mahler is always mindful of the aggressive drive. This is exemplified by her description of mood character, and of activity patterns as related to neutralization in the differentiation and practicing periods; it is likewise apparent in her accounts of the transitions from assertiveness in the differentiation period to unfocused physical aggression in the practicing period, and then to focused physical aggression in the rapprochement subphase. Lastly, she shows that the fate of the aggressive drive may be perceived in the balance of neutralized versus unneutralized (and even unfused) aggression in respect to object relatedness, to activity, and, with the attainment of representational thinking, to the child's fantasies.

As Mahler indicates, many aggressive drive manifestations converge in the rapprochement subphase when the child is faced with increasing outer and inner complexities. By virtue of her keen eye for behavioral clusters, she is now able to distinguish such factors as developing language and representational thinking, the move from automatic to signal anxiety and changed anxiety situations, psychosexual conflicts, greater physical independence, and enhanced self-awareness with its attendant ambitendency and negativism. Some of the foregoing contribute to and others are consequent to the rapprochement crisis.

At this juncture we would underscore that one can scarcely even allude to Mahler's papers on separation-individuation without special mention of the rapprochement crisis and its implications for the future course of ego and drive development in respect both to the attainment of adequate object constancy and to the patterning and texture of the child's oedipal constellation.

Although Mahler's original intent was to study the normal

separation-individuation process, she nonetheless has widened our understanding of the genesis of pathology. By observing the different children as they traveled through the different subphases, she inevitably was confronted with behavior that extended beyond the boundaries of average, individual variations. These pathological deviations include subphase distortions and especially unfavorable outcomes of the rapprochement subphase. Foremost among these untoward outcomes are persisting ambivalence and separation anxiety; and the depressive affect as this relates to the fate of omnipotence, narcissism, self-esteem and internalized aggression, with a simultaneous depletion of available neutralized energy for ego development.

In her illuminations of the different outcomes for each child in each subphase, Mahler perforce recognizes clinical configurations ranging from transitory neurotic symptomatology to that resembling narcissistic and borderline phenomena. She further relates these outcomes not only to narcissistic reserves derived from symbiosis but also to subphase adequacy and the resolution of the rapprochement crisis which in optimal instances pave the road toward object constancy. As she demonstrates, an unresolved rapprochement crisis may create unfavorable fixation points and result in a persisting intrapsychic conflict which then adversely affects the child's oedipal development and oedipal resolution. Hence it represents an antecedent, or preliminary form, of the infantile neurosis. And she also offers a way of assessing subphase adequacy by a scrutiny of the developmental course of narcissism, psychosexual development and object relations.

It is to Mahler's credit that she has systematically studied the second year of life—an area which heretofore had been relatively neglected. She furthermore, within this context, gives consideration to the father's role and reintroduces him as the "uncontaminated partner"[4] in the rapprochement struggle and as an object of identification. Her integrative gifts have not only enabled her to penetrate the complexities of this period but also, as we could see in her studies

4. Mahler thus labeled the father in the ambivalence struggles of the psychotic child as described in volume 1.

in volume 1, to synthesize a wealth of relevant data. Yet, in spite of the fact that she extracts the aforementioned data from a wide variety of sources, including academic psychology and psychiatry, she never swerves from her psychoanalytic stance. She does not hesitate to use metaphors, but rather than detract from the scientific validity of her work, they enhance the specific meanings. They are so in keeping with what she has observed that we find ourselves focusing on the latter rather than on the language in which it is stated.

We hope that our attempts in the preceding pages to highlight some aspects of Mahler's inquiries and conceptualizations convey a semblance of the scope and articulation of her searching studies, whether they took place in her consulting room or at the children's center where she conducted her research on the separation-individuation process. Her insights into early development which reached their culmination in these separation-individuation studies have opened the way for a greater understanding of those more severely disturbed patients who seem to come our way with increasing frequency. For many of us, however, her findings on the early years of life have equal pertinence for the less severe pathological formations in that they not only shed light on the oedipal problems but additionally they heighten our sensitivity to nuances of adaptation and defense, that is, to character formation. We would underscore that the essence of Mahler's contribution lies not only in the fecundity of her observations but, more important, in their arrangement. Were we to single out but one of the qualities that distinguish her as a remarkable innovator it would be her capacity to perceive relationships between phenomena which to those of us of lesser ability would appear in isolation. We believe it is this quality which has given such unity to the totality of her work.

Marjorie Harley, Ph.D.
Annemarie P. Weil, M.D.
January 15, 1979

ACKNOWLEDGMENTS

Since the publication of *The Psychological Birth of the Human Infant** an ever-increasing number of psychoanalytic writers, as well as students in auxiliary disciplines, cite that book as the almost sole repository of my original concepts. Innumerable theoreticians and clinicians have demonstrated the usefulness of these concepts. At this writing dissertations, essays, and scientific articles based on my research come into my hands almost weekly. While this is very gratifying, *The Psychological Birth of the Human Infant* does not contain all my ideas. My concepts have had a developmental progression. Inasmuch as they were formulated in papers published over a few decades and scattered throughout the literature, it is no wonder that workers in the field have found it difficult to locate the pertinent articles in which these concepts first appeared. Therefore, at the behest of some of my colleagues, and encouraged by Dr. Jason Aronson, I decided to collect and publish my selected seminal contributions in two volumes. The first volume includes some of my early papers and my contributions on infantile psychosis; the second chronicles the shift of the focus of my interest to the study of normal development.

In two previous volumes I have expressed my gratitude and appreciation to many colleagues and friends who provided help and

*Mahler, M.S., Pine, F., and Bergman, A. (1975). *The Psychological Birth of the Human Infant*. New York: Basic Books.

encouragement over more than half a century of clinical work, study, and research. I wish to repeat my acknowledgments to these co-workers, mentors, and admired colleagues, as well as to the foundations and institutions which supported our work over the years; they are named in the source notes to each chapter.

Nevertheless I cannot abstain from expressing my special gratitude to the National Institute of Mental Health and the Menil Foundation. NIMH made possible the two projects—namely, On Symbiotic Child Psychosis and On The Normal Separation-Individuation Process.

In their wisdom and foresight, John and Dominique de Menil provided the means, long after all other sources were exhausted, that allowed my work to come to its optimal fruition. Through them the Margaret S. Mahler Fund of The Menil Foundation was established. This has since become the Margaret S. Mahler Psychiatric Research Foundation.

I also wish to express my thanks to the two collaborators with whom I have worked so closely in recent years—Dr. John B. McDevitt in particular, and secondly, Mrs. Anni Bergman.

I feel that these *Selected Papers* gain immensely in value, especially for those scholars who will wish to study the source material for its place in the history of psychoanalytic thought, through the brilliant introduction provided by Drs. Marjorie Harley and Annemarie Weil.

I want to express my grateful acknowledgment to my coauthors: Drs. Jean A. Luke, Paula Elkisch, Manuel Furer, Bertram Gosliner, and Calvin F. Settlage for our work on childhood psychosis. For our study of normal child development, I wish in addition to thank my coauthors: Mrs. Anni Bergman, Drs. Louise Kaplan, John B. McDevitt, Kitty La Perriere and Fred Pine. Even though we did not write any papers together, I also owe thanks to Dr. Selma Kramer, with whom I have exchanged clinical and theoretical insights over many years.

Dr. Vann Spruiell read the manuscript in its initial state and contributed valued advice and suggestions and was always generous with his time.

For steady encouragement I owe thanks to E. James Anthony and a host of other colleagues, particularly those of the Philadelphia Psychoanalytic Society, and to scores of unnamed analysts who supported and inspired me. Among those who cannot go unnamed: Dr. Phyllis Greenacre, and the late Edith Jacobson.

Finally, my heartfelt thanks are extended to the officers of the Margaret S. Mahler Research Fund of the Menil Foundation, in Philadelphia; and to the officers of the Margaret S. Mahler Psychiatric Research Foundation, in New York. At great personal sacrifice they have made further work with the data possible. They maintain the Margaret S. Mahler Psychiatric Research Archives as well, which at present are used by workers familiar with our original studies, and which I hope, will be used by workers of future generations.

Margaret S. Mahler
New York
December 1978

Part One

EARLY CONTRIBUTIONS

Chapter 1

PSEUDOIMBECILITY: A MAGIC CAP OF INVISIBILITY

[1942]

One of the magic objects owned by the Nibelungs of German mythology is a covering for the head which endows its possessor with the power of becoming invisible. Being invisible, the wearer can be present and act in situations from which otherwise he would be excluded. Young Siegfried, the hero of the Nibelung saga, is the embodiment of juvenile strength and courage. With the help of his magic cap *(Tarnkappe)*, he commits a series of deeds which amount to conspicuous sexual crimes. He woos Brunhild in place of King Gunther, and invisibly usurps the *jus primae noctis* with the Queen in the presence of his King. These exploits do not reduce Siegfried's radiant reputation as the popular symbol of the youthful national hero; on the contrary, the invisibility provided by the magic cap is one of the most important attributes in according him the privileges of a hero.

It is well known that the essence of mythology, like the rituals and customs of primitive culture, reflect the inner psychic realities of childhood. Experience in psychoanalysis with children brought me to realize what is the symbolic psychological meaning of the "magic cap" in childhood generally, and in cases of pseudoimbecility specifically. What I wish to describe is the function of stupidity as a magic cap *(Tarnkappe)*, as a means of restoring or maintaining a secret libidinous rapport within the family. This, I believe, essential function of stupidity (not recorded to an adequate extent in the psychoanalytic literature) enables children as well as infantile adults to participate in the sexual life of parents and other adults to an amazingly unlimited extent which, overtly expressed, would be strictly and definitely forbidden.

Between child and mother there exists from the beginning a close phylogenetic bond which is unique and much more exclusive than communication by words or thoughts; it is an interrelationship through the medium of affective expressions. We know how subtle is this communication between the infant and the mother who feeds it at the breast. It is clinically and statistically proved that difficulties in feeding, as well as the general health of the infant, are much more dependent on the emotional attitude of the mother towards the child than on her organic ability to supply milk or the degree of her conscious efforts to provide hygienic nursing. The interrelation between the unconscious of the mother and the reception of stimulation of the sense organs of the baby is the prototype for a way of communication between child and adult which is not confined within the limited sphere of language.

The affective outbursts of the infant are the means by which it attains gratification of its instinctual needs, and the absence of such outbursts indicates an alarming degree of inertia (Ribble 1941). The infant's bodily functions are in direct accordance with its instinctual drives; its reactions to surplus stimuli are outbursts of temper. By these affective outbursts the infant achieves domination in the mother-child relationship; left alone it would be completely helpless, abandoned to perish. Even after the differentiation of the ego and the beginning of speech, the expressive movements and affective expressions of the entire body are used by the child as much more congenial means of communication with the environment than language. The archaic common language of human beings is and remains the language of affect. Whenever the repressed complexes of childhood are evoked, we relapse again into this unconscious affective rapport. The domination of the mother by the infant gradually becomes reversed in the course of the second and third years. While the eighteen-month-old baby, on uttering a short cry of command, is brought with eager speed to the pot, the three-year-old is threatened with deprivation of love should it fail to comply with the requirements of the adults which are, moreover, administered with large quantities of affect and aggression. The child gradually realizes that its power is waning. It has not only to renounce sensual gratifications but must in addition lose its sense of omnipotence. The language of violent affect is rendered useless as a means of communication with the parents, and the child has to renounce them in favor of speech. Tempers and crying spells are met by the parents with increasing stoicism or measures of punishment or suppression. It seems as if these affective outbursts at the age of two to three years are struggling attempts of the child to maintain the archaic common ground so familiar to it: the intensely pleasurable affective rapport with the parents, and the child's affective domination of them. This attempt is destined, like the oedipal strivings, to fail from the danger of loss of love and fear of castration.

Direct affective attacks failing, the child searches for other means to regain entrance to the Garden of Eden. This coincides in time with beginning to walk, and the process of taking in impressions of the outside world with all the senses, acquiring knowledge and testing reality. The child utilizes these newly gained discoveries to share them with mother and father and thus restore a common ground with them (D. T. Burlingham). The expressions of enchantment and affection which the parents give so abundantly at the first presentations of such fact-finding bring the child a temporary restoration of the old affective, and a new intellectual, coexperience with the parents.

But again the parents cannot allow the child to enter their lives beyond a limited distance. The common emotional and intellectual experiences infringe upon the strenuously established repressions of the adults. The small child's keen powers of observation, its bold intuition, become unwelcome. This applies especially to perceptions in the sphere of sexual exploration whose failure to reveal the secret of the sexual relationship between the parents marks the beginning of the latency period which is characterized by repression of overt sexual interests and a slowing down of development of the child's hitherto brilliant exploratory intellect.

Little emphasis has been put on the fact that twice in its early development the small child meets a rebuff in its passionate endeavor to share the lives of the parents. It learns gradually to discriminate between those perceptions and experiences which it may share with adults and those facts which are better kept to oneself as secrets. Taking advantage of the discovery that it may collect and maintain a secret treasury of libidinous experiences and knowledge, inaccessible to the adult world, the child learns to isolate these experiences from verbalization and hide its secret from the depriving adults.

The magic of such relative "stupidity" during the latency period provides for the child a partly undetected, partly tolerated preverbal libidinous channel of communication with the parents without conflict. Besides this inconspicuous, quiet, "peaceful infiltration," we meet often enough, during latency and beyond it, with innumerable forms of a kind of guerilla warfare on the part of children, well known from child analyses and child guidance practice. In all these conflict situations between children and parents we are struck again and again by the intuitive accuracy with which children are able to detect the weakest spots in their parents, and how often they succeed in gaining entrance and seducing the parents to respond in the old affective way. When this partly archaic, strongly affective rapport is restored on a preverbal level by child and parents, it escapes detection. An important part of this libidinous interchange throughout latency has been described by Lillian Rotter-Kertész (1936) with reference to the child and its father.

How the adults' secret is played off against the child's secret and vice versa was nicely demonstrated in a child's analysis. Lilly, six and a half years old, was analyzed for extreme motor inhibition and inability to play. At the root of her neurosis was, first, her accurate intuitive knowledge of how much the family regarded her a superfluous burden. Her birth was accidental. The parents were poor people who had difficulties even sharing food with this unwanted child. Second, a congenital dislocation of the coccyx had made it necessary to confine Lilly at the age of two in a hospital far removed from her mother.

Not before she had established a very good relationship with me was Lilly able to talk and reveal her secrets. She was compelled, for example, to turn and look back frantically out of the trolley car window whether coming or going because, "You never can tell whether your mother would not lead you somewhere from where you would not be able to find your way home."

This recalls the fairy tale of Hansel and Gretel, whose parents wanted to get rid of them. One night they made a secret plan to lead the children into the woods and leave them to perish. But the children, overhearing the secret of the parents at night, pretend ignorance and innocence. The magic of their apparent dumbness enabled them not only to intrude into the parents' secret (primal scene), but to keep their own secret (defense against the parents' secret) which in turn enabled them, when abandoned by the parents in the woods, to return home.

The mechanisms which lead to pathological limitation and restriction of intellectual functions of the ego have been examined by many analysts—Landauer (1929), Rado (1919), Aichhorn, Bornstein (1930), Bergler (1932), Oberndorf (1939), Edith Jacobson (1932), Maenchen (1936) and others.

The genesis of intellectual inhibition follows the general pattern described by Freud in *Inhibitions, Symptoms and Anxiety* (1936). Erotization of the intellectual functions of the ego has been shown to cause the ego to give up this function in order to escape conflicts (Bornstein 1930, Landauer 1929). It is known also that the intellectual restriction is often used to disguise aggression in order to escape retaliation (Bergler 1932, Oberndorf 1939). Pseudostupidity, in addition, has been described as a display of castration to escape fear of literal castration and the loss of a loved object (Landauer 1929, Maenchen 1936).

This paper aims to demonstrate still another essential function of stupidity: to restore or maintain a secret libidinous rapport within the family.

In an unusually impressive fashion the usefulness of stupidity was demonstrated in an eighteen-year-old pseudoimbecilic male, whom I had analyzed for almost three years when the treatment had to be discontinued. He had a whole arsenal of defense mechanisms and symptoms. Besides latent passive homosexuality, he presented definite obsessional neurotic as well as phobic mechanisms which contributed to a severe impoverishment of his ego.

Jack was one of nonidentical twins, born as late offspring of a father who, at the time of their birth, was ailing with a heart condition, and who died when they were nine years old.

Up to his death the father, always a cranky introvert and owner of a large estate, maintained in an obsessional fashion a splendid isolation for the twins in this rural environment. He projected his fears of infection and death especially onto Jack, the more delicate of the twins, who, because of his resemblance to the father, attracted his intense ambivalent love.

The father believed the boys should grow like delicate plants in sunshine and air, under the best hygienic conditions, in the country. The vegetative functions of the body should be attended to, and later, education in sports introduced. Systematic intellectual education was unnecessary, at least not worth getting at the slightest expense of clean, healthy, simple, and innocent rural life. Schooling would involve going to the city—dirty, dusty, and dangerous with its noisy traffic and effete sexuality. In the seclusion of the country the twins were protected from sexual knowledge. They were to remain inno-cent, that is, stupid and ignorant.

The patient at first presented the clinical picture of severe pseudoimbecility. He sat with arms hanging, stood up like an automaton, walked with a shuffling gait, and wore a silly smile. He stared into space, and an unshaven face completed his pathetic appearance.

All day long Jack would loiter around with a more or less absent-minded look and, whenever a task came up from which it would be hard for him to escape, he could fall asleep in almost any posture. Though he was extremely affectionate towards the family, especially his sister, the expressions of his attachment were those of a small child, with abundant exchange of caresses, kisses, and hugs. He consciously refused to be treated according to his age. He did not want to make any decisions but was eager, like an obedient child, to obey all wishes of adults as far as his conspicuously limited abilities permitted. In his social activities he was simply an appendage of his married sister, six years older, or of his twin bother John and his fiancée. They permitted him to be present like a pet animal which does no harm by its presence and neither understands nor participates. His magic cap of stupidity hid Jack so well that he was almost forgotten. He was allowed to be present during the preliminaries of the sexual relationship of an older brother and his sweetheart, a married woman. The latter was quite desperate when her attention was called to the signs of devotion which she had unconsciously aroused in Jack, and tolerated "unrecognized." He was allowed to come into the bedroom where John and his bride lay in bed, and in a more sublimated fashion he participated in the marriage of his sister and brother-in-law.

Analysis revealed that his earliest childhood memories centered around passive exhibitionistic experiences which took place in the bathroom. He remembered his twin urinating in his face when they were both in a baby carriage, and hearing the loud laughter of a couple of spectators. Then he recalled that his brother laughed at him when he was having a truss adjusted for congenital inguinal hernia. Compensation for this phallic failure centered around the pleasure which the particular attention paid to his bowel functions (probably because of his inguinal hernia) gave him. These exhibitionistic performances were his only means of keeping contact with his father and mother. When, however, his great complementary curiosity came to expression, his questions were met with stereotyped reproofs: "You should not ask about that." "It is not good for you to wonder about it." "You are too young." Thus restricted, his curiosity resolved itself into voyeurism. Everywhere that he could he would creep in secretly and spy. He was allowed to be present while his mother was bathing on condition that he kept his back turned to her.

Under the influence of an athletic instructor, who was "especially active and a right wing radical," he became quite courageous in sports. Once he fell and injured his leg. In the bathroom he took a washcloth to stem the bleeding when suddenly his father, quite contrary to his usual behavior, jumped at him, struck him, and scolded him about the danger of infection and contamination. The father then attended to the wound himself. This castration scene came up in the analysis of a cynophobia. "You never can tell about a dog," he said. "All of a sudden it can bite you in the leg, or it might run between your legs and you might fall over it."

When after the death of his father the twins were "dragged into the city to school," contrary to the wish of the father, the patient developed severe isolation and avoidance mechanisms in unconscious compliance with the requirements of the dead father. With his obsessive neurotic mechanisms he was trying to isolate himself from the temptations and dangers of the "vicious city." To keep clean in the dirty sexual atmosphere of the city, he had to avoid touching things. A head cold placed him in a predicament because he could not allow his hands to come in contact with the nasal secretions. Similarly, when for "hygienic reasons" it was necessary to masturbate, he exercised great care in avoiding contact with the ejaculate. He avoided barbers from fear of razors but went nevertheless to be shaved, experiencing a thrill which reminded him of similar feelings he had had when a doctor administered eye drops which smarted.

He wandered aimlessly through the streets in a state of chronic anxiety about the traffic. He rationalized this, as he did many of his compulsions, on the grounds of hygiene. He took evening walks which extended long after midnight "in order to sleep better." With his shuffling gait and absentminded look, seeking to avoid pedestrians as well as vehicles, he had the compulsion to creep along the edge of the pavement and achieved the exact opposite of his conscious intention. He provoked the pedestrians into colliding with him, shouting at him, or pushing him deliberately or unintentionally into the gutter; off the pavement, he was endangered by the cars and trucks. His father had hinted that something like this happened to young people in the vicious city, and he was thus proving it continually to the analyst and to himself.

Very similarly to his attitude with reference to traffic in the street, he missed no opportunity to travel and to put himself to great trouble to find occasions for it, though days before he would be sick from fear of having to use the train and of meeting strange people; and he would fall asleep while traveling. Here the same mechanism was at work: a compromise between his intense curiosity—the urge to create situations in which he could watch strange people—and his anxiety.

It was not accidental that this series of neurotic attitudes and symptoms centered for him around forbidden traffic situations in which his impulse to look on and watch overcame the compulsive and phobic defenses. Being a German, traffic *(Verkehr)*, had, for the patient, also the meaning of intercourse. Analysis gave evidence that this connection led to a hypercathexis of all traffic situations which had been prohibited in both meanings of the term by the dead father. He tried to ward off his voyeurism by absent-mindedness in the street or by closing his senses through falling asleep while traveling, while simultaneously obsessively seeking to gratify his curiosity.

To summarize, this patient, in the phallic stage, had to give up competition with his aggressive twin brother in comparison with whom he considered himself malequipped in the phallic sphere because of a congenital hernia and for other reasons; in consequence he regressed to an anal fixation. The counterpart of his anal exhibitionism was an intense sexual curiosity against which he had to maintain strong defenses because of castration threats from his father who had warned in effect: "Don't go to the city to learn about the dirty sinful life there and the dangers of traffic. Remain clean, and innocent." His stupidity served him from early childhood both as a defense against anal and sexual conflicts and as a magic cap of invisibility which enabled him to observe intimate performances of the parents in the bathroom without being noticed. In adolescence he renounced his own sexuality to escape castration but succeeded, by means of the magic of stupidity, quietly to participate in the sexual relationships of his brothers and sister. The mechanism of sexual renunciation was aided by identification and substitution with his twin, an *alter ego,* through whose phallic achievements the patient experienced the masculinity which he himself had to renounce—to say nothing of the homosexual elements involved.

Another case of pseudoimbecility is that of a thirteen-year-old boy whose stupidity was maintained in an unconscious rapport with his mother. Lyn was sent to analysis because after he had failed four times to be promoted and had been placed in a class for retarded children, the boy was found to have a normal I.Q. His stupidity took the form of chronic forgetting. This was not limited to disagreeable things nor to studies, but included every minute detail of his daily routine at home. Through this mechanism he succeeded in keeping his mother occupied with him as if he were a small child.

Lyn was the second child and elder son of a Chinese father and a Swedish mother. The parents lived in constant discord and had been unhappy at the prospect of this second child. Quarrels and gross abuse between the parents seem to have become even more marked when Lyn was about two years old. The mother had the superstitious conviction that this child would become stupid because she had had frequent contacts with a senile old man, a customer in the laundry they maintained during the time of her pregnancy with Lyn. First evidence to her of this anticipation was his development at two years of age of what seems to have been spastic stammering. The mother took this as the first sign that her son was "marked" by the elderly imbecile. While relating this, the mother could hardly contain her amusement about the funny little boy, and seemed delighted to relate that the stuttering little fool became much worse when he saw his father attacking her. Apart from his speech, the child's development was normal except for intermittent bedwetting every night for months at a time until he was eight.

About Lyn's early relationship to his father little is known except that the father liked to play with the boy and frequently took him for walks. Between the ages of three and four the boy greatly admired his father's toolbox, and was happiest when he could play with it. As the father's job kept him away from home most of the time, the mother's influence was overwhelming. Lyn's strong attachment to his mother was strengthened by rivalry with a brother born when he was five. A short time later the mother had to be hospitalized because "her blood was poisoned by my father" (gonorrhea). Shortly after her return from the hospital she attempted to commit suicide because her husband had taken to bringing his girl friends to the house. It was at this time that Lyn began to wet the bed every night. Following her attempt at suicide, and as a final weapon in her effort to win her husband back, the mother left home.

With much resistance Lyn recalled in analysis memories of this period. While pretending to be asleep, Lyn overheard many dramatic sexual scenes between the father and his woman friend. Fearful of being censured by his severe and stolid mother for hearing and seeing things which he felt he should not have seen and heard, the boy attempted to forget what he had witnessed. During the weeks of her absence the mother kept thinking that the child "must be seeing a lot of dirty sexual things." Troubled by this thought, she decided to return to her children and ask her husband to move out. Subsequently, when Lyn was about eight years old, the father deserted permanently.

In analysis the patient revealed intense sadistic fantasies about his sister which were obviously displacements from his mother. In the transference, he displayed the same excessively devoted, submissive and passive attitudes that he exhibited towards his mother, the reverse of his sadistic fantasies. Each time he divulged one of these fantasies, he reacted with an increased display of forgetfulness and apparent stupidity. In this case, severe restriction of the ego utilized the device of forgetting which had as its purpose a resolution of his fears originating in primal scenes which were linked with sadistic scenes, quarrels, contamination, "blood poisoning," and represented to him his father, sexuality, and the attitude of his mother towards both. After the father left, the boy resorted to the magic of stupidity to meet the demands of his mother. He had to forget his real father—the underprivileged, socially inferior Chinaman, the deserter, sexual and unclean—and to create instead an illusory father—stately, kinglike, nordic—in terms of his mother's characteristics. This identification with a phallic mother simultaneously assigned to Lyn the role of the castrated, servant father which meant that in the identification with the father he was subject to castration and rejection by his mother. To avoid castration, he had to forget all about sex and maintain an appearance of innocence by forgetting all the experiences in connection with his father.

The mother's hatred of this child from the time of her pregnancy with him found expression in her superstitious conviction that he would be born stupid. Hatred of the father was partly displaced to this child in attitudes of castrative depreciation from which, however, unlike his father, he was able neither to escape nor defend himself effectively. Deserted by her husband for another woman after having infected her with gonorrhea, the mother took lasting revenge for the insult in keeping this substitute for the hated husband chained to herself as a castrated, innocent fool whom she might never lose to another woman. Through the magic of his stupidity it was possible for the boy and his mother to maintain a close relationship on a preverbal level, very similar to that of a small child and its mother. But to be stupid alone did not suffice; the sexual experiences of the father and his girl, which the boy had observed, had been too conspicuously verbalized and constantly refreshed by the grudging mother to permit the appearance of sexual innocence. A more active defense mechanism of undoing, by *forgetting*, had to be established by the ego to efface the contradiction between the mother's denying attitude and the grossly overt sexual behavior of the father, which through verbalization had been brought to conscious acknowledgment between mother and son.

Another case, a girl, was brought for analysis at the age of nine. She was the youngest among four siblings. Her mother had been left a widow when the patient was two and a half years old and the mother bestowed all her love upon the baby daughter. They shared a double bed from then on, and at the age of nine, when the school intimated that the mother ought to give Betsy other sleeping accomodations, she protested: "But how can I live without my baby daughter beside me?" The intense libidinous nature of this mother-child relationship was demonstrated by the fact that I usually found them in the waiting room, Betsy on her mother's lap, in close embrace. For the mother the strong sexual attachment to the baby daughter was a definite substitute for her marital relationship with the husband. Through continual seduction the child did not succeed in the normal and necessary repression of sexuality of the latency period. The abnormal sexual stimulation led to excessive masturbation which met with violent disapproval from the mother without any insight about her part in bringing it about.

At the age of seven the child was seduced and sexually exploited by a fifteen-year-old brother following which she developed symptoms resembling psychosis. The school physician and her teachers pronounced her the strangest and most stupid pupil they had ever observed. Her I.Q. was 116. They were eager to have the child analyzed although they really believed that the child was psychotic or feeble-minded. In the anamnesis she was described as having spells of complete withdrawal, "remote staring" with expressionless eyes reminiscent of petit mal; or as "sitting in a daze" seemingly without awareness, "staring with a cowlike gaze at the others."

Analysis revealed that the sexual relationship between Betsy and her brother, who bore his father's name, was a form of prostitution, in which she was exhibited for money to a classmate of the brother, and included mutual masturbation and attempts at anal intercourse. To the analyst the child confided a passionate longing to catch a *real* bird. The bird proved to be the representation of the spirit of her father, whose death she imagined as a mysterious flying away of his soul like a great bird. In Betsy's mind only an eagle was a real bird; canaries, sparrows, and other small birds were not real birds. One of her earliest memories was her father's fondness for breeding pigeons, to which her mother objected as a nuisance, soiling the car and the house. From associations and drawings it became clear that the bird had the further special meaning of father's penis which mother disliked, feared, and wanted to destroy. In a phase of her analysis, in which she complained repeatedly that she would never catch a "real bird" herself, she contemptuously gave her mother, as a gift, a feeding board for birds. This gift was conspicuous for its awkward, misshapen, and impractical construction—as if to say that mother would never acquire a real bird either. She divulged her opinion that she would never get a penis because her mother had none to give her. Perhaps her mother was responsible for her father's death as well as for the loss of the real bird which father could have given to her; hence a preoccupation for months with bird collections, investigations of the habits and biology of birds, measurements of their beaks, tails, etc. This was analyzed as an escape from the penisless mother and a desire to appropriate the brother's penis as defenses against fears of self-injury (castration) from masturbation. The incestuous relationship with the brother relieved the grave preoedipal fixation to the mother and was also an escape from masturbation, which seemed to Betsy much more dangerous than any other sin. By pinning the guilt onto her mother, she lessened her own sense of guilt about having lost her penis through masturbation. She shifted onto her seducers, mother and brother, as adults much of the responsibility and guilt, and vacillated between overt incest with the brother and innocent, preverbal sexual communion with the mother.

After analysis had brought to light the above facts, the mother wrote me a letter confessing her knowledge of the sexual activities between Betsy and her eldest son. She asked me to talk with her grown-up daughter, obviously the representative of her conscience. She asked me in the letter to regard Betsy as the "innocent offender" rather than put too much blame upon the son. It was apparent that she was trying to excuse her own early seduction of the baby daughter as if to say that the daughter in her innocent foolishness had crept into her bed, seducing her and not the other way round. It was astonishing that she had tolerated the sexual relation between the brother and sister for years after detection. The mother's own incestuous drives towards her eldest son prevented her from safeguarding the child who, protected by her "innocence" and stupidity, was permitted an incestuous relationship with the brother in which the mother participated vicariously with little apparent sense of guilt.

This case furnishes an especially striking example of how stupidity as a device enabled both a mother and child to maintain a secret libidinous interchange on an exclusively affective level.

SUMMARY

Pseudostupidity enables children as well as infantile adults to participate to an amazingly unlimited extent in the sexual life of parents and other adults.

In my cases this maneuver of the child was emotionally fully reciprocated by a parent or sibling because it met the adult's own unconscious desire, isolated from his feelings of guilt.

This utilization of stupidity is widespread because mutual sexual desires are gratified on a preverbal affective level, without becoming conscious through word pictures, which renders repression or other defense measures unnecessary.

Thus children and parents are able to maintain a distorted but gratifying affective communion which would otherwise be limited to mother and infant.

Chapter 2

"LES ENFANTS TERRIBLES"

[1949]

The title of this paper was taken from a book by the French author Jean Cocteau. In his book *Les enfants terribles* (1930) he depicts children who do not restrict their passions. These passions are the same passions of love and hate that adults feel but exaggerated and not amalgamated. In fact, the youthful actors in Cocteau's book are held together by masochistic infatuation, self-sacrifice, and tender adoration as well as by sadistic aggression and brutal subjugation. In other words, Cocteau has chosen as a literary theme a fact, self-evident to psychoanalysts, that children and adolescents are moved by the same erotic and aggressive cravings as are adults. The children of his novel inflict physical and mental torture upon each other. Their ego condones breaking down the barriers against direct expression of the instinctual impulses set by the superego. Their grossly aggressive and erotic pursuits are not challenged by the grown-ups. The youthful actors rely upon, and anticipate an adult prejudice, namely, the superstitious, stubborn, and traditional belief in the innocence of children. Because they are children, their obviously and grossly sexual and destructive actions and relationships are not recognized as such. The children rely on this prejudice. They love and hate in entirely adult fashion before the eyes of the adults. But the adults, entrenched in their complacent superstition, do not believe this conduct to be motivated by adultlike passion, and can be fooled all the time.

Jean Cocteau's *Enfants terribles* thus are products of a peculiar emotional interrelationship between infantile and adult society. The same elements in a conflict described in Cocteau's novel with dramatic exaggeration are contained in everyday *"enfant terrible"* phenomena occurring between children and their parents. The dynamic elements of these every day phenomena, however, appear mitigated in quality and quantity by the operation of the economic principle of the comic. In fact, the most generally accepted concept of *enfant terrible* behavior can be formulated as follows: A person—usually a child—pretending innocence and naivety, shocks adults by a deliberately embarrassing remark or gesture.

A father, who was a psychoanalyst, used to amuse his friends from time to time by telling them each new crop of his small son's cute remarks and questions. The curiosity of the little chap had obviously centered upon his father's professional pursuits. He wanted to know what his father did with the patients behind the closed door of his office. He wondered whether he beat them up, etc. It was a mystery to him why he was forbidden to join his father even for a minute when the men and women could take up all his time. In fact, he was not even supposed to know the names of the ladies and gentlemen who came to pay such long visits to his daddy so regularly. He was strictly forbidden to talk to the patients—these mysterious creatures, who to his mind were surrounded with an utterly exaggerated immunity. The curiosity and resentment of the little boy grew until one day, when coming up the elevator with a gentleman who, as he had discovered, was one of these creatures, he suddenly burst out: "Are you perhaps a patient?"

In the minds of children whose mothers are analysts the emotions which this small boy indicated are even greater in intensity. An analyst mother one day overheard her little daughter shouting all over the house: "Mooommmy, come out of the bathroom, hurry up, the patient has arrived!"

Another woman analyst's seven-year-old son gives us a more

obvious example of aggressive phallic behavior. He felt frustrated and irked by having to share his mommy with all those patients. So, one morning he waited till the patient entered the hall, and with perfect synchronization opened the bathroom door, popped his head out, and shouted a mocking and spontaneously invented rhyme about his mother: "Mrs. E. G. is a piggie!"

Seven-year-old Pete, while in analysis, was taken for a checkup to his beloved pediatrician, a very tall and imposing looking man. Upon leaving the office he raved about what a wonderful doctor Uncle B. was, etc. Whereupon his mother, in her concern for Pete's "transference" to me, said to him, "But you know Margaret is also a doctor," whereupon Pete with condescending and understanding innocence retorted, "Oh sure, Margaret knows a lot about penises."

And finally there is the example of the two sons of another analyst. They entered the elevator just in time to meet one of their mother's woman patients going up to her hour, and with the most innocent expressions they nonchalantly wiggled a snake they had just caught before her horrified eyes.

I took these examples because such and similar incidents are familiar to all of us.

If we examine the immediate genesis of such *enfant terrible* manifestations as these cited, we can see that frustrating exclusion from the mysterious and enticing community of adults over a period of time augmented the youngster's curiosity and his erotic aggressive wish to participate, until the impulse gathered enough momentum to cast off the lid of educational pressure. The first little boy pretends naivety to asking the forbidden questions, "Are you perhaps a patient?" of whose identity is kept from him. The little girl achieved even more with her pseudonaive vocalization. She embarrassed her analyst mother. By her loud broadcast she revealed, "unmasked" as it were, her mother as a human being in the midst of intimate family life. By admonishing her to hurry to her professional work she put comical emphasis upon the urgency of attending to her patient—a deliberate reversal of the child's own, opposite emotions. She achieved a two-fold revenge on her mother and on the patient. In the third instance, the child actually exposed his mother in a frankly erotic, aggressive, mocking way, calling her a piggie. He was thus sure of interfering with the patient-analyst relationship. The two boys by suddenly displaying a phallic symbol quite effectively shocked the woman-patient.

And finally, in Pete's case, from my intimate knowledge of his actual emotional situation I know that by the pseudonaive remark with which he replied to his mother, he ridiculed and minimized the importance of women around him: the doctor, mother, sister, etc., who allegedly know so much about penises but who, when "unveiled," are merely vulnerable, penisless creatures.

The children of analysts, utilizing the generally accepted pretence and privilege of children to be considered cute, innocent and naive, transgressed the barrier of adult rules. In fact, they interfered effectively, if only for a moment, with the daily analytic procedure. Thus, they actually reversed the power position between child and adult. In these episodes they managed to usurp adult superiority by the very weapon of being a child.

Hence, the *enfant terrible* whom I should like to present today, turns out to be a counterpart of that specific type of pseudoimbecile child whom I described in chapter 1. Such children hide under a magic hood of apparent stupidity, and thus manage to participate undetected in the erotic life of the adult world. The *enfant terrible* on the other hand, by virtue of his subtle or bold but swift erotic aggressive attacks, succeeds in taking the adult by surprise and disarming him by throwing him off balance, and unmasking the adults' pretence of superiority.

The child with the magic hood of pseudostupidity manages to transgress the border of adult life by means of his disguise of invisibility. The *enfant terrible*, in contrast, overwhelms the sentinel by the abrupt exhibition of his naivety, charm and acuteness. He takes the risk of being castrated for mocking the adult, but relies upon the disarming magic, which the "irresistible baby", the naive child, exerts upon the average adult, over whom he thus triumphs.

I am aware that the *enfant terrible* whom I shall describe uses motility more than does the traditional *enfant terrible*. The latter depends more preeminently on his verbalizations as a weapon.

In age *enfants terribles* are not confined to the period of childhood. The person whom we call an *enfant terrible* may be an adult who utilizes the mechanism of pseudonaivety for a similar purpose or dynamic effect. The expression *enfant terrible* cannot be accurately translated into English. It expresses a bipolarity and contains a comical paradox. The epithet, *terrible,* is bestowed on the diminutive human being as an attribute pertaining to the strong and powerful adult. Thus, the French expression contains in a nutshell the principal dynamic and economic elements involved in this phenomenon.

As we have seen, *enfant terrible* behavior may be regarded as a special form of erotic aggressive unmasking and provocation of the adult in order to force him to let down for a fleeting moment the time-honored barriers between the infantile and the adult world of experiences. I shall apply Freud's fundamental concepts of *Jokes and their Relation to the Unconscious,* and refer to Ernst Kris' (1936, 1938b), Edith Jacobson's (1947a) and Annie Reich's (1949) important work on comic phenomena and laughter, in summarizing what seemed to me essential in the dynamics of *enfant terrible* behavior. The behavior of the *enfant terrible* shocks the adult audience's superego and disarms it. It carries away and seduces, as it were, the adult's ego into forsaking, albeit for a short span of time, its serene and austere reality standards, so that the adult regresses with the child into the abandoned carefree, impulse indulgence of childhood. The adult's ego, realizing immediately its uncontestable superiority, dissolves the initial shock into an amused smile or laughter. In turn, the child playfully experiences provocation of and deliverance from the danger of castration.

Inasmuch as the' *enfant terrible* mechanism is a social phenomenon, I believe we shall investigate genetically both the infantile and the adult partner's roles in this phenomenon.

Parents are thrilled to tell about the shocking and cute remarks and deeds of their small fry. This contains both an element of narcissistic exhibition and a desire to share such delightful experience with their adult friends. The parents usually take for granted the other adult's libidinous readiness for participation. Normal adults usually promote, with friendly condescension, their children's struggles and competitive effort at playing adult. Fairy tales make abundant use of the pleasurable effect of following up to victory the audacious efforts of a little boy or a youth against obstacles which seemed threateningly insuperable. There the little chap's triumph over the ogre contains the immortal topic of overcoming castration fear. In fact, the children's playful struggle in the growing-up process is an inexhaustible source of amusement to adults. This is due to their identification with the child's efforts to overcome castration fear, which the adult once experienced, and over which his ego achieved mastery. We know by observation that the adults who habitually tease children are those whose sublimation of castration fears is not solidly established.

Children, particularly boys between five and six, frequently resort to a play of hiding behind doors or underneath furniture, and startling the adult by jumping up like a living jack-in-the-box. They expect the adult to display shock and at the same time to show delight at the sudden emergence as a kind of happy reunion with the lively little man. This behavior belongs to normal phenomena of the phallic stage of development. It does not seem difficult to recognize in this sudden dashing up movement of the boy's or girl's body as a whole, the playful dramatization of an erection. Here, I think, traces of an identification of the whole body with the father's phallus can be detected as a normal transitional stage of development in both boys and girls alike. The same gestures and actions, however, may become connected with and be the expression of a conflict, and lose their playful quality through endless repetitiousness and exaggerated intensity. Incidents such as that of the analyst's child, quoted above, evoke pleasurable reactions in the adult audience only if the aggressive element is not too prominent and if repetition does not so increase the nuisance value of such behavior as to decrease the pleasures of comic condensation.

There are numerous economic and dynamic shifts in this *enfant terrible* behavior phenomenon which vary all the way from the occasional mischievous manifestations of analysts' children to harassment and continuous trickery. We can readily see how the quality of the terrible in behavior of this type may increase to such an extent that the *enfant terrible* ceases to be considered funny. Finally, the phallic aggressive nature of the *enfant terrible* behavior may become so intensified as to betray to the analyst by the very quality of its exaggeration the character of a *pathological defense mechanism.*

As illustration I should like to describe a child patient, six and one-half year old Maxie. He remained a diagnostic enigma to me until I understood the meaning of his conspicuously phallic, aggressive behavior. Before his treatment and during the first part of his analysis, Maxie succeeded in scaring away innumerable nurses whose departure had a comic quality of flight from a highly desirable position, because of a six-year-old urchin, hardly three feet tall. The only employee who stayed for any length of time was a rather old and matriarchal cook, whom Maxie's provocative behavior neither challenged nor seduced. This woman, resolute and firm, had known Maxie from infancy, and dealt with his aggressive advances by instinctively adopting his own methods of teasing and throwing him off balance by surprise actions. He was frankly scared of her, as he was of his father, a handsome, vain, and despotic young man, who seemed to lack any sense of humor. The mother was a brilliantly talented young artist, a sculptress, sensitive and narcissistic, and filled with a sincere wish to reconcile her turbulent professional, social, and marital life with her role as a mother. She felt threatened not only by Maxie's unmanageable conduct, but particularly by the increasingly apparent rivalry between her son and husband for her favors, a rivalry which she unconsciously instigated and maintained. Whereas earlier in life the little chap's precocious and pertinent remarks and gestures had filled the mother with delight, even if their timing was inopportune and embarrassing, lately Maxie had developed into a little tyrant in the home, whom neither his mother's bribes nor his father's hardness could bring to order. The youthful father's competition with his son was quite overt. He tried to suppress and subdue Maxie with his teasing, roughhousing and brutalization—including beatings. On the other hand, the boy challenged his father's privilege as his mother's erotic partner. He offered himself to the mother as a constant source of pleasure. He continually kept awake and satisfied this mother's narcissistic needs by his exhibitionistic display of his conspicuously gracious movements, by his unusual artistic skill both in drawing and in music, and by his precocious, witty intellectual brilliance. As a result, the mother considered Maxie's smile "irresistible as far as any woman was concerned." This and similar comments were characteristic of her attitude toward him.

The mother's infatuation with her son was obvious. She was one of those mothers who regard their little sons as part of their own persons (a penis) and treat him as though he were emotionally a part of her own ego even if physically separate. When the analyst once carelessly asked: "What is our child doing?," the mother was annoyed and angry.

The attitude of that type of mother and father towards their offspring is strikingly identical with the libidinous attitude which children maintain toward their own sexual organ as described by Ferenczi in his book *Thalassa* (1924), and also in his paper "Gulliver Fantasies" (1928). Ferenczi pointed out that the sexual organs, penis and clitoris, because they are reservoirs of pleasure for the whole individual, are cherished as a kind of second personality, which Ferenczi called the libidinous ego. Ferenczi also reminded us of the fact that frequently the male organ is given pet names of a very personal character as if it were an independent little personality. Bertram Lewin in his paper "The Body and Phallus" (1933), gave numerous illustrations of this tendency, among others how a phallus was portrayed clad as a little man.

It is a rather common occurrence for an adult to transfer to his child his own infantile libidinous overvaluation of the genital, especially his phallic exhibitionistic tendencies. To this erotic overvaluation the child reacts, according to the quality and quantity of the parent's attitude, and according to the stage of his or her libido and ego development. One of the possible transient results is that the child for a while indulges in the previously described body-erection play to his own and his parents' pleasure.

Maxie, at four and five years of age, was a typical *enfant terrible*. For example, when his parents had company at night, Maxie would get out of bed during the party, sneak into the living room undetected, hide behind a large chair and when the party was at its height, he would seize the most inopportune and embarrassing moment to suddenly make his appearance with a funny gesture or noise, shocking and throwing both hosts and guests off balance. He would say to Mr. X.: "You look just as funny as your necktie," referring to something which his parents had discussed disparagingly in his presence. His charm and pseudo-naive curiosity were so disarming, however, that the company felt genuinely amused by the little chap.

The older Maxie grew, however, the more annoying and the less tolerable became the repetition of such and similar behavior. The previously comical exhibitionistic behavior had changed by the time I met Maxie to a pathological defense mechanism.

My thesis is that a certain type of *enfant terrible* behavior *represents a defense mechanism in which the eroticized body*—the entire libidinous ego in Ferenczi's sense—*is identified with the threatening phallus of the father and is used to ward off overwhelming fear of castration*. This "defense by offense" reminds one of the defense mechanisms of "identification with the aggressor," described by Anna Freud (1936). I believe that the crucial failure prompting this particular mechanism of defense is a fixation of libido at the phallic stage of development. We studied in adult women patients such failures in concentrating and organizing the libido under the primacy of the genital organ because of intense castration fear. In the genesis of this mechanism, two equations seemed of paramount significance, namely, for the child, the equating of body with phallus, and for the parent, the equating of child with phallus. It would be challenging to speculate why in so many cases identification with the aggressor is used as a defense, while in my cases "pars pro toto," i.e. the erotic weapon of the aggressive male, was selected for identification.

About Maxie's early life the following could be elicited: He was a very much wanted and planned for child. Pregnancy and delivery were uneventful. He was not breastfed, because his father did not want the mother to be tied down so much and because he wanted her to preserve her youthful figure. The mother reiterated that Maxie got too much love and had his way too easily. Feeding and habit training were normal. He was showered with toys, shown off to the many guests who came to the house, almost from the day of his birth. He entered kindergarten before he was three and exerted himself to keep up with much older boys—an ambition which Maxie maintained ever since. However, there never seemed to have been any attempt to meet the child's emotional needs on his own level.

Instead he was pushed rather precipitatedly into an intense oedipal situation and his libido development was thereby accelerated toward the phallic phase. His father expressed affection by rough-housing, wrestling and using his superior strength on the boy "in a teasing way." In this area the father dealt with the boy as if he were his sibling, but on the other hand he expected his immediate obedience to abrupt commands, interrupting whatever the boy was doing. He tolerated no opposition and enforced his views by sheer physical power.

While the child was only four or five, Maxie's exhibitionistic behavior was enjoyed and tolerated. But as soon as the child used this mechanism to ward off his intense castration fear, it became intolerable to his environment.

I learned to know Maxie as an overly smooth, wiry and yet babyish-looking boy with peculiarly undifferentiated facial expression. His motor coordination, graceful movements and acquired bodily and manual skill were striking. His verbalization and all other kinds of performance ability were far ahead of his chronological age. Maxie considered his muscular strength and his *swiftness* as his main assets, and he had learned to combine this strength and speed with the startling effects of abruptness and suddenness into an unusually effective weapon. In school his scholastic records were outstanding.

After a very short period of appearing at his best in the analytic situation, Maxie played the role of the rude, sophisticated master, who orders around, abuses, and overpowers people whom he considers in any way weaker than himself. He was a bully. He accompanied his orders by shouting: "Make it snappy!" One had the feeling he was copying, trying out, and mocking, as it were, his father's methods of dealing with him.

Soon one trait became strikingly apparent in his analysis: He would play dominoes, or occupy himself with drawing in a most absorbed, calm way, and then suddenly, and with no transition, and without external cause or provocation, he would jump up with lightning speed, a living jack-in-the-box. He would start to throw things about and to work himself up with scolding and shouting. The arresting feature of such *spells* was the *complete detachment* of the child's person, which remained peculiarly aloof. Even as he proceeded in his erectile behavior, working himself up into violence, one had the impression that *his ego was not participating.* Affects came into this procedure only if he had to be restrained. Otherwise he would go back to some quiet occupation and then start the cycle all over again. The behavior strikingly suggested a dramatization of phallic erection by means of the whole body. The erection, that is, jumping up, etc., appeared a quasi automatic gesture detached from the rest of the personality.

At times, he definitely preferred exhibitionistic but *solitary* occupation. He drew and modelled. He forbade with great ado any glancing at his productions while they were in the making. When he had finished, he would jump up triumphantly and show them to me for a minute, and then usually would quickly destroy his work.

Two motives appeared in the first phase of his analysis: competition with the analyst, in which he settled any issue in his own favor either by provocative, open cheating or by "brute force."

The second apparent motive was a peculiar, erotic, aggressive provocation. Suddenly, during the treatment, in the course of some building, bombing and water play, he abruptly turned to me and said: "Undress!" In a series of sessions he would threaten and plead to see the analyst in the nude. Maxie's passionate preoccupation with nudeness seemed primarily motivated by his confusion about the anatomical sex difference. It was obvious from the analytical material that he had never accepted the fact that his mother had no "Mr. Wee-wee" as he called the penis. According to him it was hidden under the pubic hair. In this connection he also revealed his admiration for his mother, whom he considered much more efficient and clever than his father, and most of whose interests he shared, including her artistic talents. At this point he fantasied with glee, but with an unmistakable intensification of excited apprehension how he would surprise me while I was taking a bath. Thus he had to search another woman for a phallus, in order to deny castration. He was told again and again that women did not have a penis, and was given the assurance that what he needed was not to see men's and women's bodies but to tell and understand his worries about their bodies and his own. Thereafter his effort to impress me changed in the following way: His peculiar aloofness vanished. Instead, he tried to sneak under my skirt or to tickle me. He would try with a great display of charm to seduce me into giving the proof he craved which would reassure him about being a man in the face of his *desperate denial of castration.* He built himself up to a veritable miniature roué, bragging about his sexual exploits with the intention of seducing me. He lay on the floor and dreamily recited a little parody of a poem, which went like this: "The night was dark and hazy, and the Piccadilly Daisy took off her clothes, in front of me." His behavior at this point could best be described as that of a puppy in heat.

Maxie's perplexity in sexual matters *seemed intensified* by the following dilemma: The art studies which his mother generously shared with her little son, gave him an opportunity of looking at photographs of nudes, at Greek statues, etc. Here big men were represented with the genital organs of a little boy's size, and women with only a mons veneris and then again there were statues with a fig leaf which looked to him like pubic hair. His parents were progressive people who did not conceal their bodies in the bathroom, to which Maxie had free access. Maxie therefore had the opportunity of seeing and of observing his father's genital, which in size could not be compared with the organ he saw on statues, or with his own. He had ample opportunity of observing erectility—tumescence and detumescence phenomena.

Dr. Greenacre in her paper, "Vision, Headache and the Halo" (1947), pointed out the traumatic visual impression of the phallus which is at the root of the anxieties and clinical symptoms of certain patients. It is interesting to note that not only in Maxie's case but also in other cases, particularly in adults who showed the mechanism of identification with the aggressive phallus, there were unexpected visual and particularly tactile experiences of the motion and erectile tumescence of the membrum which seemed to have been the crucial traumatic factor.

Maxie tried to impress me by exhibiting his muscular strength, skill, and speed in *acrobatic stunts*. He began the following repetitious game: He piled up all the furniture in the children's room in a huge pedestal, and with catlike grace and rapidity climbed up, stood for a while and then toppled down. I was supposed to admire his ability to perform this stunt. His dramatization of himself as a huge erect penis was even more obvious.

At this time I heard from a relative of Maxie's how direct was his curiosity about the adult male genital and its size. He wanted to surprise this man in the bathroom, and to be present when he urinated. The same male relative related that one of Maxie's favorite games with his father, for which he asked again and again, was piggyback riding. He rode on his father's or uncle's neck and revelled in that elevated position. He would get quite excited and at times unmanageable. When I tried to discuss this topic with him Maxie warded it off violently. But finally he listened to my interpretation. Thereafter he began to change this manifestation and would come into the room with his fly open and a tumescent penis. He no longer needed to use only his whole body as phallus.

I now made use of a little monkey puppet to represent Maxie and started to move the monkey on my fingers. Maxie passionately tore it off my hand, and from that day on kissed and petted it as if it were something very precious and living. He came back to it for several days in the same affectionate way until he finally destroyed it by decapitation and threw the headless rag away. It was an amazing display of the little Narcissus Maxie loving the puppet-phallus. But he also castrated, and made the Maxie-monkey into a limp rag. Maxie brought out other material which revealed that he was worried about erection and detumescence and masturbation. He played with fire and showed considerable fear. His castration fears were now more clearly demonstrated.

At this time, one of his series of nurses had fainted in Maxie's presence just after she had warned him that she could no longer stand his tormenting. This and his father's ensuing anger started Maxie off on a phase of fantasies of phallic violence in his analysis. The way in which he would break into the treatment room if the doors were closed, made me fully realize that there was a graver pathogenic agent in his life than the one represented by his interest in nudes, and that while he could not see it clearly, he surmised it. It was not the bathroom, but his mother's bedroom, shut only when the father was home, which challenged Maxie. He liked to hide under his mother's bed, and despite his father's anger, he could not bear to stay hidden, but would shock his parents by suddenly appearing. It was evident from his material in the analysis that he witnessed intimacies and the primal scene.

Also, in the analysis his movements were utterly unpredictable, and because he was so small he could force his body in between and under furniture from which he would suddenly dash out. If he was held down bodily, he would yell and scream that the object of such attacks had injured him. Interpretation resulted in ferocious fantasies like the following: "I shall bring my Mexican knife, and I will cut off your head and then I will undress you." In later sessions he would declare, "When I grow up, I'm going to be a doctor" (and the analyst thought that a good sign) . . . "but I will not do doctor's work, I will undress people and pinch them, and I will be undressed myself."

This child, who developed from a charming *enfant terrible* into a little tyrant with a compulsion to shock people could no longer conceal his own anxiousness and his tendency to being excessively startled by any sudden and unexpected noise or motion. At such times he could not conceal his intense fright.

At the same time his overt sexual aggression toward the analyst changed and he began instead to fantasy about her. These fantasies he communicated to his mother. They dealt with the topic of the analyst being castrated. One day the mother called me up, utterly puzzled by Maxie's statement, "Dr. Mahler has lost an eye." This was a projection onto me of his repeated observation of one of my adult patients who had lost an eye and pointed to Maxie's fear that I was castrated and moreover that he was responsible.

In the analysis his corporal erotic aggressive attacks on the analyst were abandoned and replaced by stealing toy soldiers and other things from her and showing them off to his mother. He was told the meaning of such acts; that because I did not show him what he wanted to see, he took away my equipment instead. He reacted by beginning to play with the scissors, cutting out things, and provocatively announced that he would steal the scissors. When the analyst told him he could have them, he turned on her and exclaimed, "You are a liar," meaning, "You do not have a penis." He dashed to a desk fountain pen set and stuck the pen into the container with such fury that the point broke off.

Maxie brought out material which showed that he believed that by his magic power he had damaged all the nurses who left so suddenly. This was revealed through his fantasies about the analyst's being crippled. The episode of his nurse's fainting formed the basis of Maxie's fantasy that he could drive people crazy, make them faint and almost die. He asked me questions about death and about "being nuts," and pretended to be nuts himself. Women were castrated by the attacks of men. But in turn Maxie was afraid of the phallic woman. This became evident when Maxie fell ill with mumps and overheard or sensed concern about his testicles. He was then still behaving like an erectile phallus, abruptly jumping up and attacking people. But when confronted with an abnormally tall nurse, he gave up this performance and became subdued. After this his castration fear could be worked through in his analysis and he became calmer.

I have deliberately omitted the contributory oral and anal material in order to simplify the presentation of the specific mechanism which I wished to describe.

In concluding I would say that when Maxie's oedipus conflict reached its peak, its solution and partial repression was destined to failure because of the obstacles which stood in the way of his identifications with a desexualized image of his father, because of his intense fear of castration by him, and finally because of his mother's phallic seductive attitude. His strong identification tendencies with his mother added to the conflict. He had to resort to a fixation at the phallic level, using his entire body. This erotization of his entire body as phallic symbol was the result, as mentioned before, of special and traumatic visual, kinesthetic, and tactile experiences of tumescence-detumescence which occurred at a crucial stage of his development when latency should have set in. Narcissistic encouragement of his phallic exhibitionistic tendencies by his mother, including his ego talents, and corporal teasing and brutalization by his father, made Maxie identify not with the desexualized image, but with the sexual aggressive organ of the father and with the fantasied phallus of his mother.

Annie Reich's paper on "The Structure of the Grotesque-Comic Sublimation" (1949) describes an attempt at a solution of the castration complex through denial of castration by an exaggerated display of a damaged, and disfigured body in lieu of the genital. In the mechanism here described denial of castration is attempted by an exhibition of the erectile potency of the adult male using the body as a phallus.

In summary I would say that Maxie's case seems to illustrate with special clarity the clinical picture of those children whose latency period has been deferred because, as Aichhorn pointed out, for specific environmental reasons they were unable to identify with the desexualized ego ideal of the parent of the same sex.

Maxie also belongs to that large group of problem children whose mechanisms of defense are expressed through the function of motility (of acting out). His overt behavior when he was first referred for treatment, was such that for six months I was uncertain as to whether it indicated a possible psychopathy. To the environment the persistent motor aggression of these children has a nuisance value so acute that the ensuing reaction reminds us forcibly of Aichhorn's dictum that the term "delinquency" is more a social epithet than a considered psychiatric diagnosis.

In Maxie's case, however, the analysis of his aggressive behavior soon revealed the deep-seated anxiety for which his noisiness was a compensation. His case, therefore, might be said to have shifted from Aichhorn's category of neurotic delinquency to that of potential (latent?) delinquent neurosis as the ratio of alloplastic to autoplastic elements in his behavior changed during treatment.

Today Maxie is a well adjusted youth, attending high school where he has maintained a satisfactory record of excellent scholastic and social performance.

This history may serve as a simple illustration of a whole group of cases. It is a clinically verifiable fact that a large number of such children, who show noisy and aggressive conduct during an extended prelatency period, in later school age, develop a neurosis and not delinquency. Or else, if they undergo a successful child analysis, they later may make a good personal and social adjustment.

Part Two

PAPERS ON TICS

A PSYCHOANALYTIC EVALUATION OF TIC IN PSYCHOPATHOLOGY OF CHILDREN: SYMPTOMATIC TIC AND TIC SYNDROME

[1949]

Before we can study the tic as a psychopathological manifestation we must describe the phenomenon and attempt to define and delimit what we mean by this term, distinct from those manifestations which are loosely and interchangeably designated as "tics," "antics," "mannerisms," and "nervous habits." A tic is an involuntary motor automatism. We use the term "tic" to designate those sudden, abrupt and quick repetitious *involuntary* movements of a physiologically interconnected group or groups of muscles. These are movements which have, at the time of their execution, lost any obvious connection with their original purpose, so that their motivation and meaning is no longer self-evident. In common parlance "tics" and habitual autoerotic manipulations are not distinguished from each other. Yet there is always a grain of truth in popular language habits (Mahler 1945). It is often difficult, if not impossible, to draw the line between transient autoerotic habits, repetitious manneristic movements which are devoid of any symbolic meaning, and the true motor automatism which we call a "tic." In fact, tics in their true, "crystallized" form may be described as but condensations of the more slowly executed "nervous" motor mannerisms and gestures. In small children who are fidgety, jittery, and restless—in a word,

hyperkinetic—their inconstant and flighty nervous habit movements may develop later into swift, repetitious muscular jerks which
they are unable to control because they have become automatic, that
is, involuntary. The question then arises: Why do the transitory,
ticlike habit movements, so frequently found in small children,
disappear without residua at school age in most cases, while in others
they crystallize into the involuntary motor symptom of true tics?
Recent research on the phenomenon of tics revealed that "motor
neurosis" often originates through the interaction of hereditary or
constitutional factors and certain typical environmental attitudes,
which we shall discuss later.

The tic as a unit is a rather conspicuous and simple example of
neurotic symptom formation with an underlying conflict. In this
symptom formation the original, instinctual impulse, censored by
the superego, finds its outlet in motility through an unrecognized,
condensed ego function, that is, through a quick, more or less
involuntary, repetitious gesture or movement. The movement contains elements of discharge gratification and of punishment.

In children symptomatic tics may be observed in the process of
crystallization as a component part of those disturbances termed
primary or *reactive behavior disorders*. In such cases the tic is a sign
of an incipient neurosis, of the fact that there is an admixture of
neurotic traits in the primary or reactive behavior disorder. In
psychoanalytic terms, the fact that the "habit movements" are becoming more and more automatic and involuntary indicates a degree
of internalization of the conflict, that is to say, it marks the consolidation of the superego. From the above it follows that the tic may be one
of the symptoms of a psychoneurosis and indeed is a quasi prototype
of it.

Clinically and phenomenologically we may describe a *symptomatic tic* as consisting of a rather distinctly patterned and more or
less localized and constant single or multiple involuntary twitching.
Single or "isolated" tics, for instance, blinking and sniffing, may
mark *transient tension phenomena*. But they may also represent a
true neurotic symptom, the symbolic expression of a conflict in body
language. The tic symptom as such is classified in psychoanalytic
literature in the category of a pregenital conversion symptom.

The tic may be part of a *tic syndrome,* which belongs to an essentially different psychopathological category from the psychoneurotic tic (Pacella 1945). It is an organ neurosis of the neuromuscular apparatus. It follows the genetic and dynamic rules described by Alexander (1943) and Fenichel (1945b) as characteristic of psychosomatic disease. The *tic syndrome,* or "maladie des tics impulsifs" (Meige and Feindel 1907), consists of generalized diffuse motor automatisms of the entire striate musculature. The tic patterns appear in intermittent and migratory crops of tics, which develop frequently amidst general muscular restlessness, hyper- and dyskinetic disorders. The tic automatisms in patients with the tic syndrome may involve all parts of the voluntary (striate) muscle system, that is, the musculature of the face, neck, arms, hands, legs, abdominal wall, and the trunk. They may involve the muscles of phonation and vocalization, resulting in grunting, barking and yelling tics, which are pathognomonic of the disease, as is the automatic ideomotor emission of obscene utterances, condensed in the so-called coprolalic tics.[1] Different crops or sets of tic patterns may successively alternate with intermissions lasting days, weeks or months, particularly in the beginning of the disease. The tic automatisms may inundate the neuromuscular apparatus in such a way that the entire musculature is in paroxysmic motion practically without respite (except when the patient is asleep). Hence the condition is very often mistaken for Sydenham's chorea (St. Vitus' dance). The personality of this type of tiqueur has very constant and typical traits. It is characterized by a peculiar mixture of high intellectual endowment, emotional immaturity, and proneness to intermittent affectomotor outbursts (temper tantrums) (SPI:4; Mahler and Rangell 1943; Mahler, Luke, and Daltroff 1945).

We wish to emphasize that it is essential to distinguish between those tics which are a sign or symptom of various psychopathological conditions, and as such are only a symptom of these conditions, and the tics which in themselves represent the central and essential disturbance. In the latter case the tic pertains to a characteristic

---

1. There sometimes occur certain so-called echophenomena of motility, phonation, and speech, which are characteristic manifestations (Mahler and Rangell 1943).

psychosomatic disease of the motor system. If we do not differentiate between the tic as part of the symptom picture of a neurosis or psychosis, on the one hand, and organ neurotic "maladie des tics" on the other hand, we cannot come to uniform and valid conclusions.

Abraham (1921), for example, disagreed with the conclusions which Ferenczi put forward in his "Psycho-analytical Observations on Tics" (1921). Abraham was inclined to believe that tics could hardly be differentiated from compulsive obsessive acts. Since Abraham based his observations upon only one patient of a certain type, we may readily see how his opinions would differ from those of a number of other psychoanalytic observers, whose conclusions were based on a few patients with different types of tic. As Fenichel expressed it, "the term psychogenic tic covers a continuous series of links from conversion hysteria to catatonia" (1945a). Gerard (1946) to whom we owe a brilliant paper on this subject, also bases her conclusions upon selected cases, "which presented, as *part* of the symptom picture, a *simple tic*" [my italics] and described only those cases in which "the circumstances at the time of onset were known accurately." This selection restricted Gerard's scope of research to the symptomatic tic. It eliminated from her study, on the one hand, the generalized tics, and on the other, those insidiously developing, migrating tics, both of which are so characteristic of childhood. The present study is based on about sixty cases of tics in children of whom seven were analyzed and the rest thoroughly studied and followed up, over a period of from six months to eight years, as well as several adult cases (one of whom was analyzed by the author).

We propose to classify tics into the following categories:

Symptomatic tics, such as:

1. Passagère or transient tics, which indicate tension phenomena;

2. tic as a sign of a primary or reactive behavior disorder on the verge of internalization;

3. the tic as symptom of a psychoneurosis (anxiety hysteria, conversion hysteria, compulsive obsessive neurosis) or of a psychosis.

In contradistinction to these psychoneurotic, symptomatic tics:

4. the tic syndrome as an integral part of an impulse or character neurosis;

5. and, finally, the tic syndrome as a psychosomatic tic disease (a systemic organ neurosis of the neuromuscular system).

The last two categories of tics have a close relationship.

Most tics of adults, which we see in their frozen form, seem to have originated in childhood. Tics which we see in adults are of three kinds. There are those which as irreversible motor automatisms are the frozen traces of a psychoneurotic conflict in body language (conversion hysteria). There are those which represent a condensation and automatization of the compulsive action of an obsessive compulsion neurotic.[2] And finally, there are motor automatisms which are the residuals of a generalized tic disease of the "maladie des tics" variety.

Meige and Feindel in their classical monograph on *Tics and Their Treatment* (1907)[3] stated that "the tic subject suffers from a disturbance of motility." They also referred to the tiqueur's peculiarities of personality by such general statements as "tic is mental infantilism," and "tiqueurs are big, badly reared children who never learned to bridle their will and actions," etc. Meige and Feindel's statement that patients with tics suffer basically from a disturbance of motility, applies, according to our experience, essentially to the last two categories of tiqueurs, whereas patients with symptomatic tics, according to our experience, do not suffer from a "disturbance of motility." This would be self-evident if our thesis that the symptomatic tic is but *one* symptom of a psychoneurosis or a psychosis is correct. The tic disease, which we have described as the "tic syndrome," corresponds to the genetic, dynamic, structural, and economic principles of a systemic organ neurotic disease, with particular affinity, as it were, for the peculiarities of the infantile motor organization (*SPI*:4; Mahler and Rangell 1943). The tic syndrome, though rare in its full-fledged form, as "maladie des tics," is, in its milder form, a characteristic and specific psychosomatic disease of the loosely organized personality of the child.

A constitutional and also a predispositional deficiency of the ego in that part of its function which integrates motility, seems to be the

2. Ferenczi (1921) felt these were "accessory symptoms," demarcated appendages of the personality of the adult tiqueur.

3. Ferenczi (1921) based his treatise on tics on this monograph.

effective basis of generalized tic—the tic disease. In psychoanalytic terms the tic syndrome is the result of the ego's failure to integrate the psychomotor system into a hierarchy functioning under the ego's voluntary control. Purposeful, intentional motility should gradually gain uncontested control over the diffuse, impulsive, and affect-laden motility—characteristic of the infant and the small child (Homburger 1922, Landauer 1926). In such directed motility the ego is the central steering system, and its organic basis is the corticopyramidal part of the CNS which gradually assumes ascendency over the predominant subcortical psychomotor organization of the early years.

Ferenczi (1919) and Landauer (1926), as well as Fenichel (1928), were the psychoanalytic authors who investigated tics, automatisms and other motor phenomena in relation to the general problem of the development of motility.

The skeletal musculature is the executive organ of self-assertion and of defense. The striate musculature is the executive organ system for normal and pathological aggression in childhood (Freud 1905a). Whereas for the adult the principal organ of discharge of instinctual tension is the genital, the child's principal means of discharge is action, and thus the musculature has the leading role in preserving the libido-economic balance of the infantile personality. Fenichel in his paper "Uber organlibidinöse Begleiterscheinungen der Triebabwehr" (1928) expressed the opinion that inhibition of motor expression may cause a partial impediment of the ego's mastery of motility. As Fenichel, and recently Felix Deutsch (1947) pointed out, every suppression of the motor release of an affect leads to an increase of muscular tension.

The renunciation of instinctual impulsive acts is the essential aim of repression. The child is supposed gradually to repress the motor release of his autoerotic, object-erotic, and particularly his aggressive impulses (Freud 1911a). In chapter 4 we describe in detail how at the onset of the latency period, the psychomotor apparatus, even of the normal child, is all but overburdened by the need to prevent the objectionable oedipal cravings from being expressed in motility. The task of massive inhibition of motor expression at this period may cause a relative weakening of the motility controlling function of the ego. Ferenczi (1921) recognized this phenomenon. Many authors have shown, clinically as well as statistically, that the morbidity climax of systemic motor neuroses in children occurs between the ages of six to eleven years.

Because the child's motor system has a priority role as the executive of affective discharge, and because the child's psychomotor organization is one of a loosely integrated, hierarchic system (consisting of corticopyramidal and subcortical parts), one may say that the child's motor system seems to have a special proclivity for becoming:

a. a preferred system for primary hyper- and dyskinetic behavior disorders and repetitive impulsions in the prelatency period;

b. a preferential site of neurotic symptom formation at the school age (Ferenczi, Mahler);

c. and finally, the organ system of choice in certain cases predisposed to psychosomatic disease (hyperkinetic disease, paracortical motor syndrome [Bender and Schilder 1940], tic disease, hysteric chorea, and hysteroepilepsy).

The musculature is the legitimate discharge organ for surplus tension long after sphincter control is established, and long before the ego's mastery of motility is achieved. Before the massive repression at the age of five and six, and because of the ready response of the subcortical, more primitive motility, little children use their expressional and automatic motility in any "normal" situation in which surplus tension has to be released.[4] Repetitious, ritualistic, or autoerotic habit movements in little children are so common that hardly a child grows up without having had such transient manifestations.[5] If we were to follow the definition of "tic" proposed by Blatz and Ringland (1935), we should find, as they did, that tics occur in nearly 100 percent of children between two and five years of age.

4. Their whole body is in motion, and synkinesias are not limited to a few, agonistically selected muscles. Expressional gestural behavior is not confined to the mimetic and facial musculature (Homburger 1922, Kris 1940, Landauer 1927).

5. These habitual manipulations, loosely and falsely called "tic", may be regarded as repetitive discharge phenomena: examples are the habitual wiggling, foot-tapping, sniffing, blinking, frowning, and grimacing of little children.

These differ both phenomenologically and structurally from the crystallized true tics. They are neither so vigorous and quick in their mode, nor so spasmodic, ambitendent and intermittent in their sequence of muscular contractions, as are the true tics. They do not represent in condensed pattern conflicting tendencies (they are ego syntonic) (SPI:4; Homburger 1922). Between such habit movements there may be fluent transitions to the more complex and elaborate yet impetuous actions of little children, which we have described in former papers as impulsions. We have postulated in previous papers (SPI:4; Mahler and Rangell 1943) that there must be an organized superego plus the trigger effect of a sudden threat or trauma, or actual inner conflict in order to produce the crystallization of a true tic. As long as the superego is not solidly differentiated within the child's personality structure, tics are highly reversible semi-automatisms, and may cease if and when the strain is over.

PASSAGÈRE TICS OBSERVED *IN STATU NASCENDI*

The passagère, symptomatic tic, when observed *in statu nascendi*, is likewise susceptible to treatment. Anna Freud, in her book *War and Children* (1943) cites such a case in her beautiful description of Patrick, age three years and two months. Patrick's case illustrates the fact that under exceptionally trying circumstances and in the face of unusual perplexities, little children may be forced to condense motor actions, particularly gestural behavior, into merely symbolic expressions of the problem and conflict, which formerly they were able to play and act out repetitiously.

During analysis we followed the development of a habitual, spasmodic narrowing of the muscles around the eyes and those of visual accommodation in a little girl, Gloria, when she was four and a half and five. From the age of four the child was analyzed because of a rather severe phobia of wolves. Working herself up into a state of excitement was a characteristic feature of her case.[6] These excite-

6. Compare the case of Elmer, chapter 4.

ments usually culminated in temper outbursts and scenes or in night terrors. As analysis proceeded, Gloria's excited, diffuse motor manifestations of her anxiety gave way to more quiet, purposeful acting and playing out of her problems which centered around the question of the anatomical difference between her little brother and herself, and around the enigma of her origin. In her case this was an unusually perplexing problem since neither her mother nor her father were her original parents. The perplexities of her situation were first reflected in Gloria's frantic, repetitive play activity and compulsive questioning. After a period of repetitious questioning of her mother, which was distinguished from the usual period of intense curiosity by its frenzy and its intensity, Gloria's frantic activity became reduced. She settled down and tried to find out the answers for herself. She would sit on the window sill and ponder. She would ask, for instance, "Could I see the children who are on the other side of the ocean? . . . Why can't I look into the X's house?" Her little face would reflect the strain, the determined effort to penetrate obstacles in the way of her mental and physical vision. At such times she would contract her eye muscles, narrowing the opening of her eyelids. This ticlike habit, the straining of the accommodation of her eye, was the symbolic expression, her looking inward, her strenuous thinking. From then on, for a while, every time she wanted and could not quite understand or see, she manifested this condensed ticlike gesture.

Such a pattern of neuromuscular innervation easily could have become a psychoneurotic symbolic tic, a motor automatism, to which the ego resorts as defense under the circumstances described by Gerard (1946).[7] These and similar cases enabled us to observe the formation of the tic, which seemed to have the following genesis: The little child becomes aware of his parents' disapproval of the motor expression (in speech and behavior) by which he has been acting out certain impulses and affective problems. He then tends to suppress or disguise the free expression of these desires. He tries to hide his gestures and actions by automatically speeding up the

---

7. We may tentatively suggest that Gloria's well-coordinated, gracious motility may have exempted her from developing motor symptomatology, even if psychoanalysis had not helped her in resolving her conflicts.

sequence of motions, and/or by executing the innervations surreptitiously. Thus, acting out may become condensed to a mere symbol of motions, and since such a condensation is no more apt to relieve tension, it also loses its discharge function, and may establish a vicious circle in the child's libido-economic balance. As soon as an organized superego renders the conflict largely independent of the environment, the symbolic motion becomes a true neurotic symptom.[8]

Therefore, if the intensity and duration of such habitual movements in little children is excessive, such ticlike manifestations should concern us inasmuch as they may be the first presenting symptom of *a.* an incipient neurosis or *b.* a so-called tic diathesis, the sign of a constitutional predisposition to motor disturbances (cf. Boenheim 1930).

The question of tic predisposition

We discussed the point that the crystallization of a tic within the matrix of a behavior disorder may mark an incipient neurosis and is frequently the first sign of it. It seems that the persistence of such a symbolic tic, used as defense-innervation whenever anxiety arises, depends upon a hereditary predisposition for tics which has been found in both types of child tiqueurs by many previous observers (Boenheim 1930, Meige and Feindel 1907).[9]

We may definitely state, however, that the constitutional habitus

8. The movement sequence becomes abrupt, "ambitendent" in its selection of the muscle groups, in order to express in gesture both aspects of the conflict: doing and undoing (cf. Kris 1940). Flexion and extension, opening an orbicular muscle and closing, or narrowing it (eye, mouth, etc.) follow each other rapidly. By relegating the movement pattern to the unconscious strata of the ego and by repressing the ideational representation, or the libidinal cathexis which the motion carried, the tic becomes automatic and thus escapes from the ego's voluntary control (cf. Hartmann 1922).

9. In the histories of even the monosymptomatic tiqueurs we often found other tiqueurs in the ascendent or collateral line. Whether these children (who are characterized by their imitative, iterative and exhibitionistic traits) merely copied these examples, or whether the same hereditary taint caused the symptom in several members of the same family, is difficult to determine.

as well as the genesis of tic in our two essential categories of tiqueurs was basically different.

THE PSYCHONEUROTIC TIC SYMPTOM

Tic as a conversion symptom

Irma was the only child of German Jewish parents. Her early development was uneventful. She started school in her native country. The teacher commented on her playfulness and lack of serious concentration. The child was eight years old when reverses entered in her life. Her father was arrested and put into a concentration camp; she and her family were persecuted. She and her mother had to flee from the country to save their own lives, leaving the father behind. During emigration there was another traumatic event in that the mother forgot the keys to her trunks, so that she had to return to the border in order not to lose that modest part of their property they were permitted to take along. Irma overheard somebody cautioning her mother, "If you return to the border, they will keep you there." The child was left with relatives, and although the mother returned, she went through an agony of fear. From that time, she was terribly afraid of losing her mother, especially in the train to their point of embarkation. In still another country in Europe they met further reverses. Then Irma began to show manneristic movements with her feet, and blinking. On her arrival in this country she suffered from *pavor nocturnus;* because of this and the crammed quarters they occupied, the child managed to share her mother's bed. Her mother went to work early in the morning. The child could hardly wait for her return in the evening to tell her the happenings of the day, and could not stop her own questioning and logorrheic recounting of her daily experiences. In the morning, before her mother left for her job and while the child was getting ready for school, Irma demanded that her mother comb her long hair and braid it. She was always tempted to tell her mother just a few more things at this time in order to keep her company just a little bit longer. This upset and angered her mother. Sometimes she could not help handling Irma's braids rather roughly, so that scenes and crying were the rule—and the braids literally became the symbol of both the bond and the emotional conflict between the mother and the child. After a long while the father joined them. His return made Irma feel strange at no longer having her mother's undivided attention. She had developed a habit of slowly but repetitiously turning her head as if looking after her mother when the latter stepped out of the house. Later the head-turning became a habit, lost its obvious and actual connection with the original motivation in that it was not performed only on the occasions when someone left, but at any odd time, and the movement was repeated two or three times in a row.

Irma's mother always was rather strict with her, yet she could not persuade her daughter to leave her over night until finally, at the age of twelve, Irma herself decided to conform to the way of life of her classmates and to spend part of her summer vacation in a camp. The only obstacle to this plan was her long braids which were her pride and her family's also, and which were the rationalized focus of her dependence on her mother. This dependence, moreover, was pointed out, and she was increasingly teased about it by her aunts and other relatives: who would braid her hair in camp? Hence, in an impulsive mood, Irma decided to have her braids cut off, so as to become independent of her mother's help before going away. After this "heroic" deed Irma went to camp. There she felt very lonesome and depressed; her menstruation started at this time. When Irma returned, her mother saw with dismay that she shook her head violently. The tic was a head-turning and "braid-hitching" tic,[10] the structure of which was determined by Irma's conflicting emotional tendencies: her wish to bind her mother to herself, her defense against her dependence, together with many other overdetermining factors, such as her decision to cut off the braids, the coinciding of the menarche and her masturbatory conflict in which her mother was protector against masturbatory impulses as well as the feared agent of her strict conscience, of which she tried to rid herself.

This symptomatic tic was amenable to psychoanalytic treatment

10. This action represented a combination of Irma's former head-turning tic with another movement, namely a muscular weighing of her lost braids, a loss which she thus repetitiously reexperienced.

in the manner described by Gerard. In Irma's case the tic was a typical hysteric conversion symptom, the symbolic expression of a conflict in body language.

Tic as a condensed compulsive gesture or action

Herbert was nine years old when he first came for consultation about a rather long-standing blinking and arm tic. The latter consisted of a two-or-three-times-repeated, rapid, wiping motion of the forearm and hand. Herbert's personality was characterized by traits found in compulsive individuals. He was meticulous, circumstantial, and fussy. He set high standards for himself in terms of achievement, and was very competitive with his siblings for the favors of his parents. His habit training had been strict and he was already clean at the age of sixteen months. His parents described how early Herbert knew right from wrong, and how he argued his way through early infancy instead of fighting. He could express his aggression in temper tantrums only. Herbert left the analytic treatment before his analysis could have succeeded. However, the structure of his tics was a most instructive example of the condensation of compulsive acts. They symbolized Herbert's psychosexual conflict on an anal-sadistic and masochistic level. Both tics referred to the same topic, namely his struggle between his scoptophilic, aggressive tendencies and exhibitionistic, passive tendencies. The one tic served to show his mother the dirt one could make to spite her and also wiped it away to prevent her from seeing it. It therefore represented his defiant soiling tendency, as well as his excessively compliant cleanliness, and his great ambivalence.

The examples of Irma and Herbert illustrate the genetic, dynamic, and structural nature of the symptomatic tic. The same principles apply to the symptomatic tic in an anxiety neurosis and also in some cases of child psychosis, in which neurotic defense mechanisms are predominant (Mahler, Ross, and De Fries 1949).

The question of "Tic Diathesis" and of "Somatic Compliance"

In the cases described the tic movements were understood as the symbolic expression of a conflict. If in the course of development or through psychoanalytic treatment the ego succeeded in giving up this method of defense before complete automatization of the involuntary movement patterns rendered the tic irreversible (somatically anchored), then the tic was resolved. If not, the tic persisted, demarcated from the ego, and appeared as an accessory symptom, an appendage, as it were, and remained unresolved, even if psychoanalysis of the adult succeeded in curing the psychoneurosis (Ferenczi 1921). Whereas a certain "tic diathesis" is frequently found in the families of symptomatic tiqueurs (Boenheim 1930), *it is an entirely different kind of "organic compliance"* which characterizes individuals suffering from the *tic syndrome*, as we shall describe below. In the initial tics we still may discover some symbolic meaning.[11] In the beginning they may seem to be built according to the psychodynamic principles of the symptomatic tic.[12] But, according to our experience, in many cases in which *multiple* tics long persist or migrating crops of tics pervade the general voluntary muscle system, the ego does not get enough respite to organize the defense mechanisms necessary for the establishment of a systematized psychoneurosis of the hysteric or the compulsive type.

In "Formulations on the Two Principles in Mental Functioning" (1911a) Freud stated that the infant, as long as he acts according to the pleasure principle, tries to discharge tension immediately and experiences any excitement as "trauma" which is responded to by uncoordinated discharge movements. Overcoming this state depends on two factors. The first is the physiological capacity for mastering motility. This occurs when the intentional corticopyramidal motility gradually gains leadership over the subordinate subcortical affectomotility. This results in an exchange of the discharge role of the psychomotor system for the role of the executive system of purposeful actions. The second factor in overcoming immediate muscular discharge of tension is the growing ability of the ego to

11. Though very often the meaning in these tics is a secondary use of the movement pattern for rationalization.

12. Edith Jacobson remarks (1946, p. 343) that in some cases it is hard to define to what extent the symptoms . . . should be regarded as psychoneurotic, as psychosomatic, or as a mixture of both.

postpone immediate reaction—because reality requires it—and to accept the interpolation of thinking, that is, trial acting—between the impulse and its execution (Ferenczi 1919, Freud 1911a). Children who later develop a tic syndrome showed in their histories an impediment in each of the two factors which Freud mentioned as prerequisites for the successful transition from the pleasure to the reality principle.

Two clinical findings of the research on patients with tic syndrome are important in this connection. First, the fact that of thirty-nine patients with tic syndrome studied, thirty-seven were males and only two were girls.[13] Second, 50 percent of our boy tiqueurs belonged to the body type which one might call pseudo-Froehlich habitus.[14] They were markedly obese and had feminine distribution of the subcutaneous fat tissue. These two findings pointed in the direction of a constitutional, inherent (maturational) deficiency of the kinetic and, secondarily, the integrating function of the ego (Hartmann, Kris, and Loewenstein 1946). The theoretical discussion of these findings follows below.

In children with a tic syndrome the characteristic behavior traits in preschool age were found to be urgency, impetuousness, drivenness (Landauer 1927) and undirected violence with a lag in sustained effort and persistence. Such children showed an initial temperamental display of enthusiasm—then distractibility and readiness to quit in despair, or in fury. A lack of endurance and tenacity, coupled with pseudo-stubborn negativism was another characteristic feature of their personality. The motor automatisms, the multiple migrating and subsequently persistent tics then seemed to have set a vicious circle which caused a secondary developmental weakening of the synthetic function of the ego (cf. *SPI*:5), so that the multiple persistent tics became a part of a subsequent general "motor neurosis," in which we found the principles of a psychosomatic system or organ

13. In representatives of symptomatic tics no prevalence of the male child could be elicited.

From the thirty-nine cases all patients with organic (encephalitic) involvement were excluded.

14. Their genitals seemed undersized because of the obesity. This was spurious. Only six boys suffered from chryptorchidism at school age.

neurosis to have become operative (Alexander 1943, Fenichel 1945b). The ego's failure to master motility and action became particularly evident at the beginning of the latency period. These children's proneness to affectomotor outbursts, to temper tantrums at the slightest frustration, betrayed their state of affective tension, particularly their *suppressed aggression,* and their inability to tolerate frustration. The psychological effect of chronic suppression of aggression led to general and multifocal tension phenomena in the musculature, with restlessness, hyperkinetic or dyskinetic manifestations. When, subsequently, *early multiple tics pervaded* the general voluntary *muscle system* of the child, this marked an *ego defect* which eventually *culminated* in either *a. character neurosis* of the *impulse* neurotic type with *interwoven tic syndrome,* or *b.* in a *psychosomatic organ neurosis* of the neuromuscular apparatus: the *tic disease ("maladie des tics").*

IMPULSE NEUROSIS WITH TIC SYNDROME

We first became aware of the kinship between the clinical picture of impulse neurosis and the "maladie des tics" in the course of the psychoanalysis of a boy patient, Elmer, who showed impulsions and intermittently recurring crops of tics. Elmer had suffered from a disturbance which one could best term: impulsions or impulse neurosis. From time to time he displayed multiple tics, at other times impulsive, aggressive and obscene behavior which seemed volitional, that is, semivoluntary. Elmer's impulsive actions and his tics were highly interchangeable, so that we could study the mechanism of his hyperkinetic, impetuous versus tic manifestations like a laboratory experiment. The impression of the close relationship between the two kinds of symptoms was verified by a number of subsequent analyses and long-term psychotherapeutic observation of similar cases.

The close connection between impulsions and motor neurosis was demonstrated in the case of Johnnie, who was nine when he was admitted to our children's ward. For the past three years he had been manifesting a tic formation involving his eyes, shoulders, neck, hands, arms, and legs. These symptoms were accompanied by unruliness, unmanageable impudent behavior toward his mother and father, and overt, erotic assaultiveness towards his sisters as well as towards other girls.

Fixation at the oral level was evidenced by Johnnie's nursing from the bottle till the age of three. An attempt to wean him was made at about the age of fourteen months, but with the advent of a younger sibling the child rebelled. Consequently he was permitted to go on using the bottle until he was three. Anal fixation was due to "very difficult and prolonged" toilet training begun very early and strictly enforced. The toilet training commenced when Johnnie was about seven months old. His mother said, "He was very dirty and difficult to train. It took me about two years before I had him broken. I would put him on the toilet and then he would do nothing and then get down and deliberately defecate on the floor in front of me."

From two and a half to three and a half Johnnie began to have severe temper tantrums, and would bang his head against the wall. At the same time he had great fear of thunder and lightning. At three he successively contracted whooping cough, chicken pox, measles, and mumps. At this time he also developed a squint of the right eye. Following a tenotomy at the age of four, Johnnie's general hypermotility and restless, fearful and temperamental behavior became worse.

The child grew up in a rigidly religious environment, which from a very early age habitually called on God's justice and punishment for every misdeed.

In spite of Johnnie's violent aggressiveness it was apparent from the very beginning of his social development that he was a poor mixer and that he never liked to play with boys, but only with girls.

At the age of six he was enrolled in a parochial school. At the same time he became initiated into sexual play by another boy. He was severely reprimanded and threatened with punishment. All of the religious fears were invoked to subdue this interest. He was subsequently found exposing himself to his sisters. During his sixth year Johnnie was observed to be overtly masturbating. His parents were greatly alarmed. He was told that whenever he did a bad thing, he was nailing Christ on the cross. Johnnie's nervousness reached a peak when he was six years of age. He also developed generalized muscular twitchings, which were falsely diagnosed as St. Vitus' dance. The parents made the child acutely aware of his condition and frequently threatened him with punishment if he did not stop. From then on he went about provoking girls, lifting up their skirts and exposing himself.

We find in Johnnie's anamnesis several noteworthy features. He showed early rebellion against strict habit training, and precocious "cruel" but patchy superego development. Fixation at the anal level and precocious superego development render the person susceptible to the establishment of an obsessive compulsion neurosis. However, in Johnnie's case, other, more specific etiological factors competed with these fixations. One was the child's strong oral fixation, the other was his impetuous anal and genital exhibitionism. Concomitant with these was his narcissistic overcathexis of the neuromuscular apparatus, resulting in an increased motor urgency.

When we met Johnnie, he presented the picture of a severely disturbed boy. Only at a very superficial evaluation could his symptomatic behavior fall into the category of primary conduct disorder. The dynamics of his symptomatology placed him in the category of impulse neurosis with a mixture of anxiety symptoms and pseudo-compulsive acting-out mechanisms with interspersed tics. He gradually evidenced definitely paranoid traits with abundant use of the mechanism of projection.

Johnnie was destructive, but if attacked by the boys, he did not defend himself by adequate aggression; "If I fight, God will suffer—unless there are four to one against me." He also expressed a fear of being jailed or otherwise restrained in his freedom of action and began a compulsive preoccupation with locking and unlocking doors, taking and keeping the doctor's key, so as to have possession of the tool with which to incarcerate other people or to set them free.

When Johnnie was asked what he thought was wrong with him, he answered: "I have nerves and I shake my arms and head." He also developed the idea that if his uncle watched his tics constantly, one by one, and scolded him, they would cease. This relative was his favorite uncle and "lots of fun." This external superego and ego extension was the one to whose magic power he wished to turn for help in his predicament.

He also expressed the opinion that his involuntary automatisms might have started "the time they poured water on me. . . . They poured water on my head when they baptized me." He also related in this connection that his mother thought that whenever he did something wrong, he was nailing Christ to the cross. The next association was his liking to lock himself up into the attic room whenever he visited his favorite uncle's house, so that the "uncle would be locked out of the room." In that room his aunt kept interesting old junk, which Johnnie liked to see and play with, and his uncle was thus prevented from throwing out those things. So, on the one hand, Johnnie wanted his uncle to cure his tics by watching and scolding him, and on the other, he locked himself in to indulge in his autoerotic activities without being disturbed by onlookers. The conflict is clearly discernable between his *exhibitionistic versus scoptophilic tendencies,* his *desire to be watched and scolded,* prevented from being bad, and his *impulse to do bad things* (masturbation, etc.) *which might nail,* that is, *painfully immobilize* Christ on the cross. This alternation culminated in his difficulty to bear any motor impulse in abeyance, and finally, in his ambitendent tics.

Elmer and Johnnie used interchangeably provocative erotic aggressive behavior, consisting of intensive peeping and of swearing, bathroom language, grimacing and other exhibitionistic performances, and the condensed symptoms thereof: the tic syndrome. With the former they sought to infuriate, belittle, embarrass, and disturb people. With this provocative aggressive behavior they tried to ward off their passive submissive tendencies which were clearly understood from the analytic material. The provocative impulsive behavior was aimed at being attacked and quelled by a father figure. This was evident, for example, from Elmer's fixation to the traumatic event of his father's return from a long trip, when Elmer was about five years old. The father was told that during his absence Elmer had been a bad boy, and particularly that he was constipated. Thereupon the father overpowered Elmer and gave him an enema. During analysis Elmer fantasied and acted out his fear and masochistic expectation of being attacked from the rear. His impulsive sticking his finger into the rectum of his playmates in kindergarten was later exchanged for an inordinate revulsion against the anal masturbation allegedly practiced by his schoolmates. The counter-part to the many operations, accidents, and body traumata in Elmer's life was his cruelly sadistic fantasies and dreams about mutilated bodies, dismembered extremities cooking in boiling water, and blood and murder.

The clinical course of Johnnie's narcissistic disturbance was also characterized by the unpredictable alternation of impulsive and tic-free intermissions of weeks and months, with periods of "unruly" impulse-ridden behavior, with or without multiple tics. During their course we could observe the ego's struggle and its increasing failure in personality integration.

The impulsive, aggressive, erotic behavior was the diffuse, amorphous manifestation of the *same basic affective attitude* which we found *underlay the tic syndrome* of this type and also of the tic syndrome of the organ neurotic type.

Psychoanalysis of tiqueurs with impulse neurotic character formation revealed that these impulse-ridden children did not succeed in erecting ego defenses necessary for systematized psychoneurosis. They did not even succeed in erecting solid psychosomatic barriers, massive and organized enough for psychosomatic organ neurosis. Fenichel (1945a) pointed out that, "Impulse neurotics tend to react to frustrations with violence." The main conflict of the impulse neurotic is one between "a tendency towards violence and the tendency to suppress all aggressiveness through fear of loss of love." In the impulse neurotic tiqueur, it seems, violent oral and phallic aggression is ineffectually prohibited by the patchy superego.

Their ego was continually carried away by affective actions (Hartmann 1947) for which Elmer and Johnnie, for instance, felt guilty and expected punishment. They were torn between this guilt feeling and their pent-up erotic, aggressive impulses, which threw them into a chronic state of conflict. The ego's failure to interpolate trial acting between impulse and action, on the one hand, and impulse and automatic discharge motility (tics) on the other, had a seriously disorganizing effect upon these patients. They resorted to the abundant use of projection in order to defend themselves, and thus may have proceeded in the direction of psychosis. They were prone to paranoid and depressive moodswings.[15] One of the main

---

15. Fenichel 1945a, p. 369. Cf. footnote, p. 28.

difficulties in Elmer's analysis was the handling of his projection mechanism: Not he, but his mother ought to change, or should be analyzed. Not he, but the maid started arguments. Not he, but another pupil was responsible for the teacher's anger. Everybody was mean and unjust to Elmer.

Also, Johnnie's paranoid projection mechanisms were prominent. He could not confine himself for any length of time either to the display of his semi-voluntary grimaces and his logorrheic accusations. His mother and sisters were blamed for his misbehavior in school, etc. "My sisters are making trouble, my mother opens her big mouth, I get blamed for everything, and my father wallops me when he comes home. He has an awful temper."

In a typical psychotherapeutic interview Johnnie tried to destroy toys; he said he "just didn't like them," and began to slam the toy soldiers into the cabinet. He then pounded clay with vigor all over the room. All the while he sang shrilly, and increased the volume whenever conversation was attempted. Finally he sat down and said, "Take my mother's c——— and throw it away. It's no good." "It has hairs on it." "Can you stop me from getting any?"

Johnnie's struggle against his very marked feminine identification tendencies, his fear of growing up to be an adult man, took the above described frantic, inconsistent form. One week he acted out his conflict by unacceptable conduct in school, swearing at his sisters and mother, and attacking them violently so as to provoke his mother into having to report his behavior to his father. Then Johnnie would receive his beating. Another week a crop of tics prevailed.

His mother was alarmed by the extent of Johnnie's impulsiveness: "It comes on so sudden." Grandmother says she would not allow Johnnie in her house if he were older, for fear "he would pick up a knife." He threw a bolt at his five-year-old sister and cut her badly on the temple. It bled profusely. Johnnie was remorseful and behaved well for awhile. Then he again wrote "obscene" notes to girls in the class.

Whereas Johnnie bullies and bosses his sisters, he will not even try to join the boys' competitive games. He wants to play with teddy bears and dolls, even steals the doll out of his sister's bed after she is asleep at night.

His sexual confusion is shown by his graphic and somewhat provocative description in the presence of his aunt how a woman's stomach "gets big and hard before she has a baby."

ORGAN NEUROSIS—"MALADIE DES TICS"

The vicissitudes of the erotic, aggressive drives, the mode of the ego's defenses and the structure of ego and superego differed in the two types of tic syndrome. The change in the behavior of children with organ neurotic tics at the onset of the latency period was very conspicuous. The impulsive tiqueur continued to be hyperkinetic, obtrusive, violent and destructive, or even antisocial, beyond latency. In the organ neurotic tiqueur, however, at the latency period one usually found that the noisy aggression, hyperkinetic impulsions, the pseudoactivity and demonstrative behavior changed and gave way to an overcompliant, ingratiating affability and submissive passivity with cropping up of tics. The organ neurotic tiqueur's syndrome appeared in a markedly *hypokinetic,* inhibited, often depressed, anxious and submissive personality, which seemed impoverished in emotional modulation and expressional capacity, and which had no free locomotor and athletic pursuits and avoided the competitive games of contemporaries.

As illustration we would refer to the cases of Freddie (Mahler and Rangell 1943) and Pete (Mahler and Gross 1945), and cite the case of seven-year-old Henry.

From the time he was three years old Henry's impulsive behavior had changed insidiously into tics. They involved successive crops of automatic movement patterns of his face, neck, trunk and extremities, and the muscles of vocalization, and finally invaded the ideomotor area with coprolalic four-letter utterances. Henry, the only child of his parents, was an obese, flabby-looking little boy, awkward and timid, with few spontaneous gestures, and with signs of depression.[16] His intelligence was superior.[17] In pre-latency Henry had displayed entirely opposite behavior picture. He had been an impetuous, demonstrative, outgoing, affectionate, happy and very noisy little child.

Throughout pregnancy Henry's mother had very severe nausea and vomiting; she stayed indoors most of the time and had frequent fainting spells; in the course of one of these she severely hurt her spine and shoulder.[18] Pregnancy, delivery, and Henry's earliest infancy were uneventful. However, at three to four months he developed a severe sore throat and from that time on vomited "all of his food." This continued until he was two years of age. When he was two and a half, an A and T was performed, mainly to eliminate the cause of vomiting. That Henry interpreted this operation as a punishment was subsequently shown by his behavior. His mother said, "The removal of his tonsils did not stop the vomiting. He used to raise a scene from then on and vomit." The mother feels that vomiting was used by the patient when he encountered unsatisfactory situations. Toilet training was begun at seven months and achieved without difficulty. But in the area of anal habit training the mother also infantilized and overprotected the child. Fixation in the anal sphere was indicated by the mother's constant watching over her son's excretory functions. She used suppositories almost daily to "give him the habit of moving his bowels once a day." The patient would sit on the toilet from a half hour to an hour at a time, and even when he was seven his mother would accompany him to the toilet and forbid him to flush the water before she had inspected the bowel movement. The boy stated, "Mother always wants to see if I make

16. We may state that whereas the symptom tic is used by the ego to ward off anxiety (Gerard 1946), the impulsions and the tic syndrome (condensations of the violent impulsive actions) serve the purpose of warding off depression and deep narcissistic fear of ego disintegration (Landauer 1927, Wilder and Silbermann 1927). Cf. Fenichel (1945a, p. 369).

17. All children with organ neurotic tic syndrome (except those with organic brain damage) had an I.Q. which placed them into the bracket of superior intelligence; the impulsive tiqueurs I.Q. was somewhat lower.

18. We saw conflict about free movement in the environment of practically everyone of this type of tiqueur.

enough." By means of the same affective attitude which had produced his habitual vomiting—namely, a distorted expression of suppressed rebellion—the patient now developed chronic constipation and finally hemorrhoids, which at times resulted in rectal bleeding.[19] This established another vicious circle in the "appersonated" mother-child behavior pattern.

The mother stated that during his first three years Henry had a happy, outgoing disposition. He was very affectionate and very emotional. He talked out loud even when playing alone. He always played noisily. When cautioned, he would try to reduce the noise, but promptly forgot and became noisy again. He was alert and full of questions, but was—as far as could be ascertained—never particularly graceful or deft with his body and/or in small muscle coordinations. He was quite *highstrung*. The mother dates the onset of the child's symptoms with her own hospitalization for a perirectal abscess, when Henry was about four years old. *The mother and child's interdependence seemed to have been quite extreme at all times.* During the period in which he vomited regularly at night, he at first always gave a cry for his mother. His father hit him frequently and his mother yelled at him occasionally. At such times Henry would become quite stubborn and determined.

The first set of motor symptoms developed at three or four years and consisted of manneristic movements of his index finger, flinging his arms about and jumping up and down. These rituals were exchanged for another set of more condensed tic movements: blinking of the eyes, twisting of the legs and throwing of the head. Between the different sets of symptoms there was usually a short period when he was free of tics. However, as he grew older, each successive crop of tics lasted longer, and "lately he is practically never free of them." The formerly noisy and outgoing child had become increasingly shy and timid. "He became fearful of other children and never fights back, and he has occasional outbursts of temper tantrums" (Mahler 1944, Mahler, Luke, and Daltroff 1945).

His present condition, which we shall describe briefly, became

19. The psychodynamics of his constipation and rectal bleeding were reminiscent of principles described by M. Sperling (1946) in the case of psychosomatic ulcer formation.

more severe in connection with the mother's illnesses and a series of accidents. The mother stated, "His trouble seems to center around me. I ought to get well and then maybe he will."

The conflict between longing for personal—particularly motor—freedom versus fear of injury and loss of love, was beautifully expressed in Henry's stories and fantasies: "Once upon a time there was a boy. He was going to fall off a cliff but there was a hole near the cliff and he saved himself. He wanted to know how far it was to the bottom." We see both the conflictful sexual curiosity and the peeping tendency struggling with the fear of castration; we also see the fantasy of the danger of motor freedom. "There was a big tree which he tried to chop down. After he chopped it down he pushed it over the cliff and then he was going to go back home." He is powerfully, aggressively active in his fantasy. "In the morning he got up and went to find more trees by the cliff. On the way there he fell into another hole but he got out." The very hole which saved him once became a dangerous trap in this version. "Then he saw a big tree nearby, so he picked up a big log and threw it at the tree and both logs fell off the cliff." Why did he throw them down? "So that if he wasn't looking and went near to the cliff, he wouldn't bang into them." Banging into the log symbolized the obstacle, the father, in Henry's close relationship with his mother. Thus the obstacle and not the boy, fell off the cliff. "The next day the boy went away to the city and went to the park and started to chop down all the trees, then he started to play ball on the grass with his father."

Henry had clearly identified himself with a puppy.[20] "The next day Dick [his fantasy—alter ego] bought a puppy—his mother said he could—and he went to the park with the puppy and played ball. One time the boy threw the ball so far the puppy had to go in the pool to get it." Would Henry like a puppy? "No, well, I would like one, maybe, when I got a little bigger. I would have to keep it in my room. Mother used to sleep in my room. But now she sleeps in the dining room. So now the puppy could sleep in my room in a little bed. Mother says when I am thirteen, I can have one." We see how timid and ambivalent Henry became in his relationship with his mother.

20. In many tiqueurs we found identification with a pet animal.

Another fantasy: "One night Dick was sleeping when the dog heard a noise, so he told Dick and Dick got up and looked out the window and saw a little parrot. It was singing all night long. Dick finally shot it, so it couldn't sing any more." The sleeping arrangements in Henry's house made the auditory witnessing of the primal scene unavoidable. In his fantasy Henry kills again, in his violence toward the singing parrot.

The conflict between active aggression, motor independence and bodily anxiety is expressed in the following fantasy: "The next day Dick took the dog to the park and threw a ball for Don, the dog. Don had to run very far after it, the ball hit a tree, bounced back and hit Don on the nose. He got the ball and brought it back to Dick who threw it again, and this time Don, the dog, caught the ball right in his mouth. The next day they got up early and they heard a horse. They couldn't see where the noise came from but finally decided the horse was in the barn and someone was trying to shoot him. [Why?] They didn't like him. They were bad men. Dick brought the horse into the living room. The next day they all went to the park together—Mother, Father, Dick, and Don—and played ball together. The next day Dick was already ten years old." (Nearer to thirteen, when he will be permitted to have a puppy.) Finally the bad boy who ventured to stray away from his mother, is punished: "There was a house, and in the house lived a little boy, two dogs and a cat. The dog and cat went to hunt for food, they saw a little boy sitting in the woods. They went over to him and saw that he was sleeping. They went away, came back there the next night and hunted for the boy but he wasn't there. They looked all over the forest. He fell off the cliff. He got up, he thought it was daytime, but he had his eyes closed and he walked right off the cliff." In this version the boy perished because he had strayed away from home.

The habitual typical affective attitude of the mother and of the child tiqueur is illustrated in the following example. Henry drew a woman with a dog on a heavy leash. "He likes to run away. The dog stretches the leash when he pulls. He is pulling because he wants to run away. He likes to scare cows off the cliffs. He is a bad dog. He wants to get rid of everybody on the farm. He doesn't like the farmer. *After he gets rid of everybody he can run away.* He does not want to make friends with anybody. He likes to be free and to do everything he likes to do." What? "Go up on hills, push rocks off. Once he pushed a rock off and it hit a tree and the tree came out of the ground and fell on him. It just hurt his foot. Just a little bit." He increases the length of the leash in the drawing. "I like dogs very much. My aunt's dog, Sandy, always runs away. He pushes open the door *if it is unlocked.*" Henry's depressed mood gets more prominent.

One of his mother's chief complaints about Henry was, "He cannot stand anything around his *neck*"! It was obvious and was interpreted to Henry that he, like Sandy, sometimes would like to run away, and do what he pleases. So the dog pulls and pulls at the leash. It was even suggested that this pulling gesture of his neck might have something to do with his feeling of wanting to pull away from his mother: he feels bad about his wish to disobey his mother; thus, ever since he was able to talk he has insisted upon knowing where his mother is and what she is doing every minute of the day, and followed her like a shadow.

The form of Henry's oedipal conflict was also characteristic for the boy patient with "maladie des tics": Henry began to draw a house which filled the entire paper except for a narrow margin reserved for the sky. He then added a chimney, a door, windows on two floors, and then drew a man entering the door. He glanced up nervously at the doctor every few minutes. Who is the man in the door? "My father. He is going into a haunted house. It's haunted inside. It is his birthday and I want to scare him." He then said the two upstairs rooms are for him and his mother, and the downstairs ones for his father and uncle. He drew lines to indicate how he could gain access to his mother's room, and to escape back to his own room when the father came up to his mother's room looking for him after failing to find him in the uncle's room. He first said that he would have all the windows locked so that his father could not climb up from the outside. "He is scared of me because I like to beat him up. We play football. I tackle him. I dreamed I played football with him, and he chases me, tackles me and then I throw the ball to him. He starts running and I jump on his feet, and he falls down and I grab the ball and make a touchdown."

Henry sleeps on a cot in his mother's room. "I like to sleep in her bed. Sometimes my father sleeps on the cot and I sleep with my mother. He does not care too much. The cot does not feel comfortable to him." His mother reported, "If his father puts his arms around me on a Sunday morning, Henry jumps on top of us and tries to separate us and tells his father to leave me alone."

In the "maladie des tics" patient the passive submissiveness, the eroticized, provocative, aggressive defense attitude, is supplied from two sources: the identification with the mother (a preoedipal mother fixation) and the defense against the passive homosexual claims directed toward the father. This struggle only superficially looks as if it were an intensification of the normal positive oedipus complex.

In the first weeks of Henry's stay in the hospital his actual crop of tic patterns consisted of: a pulling tic of the neck, jerking his head forward, down and sideward, a blinking tic of the eyes, retracting motion of the lips, and a rapid upward thrusting of one or both forearms (with extended wrist and index finger as if pointing toward something, and/or admonishing someone), and he would say "f———, f———" spasmodically while quietly absorbed in some activity (e.g., reading). At times one tic predominated, at other times they alternated rapidly.

We see the difference in the structure of Henry's obscene tic automatism as compared with Elmer's and Johnnie's impulsive obscene verbal assaults and subsequent remorse. In Freddie's (Mahler and Gross 1945) and Henry's cases, release of the erotic aggressive impulse and defense against it is condensed in the ideomotor symptom. In the impulse-ridden tiqueur the *biphasic* acting out is predominant.

Elmer's and Johnnie's deliberate making faces, cursing at people, provoking them with repetitious teasing, obscene rhymes as well as notes, was the unorganized acting out of erotic aggressive impulses. Such outbursts were followed by anxiety, repentance, guilt feelings, and subdued behavior—and finally by the tic automatisms.

All these elements can be detected in a condensed form in Henry's coprolalic tics which were quite marked after he became familiar with his ward-mates' bathroom language. He felt very guilty about his coprolalic tics, and felt them to be ego-alien and overwhelming. He stated, "Some people beat children for saying things like that."

"Sometimes I can hear myself saying it but sometimes it sounds so low that I don't even hear myself saying it."

In the interview it became evident how important it was to Henry to be a good boy; also, how much afraid he was of his father. When he talked about the latter, he thrust his hands protectively toward his genitals. He also admitted having been repeatedly hit on his hands by his father. The pointing tic was then interpreted as possibly meaning an admonition to himself when he feels like being bad: "Beware, do not do, or think, or say things that are not nice."

The effect of such direct but obviously correct interpretation concerning this and scores of similar single tic patterns in organ neurotic tiqueurs was often striking and most instructive. It seemed that through bringing the meaning of a special tic pattern to the awareness of the tiqueur, they had to give up the pattern. However, as long as the basic affective attitude, causing the psychosomatic disturbance, was not worked through, the tic pattern was replaced by the use of other groups of muscles and other movement automatisms. By substituting alternate tic patterns (called paratics by Meige and Feindel) the tiqueur continued to express the pathogenic attitudes and ambivalence conflict, which previously he had vented by means of the patterns eliminated by the interpretations. Henry, for example, never again used the pointing and leash-pulling tics after the above interpretations.[21]

THEORETICAL DISCUSSION AND CONCLUSIONS

If our thesis that the tic syndrome is a psychosomatic disease is correct, we cannot expect the syndrome to be only a localized and

---

21. Following the disappearance of his pointing and leash-pulling tic, Henry's predominant tic became a vigorous backward bending of the head with a concomitant rapid, spasmodic opening of the mouth (as if commanded to let his tonsils be inspected) and a sudden violent snapping back of the head and a closing motion of the jaws, a violent oral, aggressive gesture, which had a secondary (rationalized) symbolic meaning, yet the same psychosomatic disturbance at its genetic root! (cf. Mahler and Rangell 1943, p. 20).

limited symbolic expression of a specific conflict in body language. It seemed, however, from the psychoanalysis of such tiqueurs (Freddie, Elmer, and Pete) that the "motor neurosis" as such was not entirely free of a certain unconscious meaning. The underlying unconscious fantasies were uniform. The dominant theme was concerned with movement and quiescence, attack and immobilization, paralyzation, falling, etc. Furthermore, we were able to analyze in many cases of generalized tic disease the unconscious symbolic meaning of the temporarily predominant "presenting tic" pattern. Although the meaning of this tic pattern could thus be retranslated from its body language, and by so doing dissolve the tic symptom, this did not, however, resolve the disease unless the basic affective attitude was also analyzed and worked through. Therefore it would seem that the psychomotor neurosis, the tic syndrome, follows the rules of both the hysteric conversion and the psychosomatic organ neurotic disease.

Alexander (1943) states that the conversion symptom is a symbolic substitute for an unbearable emotion, a kind of physical abreaction or equivalent of an unconscious emotional tension—it is "a symbolic expression of a well-defined emotional content . . . an attempt at relief." In contradistinction: the psychosomatic disease (which Alexander confines to the vegetative organs) " . . . is not an attempt to express an emotion but is the *physiological accompaniment* of constant or periodically recurring emotional states."

We believe that the generalized tics (and perhaps several other "motor neuroses") represent two things. They are an attempted drainage of a chronic state of emotional tension and utilize for this purpose certain variable but well-defined symbolic expressions. But they are also the physiological accompaniment of a chronic affective attitude. The tic syndrome is the result of specific emotional constellations. Furthermore the organ neurotic and the impulse neurotic tiqueur were found to be suffering from both an innate (maturational) as well as developmental ego defect revealed in the area of their motility integrating function. We described the tiqueur as impetuous, hyperkinetic, oversensitive and intrinsically endowed with an increased "motor urgency." We found furthermore that there were typical and specific environmental influences which acted on the characteristics of these children to shape them "by the blocking of certain reactions to gratifications and frustrations and by the favoring of others." (Cf. Fenichel 1945a, p. 287).

The tic syndrome (the dyskinetic disturbance of the neuromuscular apparatus) is the pathophysiological concomitant of a chronic state of affective tension: whereas the transiently predominant "presenting" tic patterns are an expression—an attempted drainage—of the emotional tension with a (secondary?) symbolic meaning (Alexander 1943, Fenichel 1945a, Pacella 1945).

By examining our material both in cross-section and longitudinally, we found strikingly constant factors and constellations:

1. In these cases there was a predominance of male children (a ratio of 9:1). We believe this to be due to the fact that in the male sex the biological function of the neuromuscular apparatus as the organ of erotic, aggressive attack and as the weapon for self-protection is prominent. The narcissistic importance and functionality of an organ—according to Freud—renders it proportionately susceptible to becoming the site of the neurotic conflict solution (Freud 1910b).

2. The children showed a constitutional increase of motor urgency. We have described the pre-tic behavior disorder of our patients which was characterized by increased emotionality, especially aggression, and "motor urgency." These characteristics made repression and reaction-formation at the onset of latency difficult.

3. Fifty percent of boy tiqueurs presented a pseudo-Froehlich habitus, known as prototypical of passive submissiveness and suppressed hostility (Levy 1944). It is not easy to determine to what extent this was a primary factor of the psychosomatic tic disease or a result of it.[22] The pseudo-Froehlich habitus of our tiqueurs was found to be spurious since the essential feature of the Froehlich habitus, true hypogenitalism (undersized organs), was not present. The obesity of the organ neurotic tiqueur may very well be the result of overeating, coupled with his characteristic hypomotility. The feminine distribution of the fat tissue, however, marks perhaps a primary endocrine

---

22. Previous authors, unfamiliar with child tiqueurs of this type, have stated that an asthenic habitus was characteristic of the tiqueur.

inclination towards passivity.[23] (Compare also discussion of points 6 and 7.)

The unconscious fantasies which we analyzed in two of our obese boy tiqueurs (Freddie and Elmer) led us to believe that their obesity represented or was the result of their wanting to have babies, to be pregnant. Elmer, for instance, maintained the theory of oral impregnation long after other children give it up. He ate ravenously, loved little children and was exultant when his white rat had a litter. His affection was boundless and he kissed and hugged the animal.[24]

4. (a) There was a high incidence of an accumulation of sicknesses which restricted motor freedom during the exercising period of locomotion and which restricted "performance motor" independence (especially in the impulse neurotic tic syndrome); and/or (b) the children showed a tendency toward accidents, they were "motility conscious" and a conflict about even indirect restriction of locomotor freedom was prominent in group 5 of the tiqueurs.

(a) There was a high incidence of cumulation of childhood diseases at the period of learning to master the independent motility function which interfered with the function (particularly in the group of impulse-ridden tiqueur). It seems that the concurrence of motility restriction plus painful and uncomfortable bodily sensations (sickness) increased the amorphous aggressive drive of the candidates for character neurosis with tic syndrome, and had a particularly disorganizing effect on the child's personality (cf. Greenacre 1944; also SPI:4, the case of Elmer).

(b) Other tiqueurs, especially those of the hypokinetic group, from early age on were prohibited from crying, shouting, running, hammering, or playing with abandon, because of overconcern for some member of the family or a neighbor. "More pathogenic still was the indirect and subtle restriction" (Mahler, Luke, and Daltroff 1945), through the mother's emotional attitude towards the son's motor independence (e.g., constant admonition about all the risks

23. The feminine distribution of the subcutaneous fat tissue may also signify a psychosomatic correlate of the feminine identification tendencies of the tiqueur, described in this paper.

24. Elmer showed a violent reaction when he had to give up the rat as he was found to be allergic to the rat fur.

connected with freedom of activity, watching over every move, etc.).
As mentioned above, we found a history of repeated accidents in the
family of every one of these tiqueurs.[25]

5. The children occupied a position of abnormally increased
importance in the family setting. In about 90 percent of our cases
tiqueurs occupied an inordinately important or exceptional position
within the family group. This position became theirs either because
they were only children or "the baby," sometimes of old parents; or
they were the first living child (in six cases, after miscarriages, death
of older siblings or habitual abortions); or they were "only sons"
among several sisters.

6. There was a prolonged appersonation by and of the mother: a
kind of emotional symbiosis between mother and son was marked by
reactive overprotection, pampering, and infantilization, particularly
in group 5 (cf. Spitz 1948).

7. The mothers of such patients showed an intolerance of "phallic
aggression," coupled with markedly high standards of intellectual
achievement.

The combined effects of their position and their mothers' neuroses resulted in an unusually strong interlocking of pathogenic and
pathognomonic affective attitudes between these sons and their
mothers—an emotional interdependence which made these children
peculiarly susceptible to psychosomatic disease (Sperling 1946, Spitz
1949). The mothers of these impulse-ridden tiqueurs were overprotective, vindictive, and extremely intolerant of any manifestation
of phallic aggression or exhibitionistic tendencies in their sons. The
fathers usually were punitive, strict, and perfectionistic. A severe
masturbation threat was frequently found to have had a trigger effect
in touching off the tic syndrome in this group.

In several papers we described the reactive and seductive overprotective attitude (appersonation) which is characteristic of the
mothers of organ neurotic tiqueurs. Pampering, coupled with intolerance of the child's activity and aggression, frustrated any step
towards their son's independence. In the *hypokinetic* group of tic

25. Or else there was an acute conflict about free movement or some motility
restricting ailment and, in one case, also epilepsy (Mahler and Gross 1945).

syndrome patients we found that separation from the mother—
amounting to not more than a gradual psychobiological separation
tendency on the part of the child—was felt as a threat and reciprocated by threats, on the one hand, and increased oversolicitude on the
other.

The organization of the kinetic function of the ego, particularly
that of locomotion, presents for the two- to three-year-old the first
serious step toward his individual, autonomous and independent
development, *away* from the mother. This part of progressive personality development, *away from the mother*, was impaired in the tic
children by the endogenous and exogenous factors described. The
children became disarmed, helpless and anxious; they were afraid
not only to show aggression, but to move about freely lest they lose
their mother's love, or hurt themselves. In these children suppressed
aggression, and particularly curtailment of adequate motor outlets
in the formative phase of independent ego development, led to a state
of *being dammed up* as early as their third and fourth years. This
state of being dammed up is comparable to the condition of adult
candidates for organ neurosis, whom Fenichel (1945a) described as
having "the disturbed chemistry of the unsatisfied person."

This inhibition of motor expression led to a partial impediment
of the ego's mastery of motility (Fenichel 1928). Children with tic
disease showed a muscular hypertension, or dyskinetic diffuse innervations (general muscular restlessness, poor coordination, etc.) of
their neuromuscular apparatus, which was the physiological concomitant, the equivalent countercathexis of their affective tension.
These multifocal, muscular sensations finally found an outlet in the
automatic motor symptoms, the multiple tics. The resulting *hypomotility*, the inhibition of the kinetic function par excellence, was
the outcome of a secondary emotional armor-plating (*Panzerung*) of
the ego via the narcissistically libidinized organ system. This system
had regressively again become an organ of automatic (subcortical)
affective discharge.

From the analysis of a number of cases with a tic syndrome
(groups 4 and 5) we found that as the semi-voluntary (ego-syntonic)
impulsions were completely or partially replaced by their condensed
involuntary derivatives, the tics, these children constantly had to

bear the experience of being overpowered by ego-alien, unpredictable forces.[26] In an attempt to counteract these compelling, muscular sensations (felt as multilocular tenseness) a particularly strong narcissistic countercathexis of the entire musculature (and also of the entire body) was set up. The neuromuscular system was compelled to revert (regress) to its role as discharge organ, and thus became the organ of the psychosomatic *"motor neurosis"* (Freud 1910b).[27] The erotization of the body made these patients susceptible to hypochondria (cf. Ferenczi, et al).

8. Both at the onset of the disease and during the course of it, an acute masturbation conflict was frequently a cardinal problem (Ferenczi 1921). The tics symbolized the child's own inner experience of being overwhelmed by the impulse (tumescence) originally brought about by working himself up to a peak of instinctual excitement (masturbation), and at the same time it was a defensive innervation against it. In concomitant behavior the tiqueur tries to reproject an internalized conflict into the outside world by accusing people or forces in the environment. The rhythmic, paroxysmic nature, and (at least in the beginning) the obvious drive toward a climax of the tic syndrome (and not only the tic symptom) showed it to be a masturbation equivalent.[28]

26. The muscular tension was felt and described as a kind of erection, reminiscent of the feeling of a tumescent penis. The children felt self-conscious and guilty about them.

27. If the massive psychosomatic "armor-plating" was ineffectual, *psychotic disorganization of the ego* occurred after puberty.

28. H.B., a nineteen-year-old impulsive tiqueur describes her tic paroxysm as follows: "If I am not in it (the tic paroxysm), it is like working myself into it, like an automobile which gets momentum going down the hill. This is more a habit now. I can stop it but then I do it out of spite when I get that pent up feeling. . . . I must have a spiteful streak in me. . . . I cut off my nose to spite my face. Sometimes I am so wound up that I just keep going. Any irritating thought that passes through my mind causes those 'spasmodic outbursts' . . . I pick those words up. . . . I get my mother and brother very nervous with those 'f———, f———, sh——, sh——.'"

In contrast, the "inhibited organ neurotic tiqueur" describes his syndrome in the following way: "I always feel it (the sensation of muscular tension) coming on and I try with all my might not to move, but then it moves anyway."

SUMMARY OF PSYCHOANALYTIC FINDINGS IN REGARD
TO THE DIAGNOSIS AND PROGNOSIS OF "TIC"

Diagnosis

Diagnosis as to which of the described categories of tics a case belongs in, needs only a relatively short period of psychoanalytic observation. We must, however, expect overlapping in "tics" as in any other area of the psychopathology of childhood. We have seen some psychosomatic cases start with single tics—they sometimes, though rarely, end with one or two strictly localized residual tics (Mahler and Rangell 1943, SPI:5). The psychoneurotic tic often shows some spreading and sometimes concomitant general muscular restlessness in the beginning. However, in the course of psychoanalysis and/or prolonged clinical observation the genetic, dynamic and prognostic differences become evident.

Treatment

We would add one more point of contrast between the organ neurotic tiqueur and the impulsive tiqueur in regard to their respective psychoanalytic treatment. The patient with the tic disease has, in our experience, been most rigid and resistive to giving up his defensive armor-plating. Children with the tic syndrome (group 5) eventually arrive at a stage when they dread any *spontaneous* innervation or move, and thus psychoanalytic treatment is very difficult with them. They not only lack spontaneity and initiative. They try to adopt the general attitude of defending themselves by over-compliance; a conformity which literally waits for and imitates[29] every move of persons in their environment (including the psycho-

29. That gives then the impression of imitativeness in these children. That is, however, actually a mechanical, a pathological imitation phenomenon, which can, if it is cathected with the repressed affect quantities, result in echophenomena, echolalia, echokinesia, and palilalia. This differs also from the psychoneurotic *and* the impulsive tiqueur, both of whom are characterized by their gestural imitativeness, their inclination and talent for play-acting, their dramatic creative imitation (SPI:4, fn. 3).

analyst), in ideational as well as in action fields. They have complied with their mother's wish for their remaining vegetative creatures, with no will and intention of their own and resist changing this defensive attitude. The impulsive tiqueur, on the other hand, like the delinquent, is artful in evading therapeutic interference by acting out and with projective mechanisms.

Prognosis

We were surprised to find in a follow-up study that the prognosis of the tiqueur with consolidated organ neurotic motor syndrome was relatively favorable compared with that of the impulse-ridden tiqueur.[30] The organ neurotic tiqueur with the defensive armor-plating of his ego was better able to withstand the potentially disorganizing effect of the psychophysiological upheaval of puberty than either the impulse-ridden child tiqueur or the patient with the tic disease, whose defenses had been broken down through ineffective deep psychotherapy. This was especially true when there had been a one-sided release of aggression and a "liberation" of erotic drives through symbolic interpretation without concomitant strengthening of the ego's synthetic faculties (*SPI*:5; Mahler, Ross, and De Fries 1949; Meige and Feindel 1907).

30. It seems that the organ neurotic tiqueur's armor-plating has a similar bracing effect against psychotic disorganization of the ego, as have some forms of obsessive compulsion mechanisms against schizophrenic personality disintegration.

Chapter 4

TICS AND IMPULSIONS IN CHILDREN:
A STUDY OF MOTILITY

[1944]

There is a great divergence of opinion on the meaning of tics. They have been variously considered as mere habits, repetitive motions, or compulsive or hysteric symptoms. Their similarity to certain features of organ neuroses and hypochondriacal states has also been noted, and Ferenczi—who pointed out the highly narcissistic make-up of certain tiqueurs—because tics suggested catatonic symptoms, wished to call them by analogy "cataclonias." Nevertheless, he also recognized isolated tics as accessory manifestations with no relationship to the rest of the personality.

It is my belief that a better understanding of the tic may be derived from a study of its pathogenesis in children. This report is based partly on the psychoanalysis of children who presented tics and other neurotic motor symptoms, partly on the clinical findings of a research project at the New York State Psychiatric Institute, and also on information regarding behavioristic and experimental psychophysiological phenomena drawn from the works of Myrtle McGraw, Gesell, August Homburger, and many others. These works have the shortcomings of any preponderantly neurophysiological experimental research. They deal essentially with surface phenomena and stress the neurophysiological aspects of behavior. However, they furnish useful points of departure for investigating motility, if this be also considered a psychodynamic resultant of the interactions of instinctual, ego, and social environmental factors.

Motility has been explored by many authors, among whom might be mentioned Hartmann (1939), Bally (1933), Landauer (1926), Fenichel (1928), and Kubie (1941). The efficiency and rationality of motor conduct is no doubt the most conspicuous characteristic of adult behavior. It was the "absolute mastery" of motility which Freud singled out as one of the main functions of the mature ego. From the psychodynamic point of view, the kinetic ego (Nunberg 1932) occupies a unique position. Better than any other system, it demonstrates the principle of multiple functioning (Waelder 1937) as well as the principle of the overdetermination of symptoms.

To understand motility and its disturbances, it is particularly useful to follow the development of the expressive or affective motor function, and the performance motor function (*Leistungsmotorik*) of the ego. The separation of these two chief elements of the kinetic function is arbitrary, yet many motor phenomena are formulable as interactions between the two aspects. Expressive motility is much nearer to the id, while performance motility develops as an integral part of the autonomous mature ego.

At the beginning of life the two divisions of motility are inseparable. Prehension, grasping, fixation, turning the head towards the mother, are expressive; yet they become the very foundation of performance motility. Later in development the two types diverge until the affective motor part is reduced to a mere synkinesis with subtle facial mimicry, or to expressiveness in speech and other organized symbolic means of communication.

To review at this point the functions of the neuromuscular system—which as an executive center *par excellence* serves the libidinal as well as the ego instincts—would entail too extensive a discussion and would overstep the limits of this paper. Let us merely recall that early in life the motor equipment primarily aims to reunite child and mother. Later, when the motor function within the ego's autonomy begins to give the child intense narcissistic satisfaction, the neuromuscular system serves distancing from mother as well. It undertakes defensive innervations which ward off threats of narcissistic injury from without, and ward off the more objectionable impulses (oral, anal and phallic, erotic and aggressive) impulses from within.

When object erotic cravings are differentiated (before there is verbal communication) the child seeks rapport and expresses his emotions and desires through both divisions of the kinetic function.

When emotional gestures are increasingly modulated, at about the age of twelve months, the infant gradually begins to communicate a wide range of affects: fear, pleasure, rage, annoyance, affection, jubilation, and the rest. Its expressive jargon is a lalia rather than a representative symbolic language.

As far as performance motility is concerned, Kubie (1941, p. 27) significantly says: "Every new skill becomes a language weighted with a steady accretion of secondary and largely unconscious meaning ... a wordless appeal for love, praise, or help, ... an expression of unformulated yearnings and wishes." We know that this holds true preeminently for the first motor achievements of prehension, of bodily locomotor skill, and of vocal skills.

The integration of erect locomotion is the greatest step in the development of the autonomous kinetic function of the ego. In the two-year-old child, simple motor skills are combined in new actions, which in normal development progressively lose their rigid repetitive tendency, with longer periods of quiet occupation and verbalization.

Finally, the fluently mastered partial skills of performance motility are pushed down into deeper preconscious layers of the ego (Hartmann 1939), which ordinarily do not require much cathexis, and thus free libido for new skills and the higher functions of the ego (Landauer 1926, 1927). In contrast to pathological striopallidar automatisms, these important normal automatisms are parts of the ego with great libido-economic implications.

Freud in his paper, "Formulations on the Two Principles of Mental Functioning" (1911a), writes:

A new function was now allotted to motor discharge, which, under the dominance of the pleasure principle, had served as a means of unburdening the mental apparatus of accretions of stimuli, and which had carried out this task by sending innervations into the interior of the body (leading to expressive movements and the play of features and to manifestations of affect). Motor discharge was now employed in the appropriate alteration of reality; it was converted into *action.*

Restraint upon motor discharge (upon action, which then became necessary, was provided by means of the process of thinking, which was developed from the presentation of ideas (p. 221).

At the age of four to five, performance motility is established firmly enough to be of great emotional value. The ego still bends towards object-related, affectionate demonstrativeness. Its total motility has become the child's most important alloplastic tool to master reality, and at the same time, through "motor-luxury" (to quote August Homburger [1923]), a way of indulging in the pleasure of acting out its emotional impulses in play or expressional communications, positive and negative, with parents and siblings. At this point the child is at the peak of his oedipal situation.

As school age is approached, the expressive manifestations of the oedipal claims, because of their overt and obtrusive quality, become more objectionable. The child's ego is called upon to repress the libidinal and aggressive tendencies of the oedipal conflict, to repress *specifically* all direct and indirect motor manifestations which had relieved surplus tension (cf. Ferenczi, Fenichel, and others). The superego now prohibits the child's seeking release in affective motility, and the ego is faced with the potential eruption of powerfully repressed objectionable impulses.[1]

There are two main possibilities of relief from instinctual ten-

---

1. A kind of theoretical and therapeutic preoccupation has crystallized around the problem of the motor release of aggression. It seems that release is considered both the main factor in alleviating anxiety and the principle agent in resolving neurotic symptoms. To me, as to so many other workers in the field, the relation between restraint, restriction, and symptom formation is far more complicated. Dr. Greenacre (1944) is of the opinion that "it is not simple hampering of motion that provokes aggressive, ragelike behavior in the young infant; indeed that consistent, moderate and general restriction may first quiet the infant." We may add that unbiased observation seems to convey the impression that beyond infancy as well, such an attitude helps the growth of the kinetic function of the ego.

sion—discharge and binding of energy. A small child unhesitatingly chooses the first of these because of his relatively weak ego and intolerance of anxiety. Children always act out if they are permitted to do so and only very gradually obtain the ego strength and maturity necessary for control.

Children successfully attain latency only when they are able to replace immediate acting out (impulsions) by trial acting, i.e., thinking. In a great many cases latency, especially where motor manifestations are concerned, is not attained.

There is no more impressive proof of the validity of Freud's basic finding that the oedipus complex is the core of neurosis, than the comparative findings concerning the function of motility. This becomes unusually clear when we study and contrast the function of motility before the peak of the oedipus complex is reached and the motor behavior of children of school age where general repression has been successfully achieved.

Though impoverished in its vivacity, the motor behavior of a child from the age of six to eleven or twelve becomes calmer and more balanced, tends to achieve a certain degree of uniformity (Homburger 1923), and does not easily regress. In those instances in which the libido economy has manifested an imbalance in early life, interactions within the kinetic function of the ego remain defective. Having been continuously submerged by id-related motor manifestations and compelled to take over vicariously surplus libido from other zones, the performance motility becomes disrupted. Play is usually deficient in purposefulness and the kinetic function of the ego conspicuously lacks flexibility; while at the same time there is a tendency to affective motor explosions (tempers). There are also the first alarming signs which indicate to the parents the need for help. In such disturbances of the libido-economic balance and of the autonomous ego function—usually manifest in the parent-child relationship—the child is obstinately seeking restitution and compensation through repetitive, impulsive actions.

The term impulsion, partly borrowed from Bender and Schilder (1940) and partly from Whitehorn (1932), is used by us to designate those instances in which the ego condones objectionable motor release with little or no inner conflict. It thus embraces the "habit disorders" and "conduct disorders" of clinical psychiatry, in contra-distinction to true motor neurotic manifestations, compulsions, and particularly tics. According to our experience, the latter crystallize in permanent form only after a powerful general repression of libido and motility exerts its highly pathogenic influence upon the motility-controlling function of the ego.

We would differentiate three groups of impulsions: The *first* group comprises repetitive, strongly libidinized simple or compli-cated motor actions, which essentially serve the purpose of dis-charge—displacements of other, more objectionable component impulses. The impulsions of the *second* group may symbolize an aggressive gesture or magic defensive motor action of the ego against intolerable tension and conflict with the outside world. The *third* group of impulsions is represented by stereotyped performances to obtain mastery of skill (autonomous ego expansion), learning, against interference (narcissistic injury).

The second group of impulsions is frequently and erroneously called "tic" in psychoanalytic literature. In our opinion, these impulsions, or pseudo tics, are preferably classified as "denial by magic repetitive gesture." They serve as escapes from unacceptable reality—or approximately what Anna Freud, in *The Ego and the Mechanisms of Defense,* has called "denial in word and act."

In the disturbed psychosexual development and parent-child relationship, we see an exceptionally violent and complex struggle between the tendency to repetitive and obstinate motor activity (the child's impulsions), and the external forces in the environment that strive to moderate and restrict.

The transition from impulsions to compulsive tics was put into words by one of my tic patients, Teddy, who repeatedly said: "First I twinkled because I saw it in the movies [he found it interesting] and because Johnnie did it, the friend of my big brother [of whom Teddy was very jealous] and later I couldn't help blinking any more." Teddy finally succeeded in replacing and warding off this first tic by developing an arm tic instead, and he was very proud of this achievement. Later, he used to exclaim in desperation, pounding the table, "I got rid of my blinking! I must be able to suppress these other habits too. . . ."

At this point, this nine-year-old boy had developed vocal tics—animal-like grunting, barking, and squealing noises—as well as echolalia and echopraxia. They appeared especially when he was in the movies. These are the forerunners of ideomotor, coprolalic tics. We know that in many cases tics of the body musculature are accompanied by vocal tics, coprolalia, and the so-called echo phenomena. The coincidence with vocal tics, verbigeration, and other echo phenomena, and later on with coprolalic tics, may be viewed psychoanalytically in the same way as the gestural tics of the body muscles. The coprolalic tics may be traced through many intermediate stages. They seem to be ideomotor condensations of the diffuse uncontrolled repetitive vocalizations (the animal sounds) that occur in early childhood, which are usually followed, even in normal four or five-year-old children, by erotic aggressive "bathroom talk" of a provocative character. Later, through the prohibition of motor release by the superego, these erotized verbalizations turn into a compulsive and repetitive motor symptom.

We see therefore how the ideomotor impulse uses the ego automatism in the intermediate phases of coprolalic tics and echo phenomena, as soon as the inner prohibition interferes with release into expression. Echo phenomena seem to be compromise solutions of the tiqueur's tendency to imitate, and of a repetition compulsion inherent in instinctual processes, which becomes exaggerated when expression is thwarted. In passing it may be noted that oral, anal, and phallic, libidinal and aggressive tendencies appear in equal proportion in the usual four letter words of coprolalic tics.

One analytic hour with Elmer, ten and a half years old, vividly demonstrates the different phases of tic formation. It also illustrates the identical psychodynamics of vocal and gestural tics and their interchangeability. Before we describe the case, it is important for us to state that logorrhea is one of the features of the child tiqueur, whom we shall refer to as Type 1. We will also see in this type a trend towards self-observation and hypochondria.

Elmer gave approximately the following associations during one analytic hour: "Today I got a tic in my right shoulder and my eye. We gave a play about Columbus in the assembly. . . . Last night I was awfully silly, because my sister Peggy always asks me why I won't go to the bathroom. She smells gas. That made me silly. I made up a joke, because she says, whenever she comes home, 'It's an awful smell.' I giggled and laughed and danced and shouted, 'Smelly gas, ballooni, furters, gas bubble, gas bubble, barrage balloons, balloons, balloons.' Mother came in and tried to stop it. She got very angry, yelled at me . . . and Peggy always complains that I belch at the table." At this point, his tics in the analytic hour were increasingly paroxysmal. He said, "Gee, this tic is very uncomfortable—the sounds I like to make. I was chewing bubble gum yesterday . . . and when I stopped I just made the noises. The teacher and other people mind the noises, but the eye tic is very uncomfortable to me. It feels better when I do it, and with my arm too . . . it feels as if my arm were stiff and it feels better if I do this, but the more I want it to get better, the more I do it. . . ." A little later he remarked contemplatively and plaintively, "Everything happens on my right side. I broke my arm on the right side, I tore the cornea of my right eye, I cut myself on my right forehead. When I broke my arm, I couldn't play football; I couldn't play anything! Since then I have always been kind of scared to skate . . . even now I am kind of scared in gymnasium."

We may differentiate three phases of tic formation in this session. Pent up pregenital and genital instinctual impulses were leading to bizarre, grotesque, exaggerated affective motor and linguistic behavior, such as appeared in his talk with his eight-years-older sister. He was provoking her through coprolalic utterances, belching and flatus, by mimicking her with gestures and imitating the sounds he heard her making in the bathroom. However, when she and his mother tried to stop his diffuse, perverse, expressive behavior, coarse affective motor acts had already inundated his ego to such an extent that he could no longer stop.

The next day, the tics which had been evident intermittently since Elmer's sixth or seventh year reappeared—but in two forms. The first was the sound tic, which he liked to make, and which he could stop rather easily if necessary. This was volitional, nearer to the pleasurable impulsions, and objectionable only to the environment. The eye and shoulder tics—the second form—were real neurotic symptoms: compulsions, conceived by us as a compromise solution of the ego between the impulse and the superego, and were strongly self-punitive rather than gratifying.

It may be worthy of note that on the previous day, Elmer was unusually excited in anticipation of an important role he was to play in the school assembly program. Elmer, as so many other tiqueurs, was a talented actor but the conflict between his exhibitionistic tendencies and the fears related to them was obvious.[2]

This boy was brought to analysis, not primarily because of his tics, but because of his inability to get along with his sister and because of his "silly" aggressive erotic behavior. He used to work himself up into states of excitement which usually culminated in crying and unhappiness. Though intellectually exceptionally well endowed, he was not able to function up to capacity: each activity engrossed him so much that he could not effect a transition from one to another. He seemed always on the go. His teachers, who liked him very much, called him "our beloved blunderbus."

Long before he started analysis, the school wrote, "Elmer is blind to all other considerations in fulfilling an idea. He frequently knocks down chairs and rushes into people in accomplishing his purpose. These personal collisions are sometimes interpreted as intentional and result in a scuffle."

Elmer was the only son, the second and late offspring of his parents, and his birth was eagerly anticipated. He had an unusually difficult childhood, however. Soon after his birth his mother became ill and he was left to the care of a nurse. In his second year he developed severe boils on his face and body, which were treated with poultices. At a time when the developmental freedom of the autonomous kinetic ego function was of utmost importance (locomotor and other skills), the baby was immobilized by pain and by medical treatment.

Due to boils on his buttocks his toilet training was delayed; he was eighteen months old when first put on the pot, which he detested, preferring to soil himself and to retain his feces. He was

2. The excess tensions brought about by such conflicts always produced a heightened emotional state and expressive motor paroxysms. Thus, the controlling function of the ego became inundated by id-motor acts. These had a definitely orgastic quality and left a subsequent emotional hangover feeling. Or else the ego finally resorted to the intermittently available compromise solution, the tic symptom.

given suppositories and enemas. From the age of eight months, he was supposed to be suffering from sinus trouble, and inhalation treatment relieved him, but in analysis it was discovered that the inhalations produced immense fears and sado-masochistic fantasies.

At the age of two, Elmer was placed in the exclusive care of a very energetic maid. With her he was well-behaved and in general healthy. His bowel control improved, but he became very excitable. There were indications that he was seduced by excessive genital fondling during this period. When the maid left suddenly, Elmer started to masturbate. This and his polymorphic perverse impulsions at home and in relation to other children became so excessive that he was sent for psychiatric treatment at the age of four and a half years.

The treatment somewhat improved his autoerotic behavior. Acting out of the most objectionable impulses was reduced. Genital and especially anal masturbation was superseded by less objectionable diffuse muscular and vocal activities with a marked masturbatory quality.

It is not easy to place chronologically the crystallization of Elmer's general jerkiness and excited gesticulative motility into multiple intermittent tics. Volitional habits and grimacing were noted at a very early age. Eye blinking and occasional head turning of the torticollis type were noted by the psychiatrist before the age of five. Impulsive repetitious coprolalia was marked from four years on. From camp and school reports it would appear that Elmer's true tics started as facial tics around the age of seven.

The camp, which he attended at the age of seven, reported: "Elmer's noises are annoying the children. His excitement in being with the group at bedtime is stimulating enough to have a destructive effect on the rest of the group. However, when he is out in space, the story is quite different. He is most constructive for a reasonable length of time. When he becomes fatigued he becomes excited and excessively dominating. His throat noises and facial contortions are still in evidence, particularly so before he goes to sleep."

One of the findings of our current research project has been that the tic and other hyperkinesias, for example logorrhea, increase before sleep. In the first stages of tic crystallization, there are initial nightmares, calling out to mother, talking while asleep, and in some cases even sleepwalking. When the ego is fatigued, the motor impulse becomes predominant. In sleep the censorship is loosened and motor release in action may result. On the other hand, both organic and functional tics always subside during sleep.

Another characteristic feature of this type of child tiqueur is poor physical coordination. In Elmer, according to the school report, this was conspicuous, and remained in striking contrast to his extraordinary skill in dramatization and manual work (observed from the beginning of his analysis till the end). The early restriction, imposed by sickness and pain upon Elmer's kinetic functions and performance coordination of the total body, led to a particularly high development and differentiation of normal manual compensatory skills and intellectual ego functions.[3]

To review our material, intermittent and permanent tics may be tentatively classified into three types.

1. Tics resulting from a conflict between a vicariously used and therefore overtaxed affective motility and the claim for control. These tics, first manifested at a very early age in a conspicuous motor restlessness and hypermotility, are characterized by great interchangeability of the movements involved. They can be stopped voluntarily by the child for a period of time when outside pressures or the demands of the superego call for temporary control. Later, usually at the age of six or seven, the impulsions and "tics" lose their volitional nature and their high reversibility potential through the catalyzing influence of the general powerful repression. This type of tiqueur never seems to enter latency.

2. Tics which seem to develop after the child has entered school and has made a fair adjustment. There is always, however, a preschool history of fidgetiness and immaturity in the sense of playful-

3. We might give a possible reason why children with a disposition to tic are commonly known as imitative and particularly talented in dramatics and otherwise. Is it not possible that in the common identification tendencies of childhood, because of the hypercathexis of the musculature, these individuals find themselves most successful when they can identify in the kinetic expressive field, whereas other children more readily identify with the ideational and perceptual qualities of their parents?

ness. An increase of instinctual tension by trauma (auto accident etc.) or a sudden heightening of a sense of guilt (holy communion, threat of the consequences of masturbation) are followed by volitional, so-called "nervous habits," like blinking, picking the nose, or rolling on the stomach. These habits, which are accompanied by an anxiety state, are usually opposed by threats of corporal punishment or of other consequences—a pressure which facilitates the eruption of the impulse. The real tic, frequently coinciding with or followed by a general bodily jerkiness, appears a few weeks after the child has given up the autoerotic activities. The first manifestation is never of a permanent pattern. On the contrary, before long other tics appear as defenses or secondary elaborations of the first manifestation. (This seems to concur with the concept of the "para-tics" described by Meige and Feindel [1907]). The generalized jerkiness, darting about, and tossing are usually confused with the symptoms of chorea minor. The differential diagnosis between tic and chorea is indeed often very difficult. It sometimes happens that children known to have had multiple tics acquire rheumatic fever and chorea many years later (Wilson 1941). We have seen in our follow-up study at least one case in which a child with severe recurrent chorea and rheumatic endocarditis finally ended up with generalized incapacitating tics of a gestural and vocal quality (paroxysms).

Another contrast between the first and second type of tiqueur may be mentioned. Whereas the children of the first type are often characterized by an abundance of expressive motility, the representatives of the second group are gravely inhibited in their voluntary expression so that it is sometimes very difficult to get them to talk or to initiate activity. In them, defense and fear of being overpowered by the impulse is uppermost.

3. Tics appearing in adolescents and in adults. These tics seem to have a more localized organ neurotic character and an obstinate local affinity to the eroticized organ, for which the tic muscle group in question is used as symbolization. Their psychodynamics is like that of traumatic neuroses. In all probability, they are those tics which Ferenczi described as single, and living a so-called parasitic life. They are isolated from the ego function and therefore very difficult to reach therapeutically.

The three categories of tics we have just described represent only a preliminary orientation. Like all other psychopathological phenomena, they usually overlap. All tiqueurs have definitely shown highly increased body narcissism as well as a tendency to hypochondriacal self-observation. It cannot be said at this point whether these are *post hoc* or *propter hoc* phenomena.

Clinical and statistical data prove the validity of Ferenczi's (1921) remark that children in the latency period appear to be particularly susceptible to tic, chorea, and other motor symptoms. This observation is in complete agreement with our developmental and psychodynamic findings. They are verified by clinical and statistical data which show that the morbidity climax, that is to say, the age incidence of permanent tics is at six or seven, regardless of whether the tic belongs to the functional or to the organic type.

As to the question of a somatic basis for tic, which Freud brings up, our work up to date seems to convey the following: In all three types of tiqueur, overstimulation and fixation of component impulses have occurred and the neuromuscular apparatus was vicariously or constitutionally hypercathected in infancy and early childhood. In addition, infantilization and absolutely or relatively increased and inconsistent restraint of the affective motor component of the ego's kinetic function was noted in the anamnesis in all three types, whereas simultaneously channeled performance motor function and compensatory ideational functions and skills were on the whole neglected. The kinetic function of the ego was especially damaged in those cases in which there was a lack of consistent and moderate general outside control to aid the development of the normal and balanced synthetic function of the ego. Due to the erotization of the neuromuscular system in these cases, motility lags in development and is not well synthetized.

According to Freud, hypercathexis, that is, erotization of a system, renders it susceptible of becoming the organ of choice for the establishment of the neurotic conflict in its sphere. Hence, as the data presented above prove, this factor of somatic compliance accounts for Freud's remark: "In the case of tics we seem to be dealing with something somatic" in that in these susceptible individuals motor symptoms serve the purpose of pathological solution of the conflict.

Chapter 5

OUTCOME OF THE TIC SYNDROME

[1946]

In October 1945, the writers of this paper published in collaboration with W. Daltroff the "Clinical and Follow-up Study of the Tic Syndrome in Children," in the *American Journal of Orthopsychiatry*.

The charts of eighteen former child-tiqueurs of the Children's Ward of the New York State Psychiatric Institute and Hospital were studied, and follow-up examinations carried out as far as possible. Eleven out of these eighteen follow-up cases were suffering from a typical and severe tic syndrome at the time of their hospitalization on the children's ward of the New York State Psychiatric Institute and Hospital. These children suffered from organ neurosis of the psychomotor system, that is, they displayed multiple or generalized tics of a paroxysmal nature, along with ideomotor coprolalic tics or their equivalents (obscenities or logorrhea) and showed the typical concomitant tic personality disorder: hypermotility, impulsions, or else a conspicuously tense (pent-up) behavior with proneness to explosive tempers, or erotic aggressive outbursts. In many cases echophenomena were also present. In selecting cases for follow-up study,

In collaboration with Jean A. Luke.

we discarded many in which there was either accompanying proven organic involvement (choreoencephalitis, etc.) or proved psychosis, of which the tic syndrome seemed to be only a complicating factor. Of the eleven follow-up cases with psychosomatic tic syndrome, ten were boys and only one was a girl. The restudied former girl patient, case 11, H.B.—the only girl in the series—presented a typical picture of tic syndrome with coprolalia and echophenomena, accompanied by severe organic choreoencephalitis with rheumatic heart lesions.[1]

The remaining *seven child-tiqueurs of the follow up material did not suffer from a tic syndrome.* They had *symptomatic* tics in association with other neurotic traits of the primary behavior disorder type for which they had been admitted to the Psychiatric Institute. (On criteria of differential diagnosis between symptomatic [psychoneurotic] tic and the psychosomatic tic syndrome, see chapter 3.)

In order to furnish the main data from which we have drawn our conclusions as to the outcome of the tic syndrome, we present Table I.

From the tabulation we observe:

1. The age of the children with tic syndrome at hospital admission ranged from 6 years 11 months to 12 years 4 months.

2. The onset of tics was given by the parents as occurring at 3½ to 9½ years of age, which would indicate the average age of onset to be about 5½ years. We must take into consideration, however, that parents rarely discriminate between true tics and those motor habits which many children temporarily display in the course of their growing-up process, and which usually dissolve without residua (Mahler, Luke, and Daltroff 1945). These habit movements have not the characteristic qualities of true tics but are inconstant, flighty and reversible. We are inclined to attribute importance to the fact that the onset of true tics (crystallized and irreversible) has been observed by many authors to occur seldom if ever before the sixth to eighth year of age at the latency period (Mahler, Luke, and Daltroff, 1945, Meige and Feindel 1907).

1. In spite of organic choreoencephalitis we had included this patient in our study, but because of the organic involvement this case was discarded from the group on which our observations on the "Outcome of the Tic Syndrome" is based.

3. The age at onset and age at admission contain tentative information regarding duration of the tics prior to hospitalization, by which we may estimate the reversibility, that is, the recency or *chronicity* of a tic syndrome. Duration of the tic syndrome prior to admission, ranged from nine months to six years.

4. Psychotherapy in the hospital and sometimes after discharge lasted from seven weeks to three years.

5. Status of the cases at discharge was: two much improved; three improved; two slightly improved and four unimproved.

6. The interval between hospital discharge and follow-up in 1943, ranged from one and a half years to ten years eleven months.

7. The ages of the child-tiqueurs at the time of the follow-up study ranged from 12 years to 23½ years. Of ten male patients seven had reached military age. Three of these seven had been classified as 4F, two for psychiatric reasons, and the third for "eye difficulty." A fourth patient, G.K., was deferred because of essential occupation, but a few months after follow-up examination, at the age of 19½, he was committed to a mental hospital with the diagnosis of schizophrenia. Two patients with tic syndrome had been accepted by the Army, and were serving satisfactorily. One patient of military age was not available at the time of the follow-up study, having moved to the West Coast, but he had been seen one and a half years after discharge at the age of 12, and considered greatly improved.

The three remaining patients were of school age, 13, 14½ and 15 years 9 months, at the time of our follow-up research.

In studying the age at onset, age at hospitalization, duration and method of psychotherapy, immediate result of treatment and long-term result at follow-up, we found no direct correlation between recovery from the tic syndrome and length or method of psychotherapy, neither did we find that thoroughness of treatment and good therapeutic results were in direct proportion, even when the syndrome was of short duration and the child was relatively young.

Case No. I, G.K., was hospitalized nine months after onset of the tic syndrome (the shortest interval between onset and admission). He was 10 years and 3 months old at admission. He remained in the hospital for sixteen months, and received the longest and "deepest" psychotherapy (continued after discharge and renewed

TABLE I

No.	Initials	Age at admission	Age at onset (years)	Duration of hospitalization	Type of Therapy and management during hospitalization	Status at discharge
I.	G.K.	10 yr. 3 mo.	9½	21 mo. + O.P.D.	Very deep psychotherapy; inadequate channelization into motility, performance or other ego activities	Improved
II.	C.R.	12 yr. 5 mo.	6-7	16 mo.	Psychotherapy with sodium amytal hypnosis, "cathartic confession" of pederastic experience; no improvement	Unimproved
III.	W.C.	12 yr. 10 mo.	7-7½	16 mo.	Psychotherapy (daily sessions) tic-exercises (which excited and upset him considerably!) Aggression release: wood-scraping with sharp knife	Unimproved

Cases I, II, and III continued from previous page

No. cont.	Postdischarge management, life circumstances, therapy, "outlets," environment	Time elapsed between discharge and follow-up study	Age at follow-up	Follow-up data
I.	Paroled to parents. Very unfavorable home situation (Lost job at 18, had nervous breakdown then, and tried to rescue himself at 19 by moving away from his parents, esp. mother. Holds a defense job since one year. Sought his former P.I. physician when breakdown, treatment once weekly past 1½ yr.)	8 yr. 6 mo.	20 yr.	5 ft. 9½; 180 lbs. Obscene incestuous phantasies very marked. Great anxiety. *Tic syndrome completely vanished.* 1944, schizophrenia, admitted to mental hospital
II.	14 months after parole discharge to father, admission to Rockland State Hosp. Sept. 1939 to April 1941. Unimproved. Paroled to excellent rural foster family. Unrestricted and organized physical activity. "Considerable improvement" at discharge from parole by Rockland, Apr. 1942	6 yr. 4 mo.	19 yr.	Slender; 6 ft., well built, muscular. Reliable, self-supporting, cheerful and happy. Tic residua not found. Accepted by the Army. Excellent social adjustment
III.	Paroled to parents—with no change in environmental conditions	8 yr. 9 mo.	21 yr. 3 mo.	Rejected by the Army. Frail, acne. Tics unchanged. Coprolalic tics controllable, replaced by volitional obscenities. Refuses work. Mental deterioration marked. *Personality changed*

TABLE I (continued)

No.	Initials	Age at admission	Age at onset (years)	Duration of hospi- talization	Type of Therapy and management during hospitalization	Status at discharge
IV.	B.S.	10 yr. 10 mo.	8-9	12 mo.	Psychotherapy aimed toward independence from pathol. mother; channelization of artistic outlets (artwork!)	Improved
V.	R.R.	9 yr. 6 mo.	3½?	12 mo.	12 months' guidance psychotherapy. Regular social work contact weekly with mother 4 months before discharge, aimed toward improving father's relation with patient	Much improved
VI.	H.G.	6½ yr.	5		Play therapy with emphasis on release of sibling rivalry	Slightly improved
VII.	R.T.	6 yr. 11 mo.	5-6	3½ mo. + O.P.D.	Psychotherapy; social work contact with mother	Improved

Cases IV, V, VI and VII continued from previous page

No. cont.	Postdischarge management, life circumstances, therapy, "outlets," environment	Time elapsed between discharge and follow-up study	Age at follow-up	Follow-up data
IV.	Paroled to parents. Physical activity, artwork and independence from mother emphasized	8 yr.	18 yr. 9 mo.	Pvt. in the Army, doing well. Possible residua of tics unknown
V.	Paroled to parents. Moved to California. Intrafamilial situation much improved. Military school, horseback riding and other sports	18 mo.	12 yr.	*Excellent health.* Friendly and at ease with examiner. Dislikes military school, but keeps up fairly well with rigid requirements. Social adjustment good. *Facial tics barely visible. Marked improvement*
VI.	Paroled to parents. Family situation essentially unchanged, both father and mother oversolicitous in a morbid way. Economic status improed. Physical exercise stressed. Father considers H. "too quickly developed, he likes girls too early."	4 yr. 8 mo.	13 yr.	Pale and puffy. Very good in shopwork. Average schoolwork. A few slight residual tics remain. Social adjustment good. Personality development fair; hypochondriacal traits
VII.	Paroled to parents. Increased activity. Boy continued in O.P.D., and mother with social worker. Very efficient father. Harmonious family. Mother aware of her role in patient's difficulties	7 yr. 3 mo.	14½ yr.	Active, well developed, cheerful. Tic residua very slight. Unusual mechanical ability. Predilection for chemistry and photography. School achievement average. Good social adjustment

TABLE I (continued)

No.	Initials	Age at admission	Age at onset (years)	Duration of hospitalization	Type of Therapy and management during hospitalization	Status at discharge
VIII.	A.C.	11 yr. 11 mo.	5½	5 mo.	Psychotherapy	Improved
IX.	M.C.P.	10 yr. 7 mo.	5	2 mos.	Inadequate therapy. Short psychotherapy, releasing completely the suppressed resentment against uncle with whom he lived, but not touching *deeper* resentment against deserting mother who had remarried	Much improved
X.	M.R.	12 yr. 4 mo.	8	7 wk.	No therapy	Unchanged

Cases VIII, IX, and X continued from previous page

No. cont.	Postdischarge management, life circumstances, therapy, "outlets," environment	Time elapsed between discharge and follow-up study	Age at follow-up	Follow-up data
VIII.	Paroled to parents who moved to rural Connecticut. Many outlets permitted (athletics, dramatics, hand-skills). Financial status of family improved.	3 yr. 10 mo.	12 yr.	Ht. 65 inches; weight 126 lbs. Still "nervous," "high-strung" but *popular*, excels in athletics and is very skillful in photography and mechanics. School adjustment fair. Some tics and lisp persist
IX.	Paroled to carefully selected foster-home—away from the punitive uncle	10 yr. 1 mo.* •3 yr. at in between check-up	21 yr. 9 mo.* •13½ at in between check-up	Rather small, slender and infantile looking, 21¾ year old male, with slight grimace. 4F draft classification. Reports wanderings to California and back, earning his living on route. P.O. clerk. Social adjustment poor. Suspicious, paranoid quality in his narrative. Reports cessation of coprolalic tics 6 years prior to follow-up examination. Adjustment: fair to poor
X.	Unknown	10 yr. 11 mo.	23¾ yr.	Rejected by his draft board because of his "eyes." Refused to appear for follow-up allegedly because "it is impossible to leave retail machinery store which he has owned and run for six months." Status of syndrome unknown. Personality adjustment seems poor, according to own statement: "Don't seem to work well with others"

at his own request one and a half years before the follow-up study). Though his tics cleared up completely, his outcome was the worst: schizophrenia.

Case No. II, C.R., in contrast, was hospitalized six years after onset, presented a no less grave symptom picture and was considered by several psychiatric consultants to have a malignant prognosis. He spent about three years in psychiatric hospitals, and was discharged on parole without improvement. Yet, with highly skillful post-discharge management, C.R. made an excellent adjustment. He was accepted by the Army and had served for about a year at the time of follow-up. He was said to be happy, contented, and doing well. The tic syndrome had disappeared.

Case No. III, W.C., had a history of five and a half years' duration of tics on admission. During his sixteen months' hospital stay he was treated with intensive psychotherapy, released of aggression through the wood-scraping method with a knife, and tic exercises *a la* Meige and Feindel, and was discharged unimproved. At follow-up examination, nearly nine years after discharge, when the patient was 21 years 3 months old, the syndrome persisted but appeared "stationary," and he showed definite signs of personality and intellectual deterioration and social maladjustment. On admission his intelligence rating had been superior.

Case No. IV, B.S., had a tic syndrome of fairly recent onset. During his twelve months of hospitalization improvement occurred gradually under psychotherapy focused mainly on freeing him from his pathological dependence on his neurotic mother and creating satisfactory outlets for his artistic talents. Progress continued during the eight years which elapsed between hospital discharge and follow-up. At that time B.S. was 18 years 9 months old, a private in the Army, doing very well.

Case No. V, R.R., was admitted at 9½ years old with a history of onset of tics at 3½ years. But we are inclined to question this history. Clinical course and result of treatment justify our assumption that his tic syndrome was not in a frozen, irreversible state at admission as tabulated data would indicate. Guidance type of psychotherapy was provided for this patient and for his family. He was discharged within twelve months, much improved, and a post-discharge check up one and a half years later revealed satisfactory progress.

Case No. VI, H.G., is the most indecisive as to long-term prognosis. His parents sought treatment for his syndrome relatively soon, about eighteen months after his tics had started; in fact, he was the youngest child-tiqueur to be admitted to Psychiatric Institute, at 6½ years of age. Sixteen months of play and release therapy effected only slight improvement. This case seems to furnish confirmation of the important influence of environmental, intrafamilial pathology in maintaining the vicious circle represented by the child's condition. After discharge he remained with his highly neurotic family. They were persuaded to allow him more physical activity, and the economic status of the home improved, but the constant apprehensive watchfulness of his parents continued. Four years and eight months after discharge, at the age of 13, H.G. was found to have improved in many respects, his tics were far less conspicuous and less constant, he was said to be a leader in athletics and dramatics, and his social and scholastic adjustment was good. But his grave body consciousness, emotional instability, and impulsiveness indicate a dubious final prognosis as far as mental health is concerned.

Case VII, R.T., demonstrates, on the other hand, simultaneous favorable influencing of the environment and adequate post-discharge management. In many respects this patient was similar to H.G. R.T.'s tics were also of rencent onset. His age was 6 years 11 months. The doctors who treated him remarked on the still highly reversible character of his tic syndrome. Play therapy for the boy and social work treatment for the mother were provided and the patient was discharged improved after three and a half months. Therapy was continued in O.P.D. On follow-up, seven years and nine months after discharge, R.T. was 15½ years old. He was practically free of tics, and was very well adjusted and happy.

Case VIII, A.C., was 15 years and 9 months old at follow-up. For him, as for cases 6 and 7, final evaluation of the prognosis should be deferred pending adolescence. In spite of the persistence of some of his rather conspicuous tics, A.C.'s total personality adjustment promises to be better than that of H.G. He is living in a rural environment with much opportunity for and strong emphasis on organized physical work out of doors, which seems to be one of the most important auxiliary factors in the recovery or improvement of the tic syndrome.

Case IX, M.C.P., is instructive in several respects. He came for admission at the age of 10 years and 7 months with a full-fledged tic syndrome of five and a half years' duration. His disturbance was attributed by the examiners essentially to the influence of a restrictive punitive uncle in whose house he had lived after his father's death. He was discharged after only two months of hospitalization. It was felt that with careful placement in a foster home improvement of his condition could be expected, inasmuch as the two months' hospitalization had resulted in marked improvement. Post-discharge follow-up three years later appeared to justify the management of his case. At that time M.C.P. was 13½ years old, was well adjusted in his relationship with the foster family and his school achievement was average. The tic syndrome showed improvement. The only negative sign was a "D" in conduct, the reason for which was not explained. On follow-up examination, seven years later, M.C.P.'s syndrome had disappeared except for some slight residua, but his draft classification was a "psychiatric 4F," and both personality and social adjustment were poor. He was restless, showed paranoid suspiciousness and wandered from job to job. It was our impression that his traveling from east coast to west coast and back might indicate a defense against psychotic breakdown.

Case X, M.R., was hospitalized for only a few weeks, and no information could be secured concerning post-discharge management. According to his own statement, his syndrome had not progressed. Judging from our telephone conversation with him, his personality adjustment is poor. He said his Army classification was 4F, due to his "eyesight."

The numerical limitation of these cases, not more than ten, do not permit more than cautiously tentative conclusions. Individual differences in the structure of the cases, lack of uniformity in psychotherapeutic methods, and variations in the personalities of the psychotherapists subtract further from the validity of comparison. Yet a lack of decisive correlation between recovery from a psychosomatic syndrome and psychotherapy alone is not surprising. It is indeed to be expected if our concept of the tic syndrome as an organneurotic disorder of the neuromuscular system is correct. In organ neurosis cure cannot be expected to result from a one-sided psychotherapeutic approach alone except in infrequent recent afflictions.

As has been described in a previous paper, the motility control-ling function of the ego is impaired in the psychosomatic form of tics; that is, there is a "veritable incontinence of emotion" (Mahler), and erotic and aggressive instinctual impulses are continually escap-ing through pathological discharge. This discharge fails to relieve permanently the instinctual tension which in organ-neurotic condi-tions is always increased (Fenichel 1945b, Mahler and Rangell 1943). This chronic state of instinctual "damming up" (*Affektstauung*) results in overcathexis of that organ or body system (in our cases the neuromuscular apparatus) (Fenichel) which is constitutionally sus-ceptible as the site of the psychosomatic dysfunction (somatic com-pliance, according to Freud). We have found a characteristic "motor-mindedness," consisting of increased motor urge, coupled with a relative insufficiency of the motility-controlling kinetic function of the ego, resulting in an inadequacy of performance and locomotor achievement. In other words, in child-tiqueurs there is a fixation of the psychosexual development in the affectomotor sphere. "It is probably this very factor which accounts for the marked lack of ego synthesis in spite of superior endowment," (Mahler). Increased motor urge (amorphous and id-related) in the child-tiqueur is not an asset but a great liability, it weakens instead of strengthening the integrative development of the total personality (in spite of high partial endowments). A vicious circle is thus established. Freud (1910b) expresses the opinion that because of this vicious circle organ-neurotic symptoms (in general) are "not directly accessible to psychoanalysis." In our experience they do not respond either to psychotherapy alone.

Our second tabulation summarizes our findings, with special emphasis on chronicity and age, the mode of treatment and post-discharge management with relation to the final results:

The most disappointing results were obtained in the cases of G.K. and W.C., for both of whom psychotherapy was especially long and "deep." The upsurging of deep unconscious instinctual material was facilitated, but the strengthening of the sound defensive forces of the ego was not the center of therapeutic attention. Release of increased motor urge in its instinctual erotic aggressive form (affectomotility) may overwhelm the child-tiqueur, and fur-

TABLE II

No.	Initials	Chronicity of syndrome	Duration of hospitalization and psychiatric treatment	Status at discharge	Post-discharge management
I.	G.K.	9 months	21 mo. and 1½ yr. private	Improved	*Inadequate*, no outlets provided
II.	M.C.P.	5 yr. 7 mo.	2 mo.	Much improved	Foster-home placement, wandering around freely, earning his living, adequate (?)
III.	W.C.	5 yr. 4 mo.	16 mo.	Unimproved	*Inadequate*, no change in enviroment, no organized outlets
IV.	M.R.	4 yr. 4 mo.	7 wk.	Unchanged	Unknown
V.	R.T.	1-1½ yr.	3½ mo.	Improved	Adequate
VI.	C.R.	6 yr.	16 mo.	Unimproved	After another 16 mos. hospitalization *very adequate* rural foster home placement
VII.	B.S.	2 yr.	12 mo.	Improved	Adequate (artistic outlets)
VIII.	R.R.	6 yr.	12 mo.	Much improved	Organized motor outlets and phys. competition, improved home sit., change of envir. moved to Calif. *very adequate*
IX.	A.C.	6 yr. 2 mo.	5 mo.	Improved	Rural enviroment; *very adequate*
X.	H.G.	1½ yr.	16 mo.	Slightly improved	Family situation unchanged, organized outlets provided. fairly adequate

TABLE II (continued)

No. cont.	Time elapsed	(a) Physical	(b) Syndrome	Status (c) Social	(d) Personality adjustment
I.	8 yr. 6 mo.	Schizophrenic breakdown	Disappeared	Schizophrenic breakdown	Schizophrenic breakdown
II.	10 yr. 1 mo.	Asthenic, infantile	Residual grimacing and tics. 4F draft classific. Post office clerk	Poor social adjustment	Suspicious, paranoid
III.	8 yr. 9 mo.	Poor	Progressive 4F	Poor	Deterioration
IV.	10 yr. 11 mo.	4F draft classific. (eyes?)	Not progressive	Poor	Fair?
V.	7 yr. 9 mo.	Excellent	Almost absent	Good	Good
VI.	6 yr. 4 mo.	Excellent	Cleared up, accepted by Army	Excellent	Good
VII.	8 yr.	Excellent	Latent or cured, in Army doing well	Good	Good
VIII.	1½ yr.	Excellent	Slight residual tics	Good	Good
IX.	3 yr. 10 mo.	Good	Collar hitching and spitting tic remains lisps, still nervous	Very good, excels and leads in athletics	Fair
X.	4 yr. 8 mo.	Fair	Slight occasional residual tic	Good	Fair (grave body consciousness remains)

ther weaken his inadequate control of motor impulses. Piotrowski (1945) has found independently in child-tiqueurs a characteristic lack of "the chiaroscuro responses" in the Rorschach test, indicating this very feature—the lack of defense in the tiqueurs' personality make-up. The mirror exercises, introduced by Meige and Feindel, likewise seem not to result in a strengthening of the defenses of the child-tiqueur but rather to increase his morbid inclination to self-observation and hypochondria. Tics are motor automatisms which the child-tiqueur considers ego-alien. Hence he constantly struggles with them by watching his bodily sensations, particularly those of his musculature, and his attitude toward his motor impulses is a mixture of awe and submission, with uncertainty as to which element will emerge victorious.

The clearing up of the tics as symptoms should not be the chief aim of therapy. Our follow-up data also show that disappearance of the tics was not always accompanied by improvement in the total personality. In some cases good general adjustment was achieved though isolated tics persisted (R.T., R.R., A.C.) whereas in two cases with poor outcome the syndrome had disappeared (G.K., M.C.P.). This concurs with the concept that (psychosomatic and other) symptoms serve the purpose of discharging dammed-up instinctual impulses in a pathologic way. Thus the tics represent a kind of morbid release, a safety valve for release of tension.

There were six patients out of ten whose adjustment was fair to good, and in whom no increase in the syndrome and no further deterioration of the personality has occurred after many years. In all these cases the common and apparently crucial factor for integrative personality development was adequate post-discharge management permitting organized physical activity and performance. The simultaneous or subsequent handling of the environment to free the patient as far as possible from pathological dependency appeared to be especially helpful.

C.R., who was one of the most severe cases of tic syndrome, and who was admitted to Rockland State Hospital two and a half years after P.I. discharge, was placed in a rural foster home in 1941, still unimproved. There he attended a rural school and had ample opportunity for organized motor activity outdoors. Two years later he was found symptom-free and well adjusted, and was accepted by the Army.

B.S., serving in the U.S. Army at follow-up and well-adjusted socially, in excellent health, had been given deliberately ample opportunity for outlets of his artistic talents.

R.T.'s improvement was very marked. We believe this was due to the simultaneous skillful social work treatment of the mother, to the wholesome marital relationship of the parents and to the excellent social and economic situation.

A.C. had been a very severe case of *maladie des tics;* at 15 years 9 months of age—three years and ten months after P.I. discharge—he was found to be doing fairly well in school and in society, excelling in dramatics, in athletics, and in mechanical skill. He had been living in a rural environment and had ample opportunity for channelling his "high-strung" active disposition, which persists, as do some mild tics.

Though in H.G.'s case caution is indicated as to prognosis, his personality adjustment at 13 years of age, four years eight months after hospital discharge, was found to be satisfactory; he was an average student, P.S. grade 8A; described as a muscular type, good in athletics and shopwork, somewhat worrisome and anxious, with an occasional, isolated residual head-jerking tic.

R.R. had ample opportunity for organized competitive motor achievement in a military school where he was sent when the family moved to California. This boy, who had an exaggeratedly close, infantilizing relationship with his mother, was given a great degree of freedom during his year of psychotherapy in P.I. His prognosis is one of the best.

Our experience bears out what Fenichel (1945b) says about the function of psychotherapy in psychosomatic disease. He notes that indirectly organ-neurotic symptoms *are* accessible to psychotherapy. We have found as regards organ neurosis of the neuromuscular system that, if the obstacles which are in the way of adequate instinctual discharge are removed through psychoanalysis or psychotherapy and simultaneous channelization of the energy into organized functions of the autonomous ego is facilitated, the vicious circle can be broken and the organ-neurotic syndrome may be relieved, if not cured. As regards the tic syndrome, our follow-up findings and our current clinical observation both suggest that it is essential to facilitate channelization of the increased amorphous motor urge into differentiated, highly organized locomotor and athletic exercise outdoors. Performance activity of the small as well as the large muscles of the body is useful, and, wherever possible, artistic outlets should be encouraged.

The considerably better results in our current cases of tic syndrome may be ascribed, we believe, to insight gained from the follow-up study: It seems to us that deep psychotherapy with undue emphasis on release of aggressive and erotic material further weakens the controlling powers of the child-tiqueur (G.K., W.C.). The aim of therapy should be to give the child's ego an opportunity for gaining perspective concerning those impulses, and the necessary strength to cope with them. Continuation of so-called "deep" psychotherapy throughout adolescence is contraindicated. Experiences in our current tic study concerning therapy encourage us to say that, provided a child with tic syndrome (nonorganic) is treated before severe rigidity of the motor automatisms has occurred, the condition has a fairly favorable outcome. On the other hand, we do not think that a tic syndrome if "left alone" can resolve and result in a self-restitution of the personality. If the disappearance of a tic syndrome is occasionally seen in adolescence (Pacella 1945), it is usually replaced by a severe personality maladjustment.

Part Three

ON CHILD PSYCHOSIS

Chapter 6

ON SYMBIOTIC CHILD PSYCHOSIS: GENETIC, DYNAMIC, AND RESTITUTIVE ASPECTS

[1955]

It was not until many years after ego psychology had gained its proper place within the framework of psychoanalytic theory that psychoanalysts began to scrutinize the available data of the first fifteen to eighteen months of life (Ribble, Fries, Spitz, and others). Even then the beginnings of the verbal stage of development, the period from eighteen months onward, were little studied, except by Anna Freud, Burlingham, and Bowlby. However, Ernst Kris and his co-workers at Yale are now [1955] engaged in systematically studying this period of life.

In the second year of life the infant gradually changes from an almost completely vegetative being, symbiotically dependent on the mother, into a separate individual. He still commands, and obtains, the executive services of this external ego (Spitz 1951). But he becomes increasingly aware of his own capacities as well as of his own separateness. This apperception is, however, still a very precarious one at twelve to thirty months of age.

During the second year of life it is the maturational growth of locomotion which exposes the infant to the important experience of

In collaboration with Bertram J. Gosliner, M.D.

deliberate and active bodily separation from and reunion with the mother. Furthermore, the normal toddler of one and a half to two and a half years, delights in exploring his environment, however indiscriminate his efforts. From so doing he derives sound narcissistic satisfactions. He discovers and masters ever-increasing segments of his physical surroundings, provided he feels his mother's encouragement and availability. This is that second eighteen-month period of life in which pregenital libidinal phases progress in a rapid and overlapping procession. Yet, this same period is no less fateful as far as the infant's ego development and object relationships are concerned.

Let us, for the sake of brevity, call the period from twelve-eighteen to thirty-six months the *separation-individuation phase* of personality development. It is our contention that this separation-individuation phase is a crucial one in regard to the ego and the development of object relationships. It is also our contention that the characteristic fear of this period is separation anxiety. This separation anxiety is not synonymous with the fear of annihilation through abandonment. It is an anxiety which is less abruptly overwhelming than the anxiety of the previous phase. It is, however, more complex, and later we hope to elaborate on this complexity. For we need to study the strong impetus which drives toward separation, coupled with the fear of separation, if we hope to understand the severe psychopathology of childhood which ever so often begins or reveals itself insidiously or acutely from the second part of the first year onward.

This separation-individuation phase is a kind of second birth experience which one of us described as "a hatching from the symbiotic mother-child common membrane." This hatching is just as inevitable as is biological birth (Mahler 1954b).

In animals the absolute dependency on a mother animal is brief. Yet one can observe that pups prematurely taken from the mother are insecure and are considered somatically and dispositionally less stable. Dog breeders furthermore advise that if one has the choice of the litter, the procedure by which he can be sure of getting the best pup is to watch the bitch with the litter and pick the preferential pup. However, even with her preferential pup, as with all the others, the most motherly and devotedly nurturing bitch seems to get bored and obviously annoyed by the nursing process in a comparatively short time. She still plays with her pups for a while longer, and seems to enjoy them, but will soon leave them to their own devices. If she happens to be a hound, for example, she will leave them in favor of her phylogenetically inherent individual instinct gratification, her hunting, for long stretches of time. As for the pups, they will follow her in hunting when they are good and ready.

This rapid individuation process of the pup is duplicated in the case of the human infant with his mother, as in a slow motion picture. Both the symbiotic and the individuation phases are greatly prolonged. However, in humans some emotional tie to mother persists "up to the grave."

A strong and adequate symbiotic phase is a prerequisite for subsequent successful disengagement of the human infant as well. Only if symbiosis has been adequate, is he ready to enter the phase of gradual separation and individuation. The aim and successful outcome of this individuation process is a stable image of the self. As Edith Jacobson (1954) has described, the stable image of the self depends upon successful identifications on the one hand, and distinction between object- and self-representations on the other.

We shall discuss neither the normal symbiotic nor the normal individuation phases in full. However, we cannot avoid giving a brief resume of those events in the two phases, which we believe are essential to understanding the psychotic breakdown, the prepsychotic phase, and remissions in symbiotic child psychosis.

The newborn's waking life centers around his attempts to reduce tension. To ameliorate his unpleasure the infant has two avenues: his own body (Hoffer 1949), and his mother's ministrations. The effect of his mother's breast and ministrations in reducing the pangs of need-hunger cannot be isolated or differentiated by the young infant from tension-reducing attempts of his own, such as urinating, defecating, coughing, sneezing, spitting, regurgitating, vomiting— all the ways by which the infant tries to rid himself of unpleasurable tension. The effect of these expulsive phenomena as well as the gratification gained by his mother's ministrations help the infant, in time, to differentiate between a pleasurable and good quality and a painful and bad quality of experiences.

When the mother is a source of satisfaction, the infant responds positively to her, as may be observed by tension reduction manifested by quiescence and sleep. When body tension or mothering manipulations are a source of pain and displeasure, the infant deals with it as he deals with noxious stimuli in general: he draws away from it, tries to expel it, to eliminate it. In other words, the infant's first orientation in his extrauterine life is according to "good-pleasurable" versus "bad-painful" stimuli. Since hunger is the most imperative biological need, these qualities of "good" and "bad" seem to become equated with "edible" versus "inedible" substances.

Through the inborn and autonomous perceptive faculty of the primitive ego (Hartmann 1939), deposits of memory traces of the two primordial qualities of stimuli occur. We might visualize that these scattered foci of memory deposits form little islands within the hitherto oceanic feeling of complete fusion and oneness with the mother, in the infant's semiconscious state. These memory islands, containing imprints of "pleasurable-good" or "painful-bad" stimuli, are not yet allocated either to the self or to the nonself. We further may assume that these primitive memory deposits are cathected with that primordial undifferentiated drive energy, which Fenichel (1935) and Edith Jacobson (1954) have described. The young infant is exposed to one rhythmically and consistently repeated experience, namely, that hunger and other need tensions arising inside the body cannot be relieved beyond a certain degree unless relief is supplied from a source beyond his own orbit. This repeated experience of a need-satisfying good outside source to relieve him from a bad inside tension eventually conveys to him a vague affective discrimination between "self" and "nonself." It is at this point of differentiation that the predominantly "good" and predominantly "bad" memory islands become vaguely allocated to the self and nonself. The qualities of "pleasure-giving" or "pain-inflicting" become anchored to the mother, but also to the primitive memory islands formed through "pleasurable" and "unpleasurable" sensations from within his own body. This seems to be the beginning of the formation of scattered part images of the object and part images of the body-self as well (Jacobson 1954). We wish to emphasize that the self-images are endowed with the same qualities of prevailingly "good" and predominantly "bad," as are the scattered part images of mother.

We would propose that from the primordial undifferentiated drive energy, libido and aggression differentiate *pari passu* with the infant's primitive reality orientation according to the above-described differentiation of the "good" and "bad" scattered part images of mother and self. "The mother in the flesh," as Bowlby (1952) calls the real mother, is both a source of pleasure and a source of unpleasure, just as is the infant's own body. To "bad" stimuli coming from inside or outside, the infant reacts with impetuous aggression, by ridding and ejective mechanisms; to "good" stimuli coming from inside or outside, the baby reacts with quiet bliss, and later on, with reaching out. Both pleasure and unpleasure manifestations, however, are overshadowed by the still more undifferentiated and unneutralized impetuous drive of aggressive, indiscriminate incorporation of good and bad, which reaches its peak at the period of oral aggression.

The infant has the tendency to suck in, to mouth, to incorporate, to devour, as much of the outside object as possible. His expulsive, ejective, ridding tendencies alternate with this tendency to engulf.

The vicissitudes of primitive aggression are of particular importance, as Hartmann (1939, 1953), Hartmann, Kris, and Loewenstein (1949), Anna Freud (1949), Hoffer (1950a), Bak (1954), and Mahler (1948) have emphasized. The generally accepted psychoanalytic hypothesis that the infant relegates unpleasurable feelings to the non-self, to the outside world, is difficult to demonstrate. Negative hallucination in the infant is even more difficult to observe than its positive forerunner. What we can observe are the two distinct groups of phenomena just described. The infant tries to expel, to sever from his own body orbit, all painful stimuli, irrespective of whether the painful stimulation has originated from the outside or from the inside. Secondly, we can also observe, particularly from five to six months on, an indiscriminate incorporative tendency, which is familiar to all of us. In both observable groups of phenomena the surplus of unneutralized aggression versus libido seems evident.

Hoffer (1950b) drew attention to the fact that deflection of the surplus unneutralized aggression from the body ego is of utmost importance for normal body ego development.

Libidinal cathexis, on the other hand, should gradually shift from the visceral, particularly abdominal, organs in cranial and peripheral direction (Ribble 1941, Greenacre 1945a, Mahler *SPI*:7). With the libidinal shift of cathexis to the sensory perceptive system, great progress is achieved, and clearer demarcation of the own from the mother's body thus evolves.

We may assume that confluence and primitive integration of the scattered "good" and "bad" memory islands into two large, good and bad part images of the self, as well as split good and bad part images of the mother, do not occur before the second year of life. This is attested to by the normal emotional ambivalence which is clinically discernible at this age.

Only now, from twelve-eighteen months on, in the subsequent eighteen-month period of separation-individuation, are the rapidly alternating primitive identification mechanisms possible and dominant. We owe their description to Melanie Klein (1932).

In the further course of normal development there is unification of the split images of objects and of the self, and a unified object representation becomes demarcated from a unified self-representation.

Solid integration, in which there is a blending and synthesis of "good" and "bad" mother images, even in normal development, is not achieved either during the symbiotic phase of mother-child relationship, nor is it completed in the next eighteen-month period of life, during the separation-individuation phase. If the symbiotic and the separation-individuation phases were normal, however, from three or three and a half years on, the child should increasingly be able to respond to the "whole mother," to realize that one and the same person can both gratify and disturb him. With the advent of the latency period the child should not only clearly perceive and recognize that mother is separate and complex, but that other important love objects and he himself are separate and complex as well. He should also begin to be able to modulate feelings within himself, appraise good and bad by trial acting (i.e., thinking).

We could not help delving into these descriptions because during the disorganization-regression process of symbiotic psychosis all these earlier stages again become dominant.

For purposes of understanding our points, we propose focusing on the position of defense of the eighteen to thirty-six-month infant, to defend his own evolving, enjoyable and jealously guarded self-image from infringement by mother and other important figures. This is a clinically important and conspicuous phenomenon during the separation-individuation phase. As Anna Freud (1951a) has pointed out, at the ages of two and three a quasi-normal negativistic phase of the toddler can be observed. It is the accompanying behavioral reaction marking the process of disengagement from the mother-child symbiosis. The less satisfactory or the more parasitic the symbiotic phase has been, the more prominent and exaggerated will be this negativistic reaction. The fear of reengulfment threatens a recently and barely started individual differentiation which must be defended. Beyond the fifteen- to eighteen-month mark, the primary stage of unity and identity with mother ceases to be constructive for the evolution of an ego and an object world (cf. Loewald 1951). In boys as well as in girls, around eighteen months (in some cases even much earlier), the father has become an important object. This relationship ordinarily has the advantage that the inner image of the father has never drawn to itself so much of the unneutralized drive cathexis as has the mother's, and therefore there is less discrepancy between the image of father and the real father. (See also p. 124, below; and Bowlby et al. 1952).

From the very beginning, the infant creates the world in his own image, wherein the symbiotic partner is the indispensable catalyst and beacon of orientation. Early painful or distressing bodily injuries, traumata or illness disrupt this process of self-differentiation and object creation. In his paper on "Repression," Freud (1915) gave us a description of how such disruption comes about. The infant is unable to eject, or later on repress; in other words, to eliminate too massive or continually harassing painful noxi. His impetuous ridding mechanisms may merely lead to exhaustion and apathy. Then regression to a more archaic stage occurs in which the budding self-awareness as well as apperception of the "good" part image of the mother is drowned (Mahler and Elkisch SPI:11). Inasmuch as all happenings in the symbiotic phase are dominated by orality, the infant furthermore loses the necessary and normal delusional experience of incorporating and thus having the good mother in himself, restoring the blissful state of omnipotent fusion with the mother (Lewin 1950). Instead, he struggles in impotent rage and panic, with the catastrophic fear of annihilation, by introjected bad objects, without being able successfully to invoke the good part object, the soothing breast, or the ministering mother. (Compare p. 122, below).

It is obvious that such factors as early and prolonged illnesses or pain interfere with the fusion and blending of good and bad images of objects and self. Instead, fused and confused faulty couplings of part images of self and object occur. These hinder reality orientation. In constitutionally oversensitive and vulnerable infants the pathogenic effects of the described intrapsychic events are enhanced and a prepsychotic stage may be set, if fixation to the symbiotic phase is reinforced during the individuation phase. These auxiliary events occur in the case of mothers who are overstimulating, overprotective, anxious, or emotionally unavailable symbiotic partners.

The children suffering from symbiotic child psychoses described in this and other papers (SPI:7) are not to be thought of as normal children in whom a psychotic process is induced by an emotionally disturbed mother. These children are constitutionally vulnerable and predisposed toward the development of a psychosis. It is the very existence of the constitutional ego defect in the child that helps create the vicious circle of the pathogenic mother-child relationship by stimulating the mother to react to the child in ways that are deleterious to his attempts to separate and individuate.

The pathogenic effect of the attitude of the symbiotically overanxious mother is particularly increased if that mother's hitherto doting attitude changes abruptly at the advent of the separation-individuation phase. Coleman, Kris, and Provence (1953) have drawn attention to the important fact that the attitude of mothers to the same child in different phases of his development may undergo radical changes. A complementary pathogenic factor is the well-known parasitic, infantilizing mother who needs to continue her overprotection beyond the stage when it is beneficial. This attitude becomes an engulfing threat, detrimental to the child's normal disengagement and individuation from his second year of life on. Another type of symbiotic parasitic mother cannot endure the loss of her hitherto vegetative appendage, but has to, emotionally at least, slough him off abruptly.

A case in point was that of Aro, who was brought by his pediatrician for consultation at the age of nine and a half, because of his incapacitating seizurelike paroxysms of generalized tics. He had been having tics with intermissions since the age of six. The referring pediatrician stated that Aro had been hypertonic and hyperkinetic from birth on. He had suffered from pylorospasm. Yet he is said to have been a happy, outgoing infant till the age of about two and a half. As an infant he smiled at people, cooed, played pat-a-cake, how big, etc., which is noteworthy as differential diagnostic criteria to rule out early infantile autism (Mahler *SPI*:7). At closer questioning the mother recalled, however, that Aro never could tolerate frustrations. He insisted that the mother or the nurse be closely at hand at all times. When, at the age of one and beyond, Aro was put into a playpen, he would throw a temper tantrum. In retrospect this was the first manifest sign—we believe—of a progressive disturbance in the neutralization of aggressive drive energy. This assumption is borne out by subsequent disturbed behavior: as soon as Aro could stand on his feet and walk, he manifested a "deadly" hostility toward his five- and seven-year-older siblings. He threw forks and knives and spit at them. This behavior, in turn, brought about a radical and abrupt change in the mother's attitude toward Aro. She was indignant and completely intolerant in the face of the small boy's bold, and what seemed to be vicious attacks upon his so much older siblings. The mother unhesitatingly and completely sided with the older siblings. Aro was often severely restrained, reprimanded, and ostentatiously left behind. Yet there were objective signs and symptoms of constitutional vulnerability of the ego, such as hypertonicity, in Aro's case.

At ten weeks Aro developed a severe pyloric stenosis. He would eagerly take his bottle and keep the milk down for a few moments. Then there would be contractions of the stomach, observable through the abdominal wall. Unmistakable expressions of pain accompanied these contractions, and the milk was expelled by violent projectile vomiting. Very soon after the vomiting Aro would be given another bottle; and if he vomited again, this was followed by forced feeding. He was weaned from the bottle to a cup at five months. From that moment to the present he has put fingers, toys, and various objects indiscriminately into his mouth.

Attempts at toilet training were started unbelievably early by a strict nurse. About the age of four Aro began to retain his feces for a week at a time, complaining that it hurt to defecate. The mother gave the boy frequent enemas against his struggling protests.

Aro began school at five and a half; a year after this, his tics began. At this time, the mother's father, who was devoted to the boy and to whom Aro was most responsive, died. A short time after the grandfather's death, Aro became depressed, his tics became violent. Most disturbing to the family was a loud yelling tic. (Later, during a psychotic break Aro was to say that he had a yell that could be heard around the world, that could bring the dead to life.)

At school Aro was unable to work up to grade, in spite of his normal I.Q. At nine Aro suffered his first psychotic breakdown which lasted six weeks. Aro insisted that he would not leave his room until his tics stopped. He would shriek prayers to God and announce that he and his daddy had a secret. "I'm practicing the loudest yell in the world. When I give that yell everything will come to life—even the pictures in the room." Later, in his analysis, Aro elaborated this fantasy. In addition to the obvious wish to revive the dead grandfather, Aro fantasied that in response to his yell the most ferocious tigers in Africa would come to Aro, protect him, and kill Aro's enemies.

The details of the onset of the psychotic breakdown are revealing. It happened in the midst of psychotherapy with a therapist Aro shared with his mother. The morning of the onset Aro was to be taken to the psychiatrist, and the mother noticed that Aro was crawling like a baby on the front lawn and that he was masturbating. She harshly reprimanded him. They then waited in their car for a friend. She remembers fearing an accident. Aro, who always was affected by his mother's moods, appeared tense and worried. The friend, a teacher, finally arrived and dramatically explained the reason for being late. One of her pupils badly cut her knee and they had to stop the bleeding. At that moment Aro slumped to the floor of the car, writhing about and uttering inarticulate cries and groans. His body appeared completely out of control and his clothes were drenched with sweat. The psychiatrist gave Aro a sedative which was ineffective, and following this Aro refused to leave his room. The friend's tale of the bloody accident that happened to the child, triggered Aro's psychotic breakdown. At that time the child was suffering with intense castration anxiety. His excessive masturbation indicated that repression of his oedipal strivings had not been successful. The mother's harsh reprimand, the fear of an accident, the bleeding accident of the pupil, and particularly the impending visit to the psychiatrist who belonged to mother and represented the punishing father, added to Aro's mounting terror. His psychotic breakdown represents a refuge for his disorganized ego from castration anxiety, a reunion with the good object on a regressive level. The almost totally disorganized child sought to obtain strength and nourishment from the higher good powers (God, father, etc.). Only the good objects are ego-syntonic and can be tolerated within. Only by constant alternation by ejection of the bad and incorporation of the good object, can Aro succeed in replenishing his empty and disorganized self. It seems that during his psychotic episodes Aro's regressive behavior, entailing alternating primitive introjective-projective mechanisms, is similar to the patterning of the relationship between the normal symbiotic infant and mother, in which incorporative and ejective mechanisms alternate. The autism, with its attendant megalomania, connotes union and fusion with the good mother, the tic paroxysms signify the loss of control in the struggle to eject the incorporated bad object.

Aro, an emaciated child of about ten, usually was brought to the office by his mother, who sat down in the waiting room with an apologetic smile. Aro would sit as far away from her as he could get, and gaze away from her at the ceiling or wall. Frequently he would dart a look at her and then quickly avert his gaze. His body was racked with involuntary movements of arms, torso, neck and face. The movements were particularly predominant in the mouth and jaw. We will not give a detailed description of his tic paroxysms. Frequently loud, guttural vocalizations accompanied the tic movements. The boy would appear terrified and anguished during these episodes. At the completion of the tic paroxysm Aro would repeat it volitionally in an abbreviated form, with a look of nonchalant mastery. He might, during this purposive repetition, hum a little tune and move his body, as if in response to the rhythm. At these times he would attempt to maintain a contemptuous, mocking attitude which he would preserve until he was overcome by the next attack.

Applicable to Aro's tic syndrome is the description by Mahler and co-workers (1945, *SPI*:3) of the tic syndrome as a loss of control of and struggle against introjected objects, ego-alien demoniacal inner powers. To our patient it was as if these powers gained possession and reduced the self to the status of a puppet. The voluntary repetition of the tic seizure indicates that ejecton of the demon has been successful and that the ego-alien inner force has been banished. The child for the moment is once again in command. His air of mastery during the volitional repetition of the tic movements, the rhythmic response of his body to his humming, indicates that his self-mastery is dependent upon the introjection of the good mother; he rocks and soothes himself.

Aro's defective ego alone is incapable of dealing with his inner needs. He constantly attempts to obtain strength and gratification from the outside by means of incorporation. His regressed patterning is that of an infant indiscriminately sucking in supplies from the outside. A consequence of this avid incorporative striving is that the bad and painful as well as the good and pleasurable are ingested and introjected.

This cycle in the tic paroxysm—need, inner turmoil, loss of body control, on the one hand, and the attainment of gratification and quiescence through introjection, on the other—brings to mind Aro's experiences with his pylorospasm. Then at ten weeks the ingested food caused actual pain and culminated in expulsion through vomiting. The vomiting was invariably followed by a fresh bottle until the infant attained satiety, even though at the expense of forced feeding. Or else quiescence through exhaustion ensued.

The fear of reengulfment on the one hand and separation anxiety on the other is graphically demonstrated by the relationship of Aro and his mother. It was the mother who would ring the office and elevator bells, open the doors, greet and say good-bye to the analyst. There was never conversation or physical contact between mother and son. On occasion, when the mother came too close to him, Aro would suddenly lash out with his fist, striking her sharply on the breast.

Although mother and child did not converse, there was much communication by means of gestures, body movements, and facial expressions. The mother was particularly adept at remaining at what for Aro was an optimal distance from him. He would indicate by tics or mouth-fingering, etc., when she was too far away and, as mentioned before, would strike her when she came too close.

The communication without words between Aro and his mother is illustrated by the following: In the waiting room on one occasion Aro lurched to his feet, looked over at his mother, then looked toward the bathroom. He made a gesture toward his penis. His mother quickly arose, opened the bathroom door, and switched on the light. Aro urintated with the door open, looking back at his mother and chuckling happily. The mother flushed the toilet.

From the beginning, Aro willingly came into the consultation room alone. Without a sign of recognition he would move past the analyst with a curious propulsive gait and run through the open doors to the playroom. The social amenities were never responded to. He would cringe and shrink away from the slightest physical approach on the part of the analyst. Often Aro would look to the side, mutter to himself and then laugh wildly, without contagion. At such times he appeared to be responding to purely inner ideas or stimuli. His being out of control, violently hitting at the chair or the wall, his body being thrown about by his paroxysms of laughter, appeared frankly psychotic.

Aro would listen intently to the sound of the elevator taking his mother down. As soon as the noise would cease, Aro would roam about the room investigating its contents. He would look, touch and retouch, smell and mouth the objects and compare their weight. He would both taste and bite them.

He would question the analyst: "What is it?—How long have you had it?—How old is it?—What's it for?—Which is best?" etc. Such questions were repeated over and over again, in a nagging, querulous voice. Attempts to answer them were drowned out by Aro's loud vocal tics and by Aro repeating the first few words of the answer. When an answer was finally completed, Aro would repeat the answer over and over again, each time with a different tone and inflection so that the answer would range the gamut from a simple

statement to puzzled, disbelieving, astonished, angry, scornful affects.

Aro's restitutive attempts to orient himself in the environment are
successful with inanimate objects. Because of their stability and
constancy, and because he can explore them at his own speed, he can
make them a part of his own experience. He is able to categorize them
as to good or bad. Aro is unable to blend, modulate, or synthesize.
There is no grey—only black or white. Cars made by General Motors
are good—all others are bad. Aro cannot discriminate or grade
within either group. There is no difference between Cadillac and
Chevrolet. They are both General Motors and hence both good.
Unlike himself, inanimate objects do not change rapidly in an
unpredictable way and thus serve as a frame of reference to the child
struggling to control in a chaotic world.

Aro's attempts at orientation by means of questioning succeed
less happily. The answer provoked by his question is not predictable,
either in terms of its final form, its ultimate meaning or its effect on
him. Aro, constantly threatened with loss of self-identity through
ego-alien powers gaining ascendency, must maintain a dominance
and control over the answers his questions provoke. His interrup-
tions, mimicry, etc., serve this end. He is careful not to be taken by
surprise and not to be emotionally stirred. An emotion which arises
unbidden and which takes an unpredictable course is experienced by
Aro as if it were a foreign body, threatening the integrity of his ego.
Because he cannot synthesize and modulate, Aro has to employ the
above-mentioned maneuvers—to "tame," as it were, the answer and
thus to achieve mastery over it. He makes it his own through a
process of alternating ejection and incorporation.

The transition from one situation to another was very difficult for
Aro. This was demonstrated by his behavior when he heard the
elevator's noise, indicating the return of his mother. He would tic
violently, run to the door, run back to the center of the room, repeat
this several times, and ask repeatedly, "Is it time—is it time?"

Most striking in Aro's relationship to his mother is his endeavor
to remain at an optimal distance, spatially and emotionally, from
her. The boy seeks to attain an equilibrium between the need of his

weakened ego to obtain constant supplies from her and the threat of being engulfed and losing his self-identity to her.

He is unable to go more than a few blocks from home. He will scream in protest if she plans to leave the house and if she persists he will gag himself and retch. The father who, particularly in the preanalytic period, used to baby-sit with Aro, relates that shortly after the mother would leave, Aro would stuff himself with food. He would eat an inordinate number of hot dogs and gulp down unbelievable amounts of soda pop. He would then, in great distress, turn to his father, and through frantic gestures implore help in getting rid of the ingested pain-producing food.

Aro will permit no intimacy. He will not suffer his mother to kiss or get close to him. He is abusive and hostile to her and takes a particular delight in uttering obscenities in her presence. He hits her, tells her she is ugly, and frequently orders her to leave the room. His fear of engulfment and his separation anxiety are dramatically illustrated by a frequent occurrence.

Aro will call to his mother in a piteous and pleading whine, "Mommy, Mommy," and will start toward her. He will then stop but continue to call, entreating her to come to him. When she comes to him he lashes out, hits her and screams, "Get away, bitch." If she retires, he calls her back. When she finally refuses to come to him, he implores her, breaks into sobs, sticks his fingers down his throat until he gags or retches.

It appears that Aro's ambivalent behavior is a result of his inability to create a fused and blended representation of his mother, as well as of his own self. Because of an inner need, it is toward the good mother he moves and it is she whom he so imploringly calls. The mother who comes cannot be reconciled with Aro's idealized mental image of the all-good mother, and Aro reacts to her with violent warding off, reminiscent of the primitive ridding mechanism of the baby in the symbiotic phase—the gesture with which that baby tried to expel the introjected painful stimulus.

As Aro undoubtedly entered the oedipal phase (the passive negative aspects of which were prominent in the analytic material), the father somehow became the helping, glorified figure—basically a "good object." On the other hand, Aro's oedipal strivings toward the mother maintain his image of her as mainly bad and threatening. Because of castration anxiety, the "ugly, castrated" mother must not come too close physically or emotionally; that is, she must sit in the back of the car when he sits in front with his father, etc. Intimacy with the bad mother would result in reengulfment, in a shattering of Aro's ego organization. The fear of being eaten and castration anxiety receive additional impetus from the boy's terrifying tic seizures. The involuntary movements are a loss of control of a part of the body and a loss of that part of the body from Aro's self-representation to an evil and stronger force, the bad mother and perhaps the oedipal father.

In Aro's case the psychotic mechanisms exist side by side with neurotic ones. By virtue of appersonation of the mother's executive functions as external ego (Spitz 1951), Aro is still able to function on a regressed and constricted level. Though he has had several frankly psychotic episodes, his break with reality is not final and not complete. The main difference between cases like Aro's, where remissions are predominant, and others where the loss of reality seems permanent and irreversible, is whether representations of outside love objects remain partially cathected or cathexis has been completely withdrawn.

Bowlby (1952) has described that in the course of actual separation of the small child from his mother, both the good and the bad image of the mother undergo rapid changes. The good mother becomes glorified and the bad mother a hateful image. He has documented in his well-known film that, at reunion after separation, even the normal two-year-old temporarily has some difficulty in identifying either of his inner images with the real mother. Bowlby's case displayed a fleeting blank response when confronted with the "mother in the flesh." (Significantly, with the father the girl's reactions even at a second separation within half a year showed practically no lasting adverse effects—unlike the disruptive near-detrimental effect which the second separation had on the mother-child relationship.)

An effect similar to that produced on the normal two-year-old by actual repeated separation from the mother occurs, even without actual separation, with a symbiotic child for whom, through the factors previously enumerated, the prepsychotic stage had been set. A psychotic break may occur in response to any additional trauma, during the relative strain of the process of individuation. Experiences of disappointment in the course of the oral, anal, but particularly the oedipal phases of psychosexual development, harbor the threat of castration which in turn reinforces the threat of oral attack in these children. The fantasies of being robbed of the contents of the body and finally of being engulfed and eaten up dominate. This latter, we repeat, is the projected counterpart of the avid tendency of these children to suck in, to gulp—good and bad objects alike.

We know, in retrospect, that integration of the good and bad mother images, as well as clear differentiation of representations of the part objects in the outside versus the part images of the self, has been defective in the cases in question. Hence, at the point when fear of reengulfment, a fear amounting to fear of dissolution of identity, accumulates simultaneously with its apparent opposite, that is, separation panic—the two overwhelm the ego. This occurs with such intensity that the progressive integration and gradual unlocking of couplings of scattered part-image representations of the self and object are prevented. There is regression to the stage in which unneutralized libido and aggression were vested in the symbiotic system within the child's inner delusional reality. At this point the real mother ceases to exist as a separate entity. The introjected split objects dominate the psychotic child's world. These are then the extreme cases which do not seem to respond to outside stimuli but which seem to be continuously in communication with the introjected objects, as shown by bizarre posturing, giggling and stereotyped activities. Very often the introjected objects gain symbolic personification by means of exclusive preoccupation with a piece of carboard, hallucinated bell, an adored extremity, a toy animal, and the like, to which the patients address passionate endearments. If they are told that the psychotic fetish is in danger, or if it is symbolically removed, they fall into an abysmal panic. At such a stage the patient may no longer show any signs of missing his real mother. It is at this stage that these children are routinely misdiagnosed as autistic cases.

To illustrate the genesis and dynamics of a complete psychotic break with reality we should like to sketch, in addition, very briefly the following case. B.S. was six years old when he was admitted to the Children's Service of the New York State Psychiatric Institute. He was extremely hyperactive and destructive. He not only displayed blind aggression toward other children but mutilated himself by biting and scratching, so that big brown calluses covered his two forearms and his left hand.

His illness began at two years of age. B.S.'s first year of life was marred by illness, chronic diarrhea. He was so weak and debilitated that his early maturational growth was gravely delayed. He would lie quietly by himself, flat on his back, and make no demands on his mother who attended to his physical needs. He made no response to his brother or father; he did not seem to know them. When he was two years old, his mother developed pleurisy and was hospitalized. The child's reaction to this was not recorded, but when at two and half the child did start to walk the hitherto overly placid child became hyperactive, would bang his head against the crib, tear his hair out in bunches, and displayed increasingly bizarre behavior. He would withdraw from people but would use his carriage blanket as his constant companion. He rolled it up and talked to it and appeared to be "in a different world." He continued to be a grave feeding problem and took no food unless his mother spoonfed him. He attacked younger children and when prevented, bit and scratched himself.

On the ward he would talk only to his fetish in a continuous babble, frequently simulating his mother's talking to him. In this monologue with the fetish, it obviously represented himself.

B.S., like Aro, seemed possessed by unneutralized, destructive aggression which manifested itself, at times, in catatonic agitation and violence toward objects and his own body.

The actual break with or withdrawal from reality rarely occurs before our eyes. Such observation as described by Kubie and Israel (1955) in their beautiful communication, "Say You're Sorry," is exceptional. In this case the little girl's acute psychotic regression was triggered by the loss of the good substitute mother figure, represented by the supportive houseworker concurrent with severe corporal punishment by the good father.

We believe the stable image of a father or of another substitute of the mother, beyond the eighteen-months mark and even earlier, is beneficial and perhaps a necessary prerequisite to neutralize and to counteract the age-characteristic oversensibility of the toddler to the threat of reengulfment by the mother.

We have mentioned the dread of reengulfment versus separation panic in the phase of individuation. We tend to think of the father too onesidedly as the castrating figure, a kind of bad mother image in the preoedipal period. Loewald (1951), to our knowledge, was the first to emphasize that, "Against the threat of the maternal engulfment the paternal position is not another threat of danger, but a support of powerful force." If there is a relative lack of support on the part of either parent (or the "uncontaminated" mother substitutes as Dr. Ernst Kris pointed out in his discussion of this paper), a reengulfment of the ego into the whirlpool of the primary undifferentiated symbiotic stage becomes a true threat.

The toddler in the second eighteen months of life, whose ego is constitutionally vulnerable, symbiotically fixated, and now during the separation-individuation phase is additionally traumatized, may regress to even earlier archaic stages of personality development. A lapse into the archaic objectless, autistic stage may be the only solution. The child may suddenly or gradually lose his individual identity and his contact with reality.

This occurred to five-year-old M.C., for whose mother "all my children seemed to be the same." Although there are no detailed data of the symbiotic stage of M.C.'s development, from the mother's actual behavior at the time of M.C.'s hospitalization when five and a half years old, we can readily reconstruct it. At this time he was still exclusively on bottle feedings. The mother had made no attempt to foster the growth of independence in other areas either. M.C. was never permitted or encouraged to dress himself, nor to develop any spontaneity.

Shortly after M.C.'s birth, the father began to indulge in alcohol, at first only moderately, but gradually to an ever-increasing degree.

During the earlier phase, well beyond M.C.'s second birthday, the father remained a moderately devoted father, caring for the infant and tending to his needs. In time, however, the father's behavior came to be more and more unpredictable. When intoxicated, he was frequently physically abusive toward the mother. This eventually culminated in a particular episode when the patient was four and a half years old. The father's behavior was so threatening toward the mother that she called the police, who then proceeded to arrest the father. M.C., who had witnessed the entire episode, was extremely disturbed, not only about the father's physical abuse of the mother but particularly about the rough treatment which the father received at the hands of the policemen. When the father was subsequently removed by the police, M.C.'s agitation and distress were very great. He cried repeatedly, "Where are they taking my Daddy?" His mother was obliged to take M.C. to the police station and there obtain her husband's release. It was following this experience that M.C. gradually regressed: his speech, which had been age-adequate, eventually became limited to two words. He reverted to urinating wherever the urge overpowered him, and defecated in closets. An earlier phase of father-child communication was used as stereotyped patterned behavior. The father's throwing the child, half-angrily, half-playfully, to the bed or ground, became a pattern of behavior in which M.C. would slump to the floor and lie there quietly and unresponsively with vacuous stare. This was only one evidence of his withdrawal from reality into his self-created inner world.

We have seen that Aro is functioning (to a great extent) on the level of the symbiotic infant and the toddler between eighteen and thirty-six months. He uses his mother as his external ego. He also wards her off with autistic defenses for fear of complete dissolution of his individual entity. We feel that Aro's case, as well as the complete autistic withdrawal into a self-sufficient autistic inner world in cases such as B.S. and M.C., show that autism, this psychotic form of negativism, is an attempt at reactive restitution. The break with reality and withdrawal into an inner world serve the function of survival when the good images in the outside world are insufficient or unusable to counteract the menace of demoniacal inner powers that harass, attack, and almost annihilate the ego from within (as in the case of tiqueurs); or if both parental images become completely deflated and useless against castration threat (Jacobson 1953); or if, against consuming introjected bad objects and the hostile world (police, dangerous psychotherapist, death of grandfather, etc.), no object image in the outside world can be depended upon. We designate this *per se* regressive psychotic defense, this secondary autism, a "reactive restitution" because the ego thus restores, albeit regressively, the blissful oceanic feeling, the oneness with "the object," which seems the delusional substitute for that child whose ego is unable to endure the second hatching process, the actual separation from the good object.

Chapter 7

ON CHILD PSYCHOSIS AND SCHIZOPHRENIA:
AUTISTIC AND SYMBIOTIC INFANTILE PSYCHOSES

[1952]

It seems that psychosis is the sad prerogative of the human species. It is not confined to adults alone. Animals are born with well-developed instincts which guarantee their independent individual survival soon after birth. In the human young, however, these animal instincts (in terms of sense of track) have atrophied and become unreliable and, as Freud stated, the ego had to take over the role of adaptation to reality which the id neglects. The somatic corollary of ego development is the central nervous system, which is in a very immature state at birth. The neonate appears to be an almost purely biological organism with instinctual responses to stimuli not on a cortical but essentially on a reflex and thalamic level. There exist only somatic defense mechanisms, which consist of overflow and discharge reactions, whereby cortical inhibition is undeveloped. Thus, we may say, that at birth there exists only a rudimentary ego, incapable of retaining stimuli in any degree of tension, or else, that prevalence of the undifferentiated phase of personality development persists for a comparatively long period of extrauterine existence (Hartmann, Kris, and Loewenstein 1946). Yet the psychobiological rapport between the nursing mother and the baby complements the infant's undifferentiated ego. This normal empathy on the part of the mother is the human substitute for the instinct on which the animal can rely for survival. In a quasi-closed system or unit, the mother executes vitally important ministrations without which the human young would be unable to survive. The intrauterine, parasite-host relationship within the mother organism (Deutsch 1945) must be replaced in the postnatal period by the infant's being enveloped, as it were, in the extrauterine matrix of the mother's nursing care, a kind of *social symbiosis*.

The young infant is readily thrown into affectomotor storm-rage reactions which, if not relieved by the mother's ministrations, may result in a state of organismic distress. This organismic distress is phenomenologically quite similar to the panic reactions of later life. As a second stage of his homeostatic insufficiency, the young infant may exhaust his life energy and may lapse into a kind of semistupor, reminiscent of his fetal existence (Ribble 1941). The newborn and young infant gradually must be brought out of this tendency toward vegetative splanchnic regression, out of the tendency to lapse into this exhausted semistuporous state, into an increased senory aware-ness of, and contact with, his environment (Greenacre 1945a, Spitz 1946b). In terms of energy or libidinal cathexis this means that a progressive displacement of energy quantities from the inside of the body (particularly from the abdominal organs toward the periphery of the body) has to occur so that the perceptual conscious system, as Freud calls the surface of the body, the peripheral rind of the ego, containing the sense organs, may receive cathexis. The turning from predominantly proprioceptive awareness to increased sensory aware-ness of the outer world occurs through the medium of affective rapport with the mother. The baby's libido position thus proceeds from the stage of fetal narcissism to primary body narcissism, a stage in which representation of the mother's body plays a large part. Thus, to repeat, the infant's rudimentary and very vulnerable home-ostatic equipment after birth must be enveloped by the now extra-uterine matrix of a mother's or a mother substitute's nursing care.

THE BODY EGO IN INFANTILE PSYCHOSIS

The core of ego development, the first orientation toward exter-nal reality, is the differentiation of the body image, which is the psychic representation of the bodily self (Schilder 1935). Through the rhythmically recurring experience of painful accumulation of tension in the inside of his own body, followed by regularly repeated experiences of gratification, which the infant cannot provide for himself hallucinatorily beyond a certain point, the infant eventually becomes dimly aware of the fact that satisfaction is dependent on a source outside of his bodily self. Thus the infant recognizes an orbit beyond the boundaries of the self, that of external reality, represented by the mother. Bodily contact with the mother, that is, fondling and cuddling, is an integral prerequisite for the demarcation of the body ego from the nonself within the stage of somatopsychic symbiosis of the mother-infant dual unity. Under normal circumstances infants do not only treat parts of the mother's body as if they were their own, but, as Anna Freud and Dorothy Burlingham (1944, p. 7) pointed out: "We assume on the basis of much evidence that the child's feeling of oneness with the mother's body has a parallel in the mother's feeling that the baby's body belongs to her." In terms of libidinal and aggressive cathexis this implies that the baby's instinctual drives vicariously aim at the mother's body, particularly her eyes, mouth, hand, face and breast, as if they were his own. He experiments with the feel of the mother's body, comparing it with the feel of his own. However, this learning about one's own body contour as separate from the mother's represents a relatively high degree of ego differentiation, and ability to neutralize and direct aggresion, and a relatively advanced sensory perceptive awareness of the environment. Even this vague sensory discrimination represents a degree of development of the sense of reality—a stage which is by no means reached or maintained by all cases of infantile psychosis.

IN EARLY INFANTILE PSYCHOSIS GRAVE DISTORTION OF THE MOTHER-CHILD RELATIONSHIP SEEMS THE ESSENTIAL CAUSE FOR "EGO ALIENATION FROM REALITY"

Freud (1924a) considered the ego's alienation from reality the pivotal disturbance in adults' or adolescents' psychoses. Ferenczi (1913) has described how the infant's sense of reality proceeds—

through the stages of magic hallucinatory omnipotence—toward gestural and word magic—until, very gradually, he is able to accept and to master realistically his expanding external orbit. It seems obvious to those who have the opportunity to treat deeply disturbed children that the infantile ego's alienation from, or arrest of recognition of, reality is an occurrence inherent in the brittle and weak organization of the infantile personality (proclivity to ego fragmentation). To understand the dynamics in infantile psychosis, observation and study of the most important transitory step in the adaptation to reality is necessary; namely, that step in the development of the sense of reality in which the mother is gradually left outside the omnipotent orbit of the self. This step is preliminary to, and perhaps alternates with, the process of endowing the mother with object-libidinal cathexis. The toddler gradually delimits his own individual entity from the primal mother-infant symbiotic unit. He separates his own self (and his mental representation) from that of the mother. This stage in ego development is a very vulnerable one, particularly in children in whose early life the somatopsychic symbiosis has been pathological (cf. Spitz 1951).

THE IMPORTANCE OF CONSTITUTIONAL (INTRINSIC) FACTORS IN THE GENESIS OF INFANTILE PSYCHOSIS

In regard to the question of heredity versus early frustrational and traumatic etiology of infantile psychosis, we may say that it is very difficult to ascertain whether the grave disturbance in a case of early infantile psychosis has been caused by the mother's pathology and lack of empathy, or by the infant's great innate ego deviation, be it an inherent lack of contact with his living environment, or an inordinate need for symbiotic parasitic fusion with the adult. It is a fact that time and again we see schizophrenic children whose mothers appear not to lack warmth, genuine love, or acceptance of the individual child, nor do they appear to be exceptionally possessive, infantilizing and restrictive.[1] Human nature provides a mutuality between the

1. Compare Anna Maenchen (1953) who did not find unequivocal types of mothers pertaining to the severely disturbed children's cases about whom she reported.

infant and his mother by which, on the one hand, severe traumatization, chronic emotional starvation on part of the environment, seems to damage a constitutionally sound baby only if the baby is very young; on the other hand (as the famous Dennis experiment has shown and as everyday life experience demonstrates) the constitutionally sound baby, beyond the fourth, fifth, and sixth month automatically coerces the adult's empathy (Greenacre 1944). The infant's contact-seeking gestures appeal to woman's most basic biological longing. Hence emotional gratification as well as food are readily given unless maternal psychopathology has rendered the adult partner unable to respond. In other words, it seems that such basic damage to the ego which results in infantile psychosis, occurs in children who have a hereditary or constitutional *Anlage* for it, or in whom an intrinsic factor is prevalent. There *are* infants with an inherently defective tension-regulating apparatus which probably cannot be adequately complemented by either the most quantitatively or qualitatively efficient mothering. It seems that there *are* infants with an inherent ego deficiency which from the very beginning—that is to say, from the stage of the undifferentiated phase—predisposes them to remain or become alienated from reality; there are others whose precarious reality-adherence depends on delusional symbiotic fusion with the mother image.

AUTISTIC INFANTILE PSYCHOSIS

From the points of view of object relationship and development of the sense of reality, we may describe two clinically and dynamically distinct groups of early child psychosis: in one group of early child psychosis the mother, as representative of the outside world, never seems to have been perceived emotionally by the infant, and the first representation of outer reality, the mother as a person, as a separate entity, seems not to be cathected. The mother remains a part object, seemingly devoid of specific cathexis and not distinguished from inanimate objects. This type of infantile psychosis was first described by Kanner (1942, 1944, 1949) and given the name of *early infantile autism*. In autistic infantile psychosis there are no signs of affective awareness of other human beings. Behavior which would point to affective perception of ministrations coming from the mother—from the outside world—is absent. In the anamnesis of these children one finds descriptions of the earliest behavior, which betray that there was no anticipatory posture at nursing, no reaching-out gestures, and no specific smiling response. One finds the following data: "I never could reach my baby."—"He never smiled at me."—"The minute she could walk, she ran away from me."—"It hurt me so when I saw other babies glad to be in their mother's arms; my boy always tried to creep away from my lap as soon as he could."—"He never greeted me when I entered, he never cried, he never even noticed when I left the room."—"She never was a cuddly baby, she never liked caresses, she did not want anybody to embrace or to kiss her."—"She never made any personal appeal for help at any time."—This last remark of a very observant mother of one of these autistic children described the disturbance as seen in terms of social behavior.

My little patient Lotta, aged three years and four months, suffered from an *inherent* autistic disturbance. She provoked multiple traumatizations by a mother who herself lived in a hateful dependency on her own mother. There were severe feeding deprivations; a lip injury at spoon feeding occurred at a very early age. There was a strict and unloving regime of precocious toilet training. A vulvovaginitis followed the first signs of Lotta's beginning to "touch herself." Thus, traumatic overstimulation crowded out normal zonal libidinization in all areas of psychosexual development. Yet these traumatizations, I believe, could not have occurred, if there had not been great intrinsic ego pathology. Daily struggles over constipation, with digital removal of the feces, was just one indication of the kind of atmosphere which prevailed. At the age of three and a half Lotta had no language, no gestural communication, no hand, mouth and eye integration (Hoffer 1949). She neither fed nor handled herself and she showed a terrified startle reaction at any chance touch *of* or *by* another person. By the usual intelligence rating she would have ranked among the lower imbeciles. However, Lotta's habits were compulsively neat, her motor and manipulative skills were age-adequate, her knowledge of, her memory for, her static inanimate environment were phenomenal.

During therapy, by using every conceivable device, she was slowly brought to sensory perception of the outer world, by gradually accepting contact with the analyst's body. Yet no normal identification occurred but instead there was extensive mirroring and parrotlike word formation. Word formation was autistic and speech was not used for intercommunication, but only for commands and signals—and it was used toward objects as freely as toward the analyst.

She seemed to catch up rapidly with isolated fragments of her arrested ego development. She went through repetitious aggressive exploration of her inanimate environment—banging the doors, switching the lights on and off, and fingering everything like blind people do.

There were bizarre discrepancies of body ego integration, as the disconnected fragments of her personality forged ahead at fantastically uneven rates. Let me give you an illustration:

At the stage of treatment when Lotta went through repetitious testing of her environment, she would indeed tax the patience of her mother—a little flashlight was provided for her by the analyst in order to drain away some of the disturbing behavior from the overstrained home situation. She became quite attached to the little flashlight. At the same time Lotta started to put everything she liked into her mouth. Thus she mouthed the little flashlight like a teething baby. When driving from the office that time, her mother, as usual, used the automatic lighter to light her cigarette. Lotta, unnoticed, got hold of the glowing lighter and put it to her mouth, causing severe scorching of her lips.[2] She showed practically no reaction. Her pain sensitivity seemed grossly below normal. This, among other signs, is, I believe, an indication of the lack or deficiency of peripheral cathexis in autistic child patients. In contrast, proprioceptive stimuli, visceral pain, was keenly felt and reacted to (Mahler 1950).

To repeat: it seemed, in Lotta's case at least, unavoidable that autonomous ego functions emerged, were put together and existed simultaneously, like a patchwork of loosely connected parts, held

2. Compare Hartmann, Kris, and Loewenstein (1949).

together in a static way, without the specific matrix of "affective correlation" in the course of treatment.

This bizarre picture of scattered ego functions and the clinically clearly discernible lack of peripheral cathexis make us realize that in autistic infantile psychosis the vicissitudes of libido and aggression cannot be traced merely in terms of the hierarchy of zonal stages. Instead, we can in some cases trace during treatment the course of libido and aggression from the splanchnic-visceral position through progressive cathexis in cranial direction, outward onto the periphery of the body, the skin, and the sense organs, i.e., the perceptual conscious system (Mahler 1950). The instinctual forces, both libido and aggression, exist in an unneutralized form, due to the absence of the synthetic function of the ego. There is an inherent lack of contact with the human environment.

Whenever Lotta was in great distress, her whole little body shook with tearless sobs, yet she neither sought nor accepted help from anyone, but threw herself flat on the floor and pressed against the solid support of it. Likewise she would cling to the familiar high chair, but not to father or mother. This autistic psychotic child was characterized (as were all those whom I observed) by a peculiar inability to discriminate between living and inanimate objects, even in a perceptual sense (cf. Stirnimann 1947).

SYMBIOTIC INFANTILE PSYCHOSIS

There is, however, another group of infantile psychosis in which the early mother-infant symbiotic relationship is marked, but does not progress to the stage of object-libidinal cathexis of the mother. The mental representation of the mother remains, or is regressively *fused with*—that is to say, is *not* separated from the self. It participates in the delusion of omnipotence of the child patient.

Children of the symbiotic group rarely show conspicuously disturbed behavior in the first year of life, except, perhaps, disturbances of sleep. They may be described by their mothers as crybabies or oversensitive infants. Their disturbance becomes apparent either

gradually or fulminantly at such crossroads of personality development, at which maturational function of the ego would usually effect
separation from the mother, and would enable the child to master an
ever-increasing segment of reality, independently of her. As soon as
ego differentiation and psychosexual development confront the
child and thus challenge him with a measure of separation from and
independence of the mother, the illusion of the symbiotic omnipotence is threatened and severe panic reactions occur. These reactions
usually manifest themselves in the third or fourth year, or else, at the
height of the oedipal conflict. In other words, it would seem that a
break with reality is touched off by the maturational growth of motor
coordination which harbors the inherent challenge of motor independence, or else, the complicated and differential emotional demands of the oedipal situation throw the symbiotic psychotic child
into the described affective panic. In symbiotic child psychosis,
unneutralized libidinal and aggressive forces have remained narcissistically vested in fused systems of mother-father-child unit,
reminiscent of the primary unit (mother-infant). Landmarks of
fragmentation of the ego are traumatizations through sickness,
separation (for instance, placement in a nursery school), birth of a
sibling, but also all kinds of changes of a minor nature, which upset
the precarious psychobiological balance of such children. Thereby
the cumulative effect of previous traumata very often plays a role.
The world is hostile and threatening, because it has to be met as a
separate being. Separation anxiety overwhelms the brittle ego of the
"symbiotic psychotic child." His anxiety reactions are so intense and
so diffuse that they are reminiscent of the organismic distress of early
infancy. Clinically, such children show all the signs of abysmal
affective panic. These severe panic reactions are followed by restitutive productions which serve to maintain or restore the narcissistic
fusion, the delusion of oneness with the mother and/or father.
Restitution in symbiotic psychosis is attempted by somatic delusions
and hallucinations of reunion with the narcissistically loved and
hated, omnipotent mother image, or sometimes by hallucinated
fusion with a condensation of father-mother images. In the symbiotic infantile psychosis reality testing remains fixated at, or regresses
to, the omnipotent delusional stage of the symbiotic mother-infant

relationship. The boundaries of the self and the nonself are blurred. Even the mental representation of the body-self is unclearly demarcated. These are the cases, I believe, of whom Bender (1947) was thinking when she described their body contour melting in one's own. The autistic child's body, in contrast, is uniquely unyielding, and feels like a lifeless object in one's arms (Rank and Macnaughton 1950).

A peculiar hypercathexis of one part of the body is often encountered in symbiotic psychotic children. It seems to occur in those cases of symbiotic infantile psychosis, in which parental psychopathology—the extrinsic factor in the genesis of the symbiotic psychosis— is rather prominent. In these, but by no means in all, symbiotic cases the adult partner very often seems to be able to accept the child only as long as it belongs as a quasi-vegetative being, an appendage, to her or his body.

Steve's mother, for instance, had a good deal of insomnia during pregnancy, due to her fears lest the baby be a boy, because her own brother had turned out so badly. Steve did not sleep enough to suit his mother. Whenever his eyes were open, she would hold him tightly in her arms for hours, and would walk up and down with him until her arms were aching and numb and she could not feel her arms any more.

Is it a mere coincidence that Steve's most conspicuous symptom was going about, compulsively asking everyone and also himself: "Are these my hands?" "Are those your hands?" "Can these hands kill?" "I am many people?" In his weird histrionics he compulsively enacted many characters all day long.

At four and half years the child's extreme dependency—which his mother had previously enjoyed—so harrassed her that she placed him in a boarding school, though he was still wholly dependent on her. At that time, overt and continual masturbation seems to have been the last straw to break the camel's back, as far as the mother was concerned.

In the case of one of my schizophrenic patients the mother was pictured by the child in analysis as a "multi-pronged monster," a "giant medusa or spider," who would "wind her fat legs around my body and squash me," with all the manifestations of horror that only a schizophrenic patient can display. At the beginning of the treatment the mother lived in another country and thus had no contact with me. Later, when she came for an interview with me, she sought my reassurance against her excessive guilt feeling, because Babette's condition might be due to the "terrible thing I did with her when she was a small baby." She went on to relate then that, since her husband frustrated her and treated her very badly, she would compensate her sensual needs—as she put it—by taking the chubby, smooth little baby between her legs, and masturbating, rubbing the little body up and down her genitals.

A psychotic child's father, whose own legs were crippled (and whose death wishes toward the son were quite overt) related to the psychiatrist that he would sneak to the crib of the infant boy, night after night, and examine his legs in the fear of finding something wrong with his baby son's legs. This schizophrenic child's main somatic delusions centered upon his legs.

It seems to me that these strange coincidences—this precise dovetailing of the somatic memory traces in these pathological delusional body sensations of the symbiotic child and the way in which the aggressive erotic appersonation was effected by the parent partner—cannot be without causal connection. The peculiar hypercathexis of one part of the body, which we encountered in many symbiotic children, often corresponds to the type of overstimulation which occurred during symbiotic relationships. This finding is noteworthy and deserves further careful investigation (Greenacre 1944).

CONCERNING THE QUESTION OF "CHILD SCHIZOPHRENIA"

I now wish to take up a point implied by the title of this paper. I believe that all clinical evidence disproves the contention of certain psychiatrists and psychoanalysts, that schizophrenia does not occur before puberty, because the schizophrenic picture is based on the psychotic elaboration of the homosexual conflict. First of all, I believe that the main cause of proclivity for alienation of the ego from reality and fragmentation, is the above-described grave disturbance—a specific conflict of the mother-child relationship, be it autistic or symbiotic. Second, I believe—and have much clinical evidence to show—that bisexual conflict can be, and often is, prominent in the symptomatology, the production, and even the immediate genetic cause of the psychotic breakdown of the ego in childhood.[3] To establish the latter point, I would like to give two very condensed case reports.

George was just under seven when admitted to our Children's Service with fulminant symptoms of delusions and hallucinations. He had developed fairly normally to the age of three, when a sister was born. He began to have night terrors. At about the same time he began to have what his mother aptly described as "talking tantrums." He would pace the room, talking angrily to himself about something which seemed entirely irrelevant to his environment. He would mumble: "I'm a pussy cat. I'm a pussy cat. Elaine is big. I'm a pussy cat." Shortly after the baby came, he wanted to wear her clothes, and often wanted to wear his mother's. He insisted that he wanted to be a girl, preferred female animals and asked his mother perseverative questions as to why he should not be a girl. At about the same time he began to be afraid of the holes in a fence which he passed, or wherever he encountered any. His father frequently used this fear as a threat, often telling him he would put him in a hole. He tried to get reassurance from his father by asking frequently: "Do you love me?"

George became a very good but asocial student. He often spoke of his sister, and again and again of his pet kitten in school. "I have a cat

3. Dr. Greenacre in a personal communication, originally designated as discussion remarks to this paper, said the following: "In children suffering from severe and early traumata there is a condition of increased plasticity of the body responsiveness which may under certain conditions produce a severe bisexual identification. There are then bodily hallucinations of bisexual nature which persist and play an important part in the child's fantasy during the early latency period. . . ."

at home. It's a girl cat. I like my cat. I'm a girl cat." His fear of, and wish for, castration could be traced back to his mother's pregnancy. First he developed a strange interest in barrels. He stopped and touched barrels and looked at them with extreme interest. After his preoccupation with barrels he became fascinated by pipes of all sorts, which again he would have to stop and touch, commenting on their size, shape, or other characteristics. He would play with his father's pipes for long periods. After a few months he developed a similar preoccupation with electrical appliances. He would endlessly pretend to be plugging in a cord into a socket. Later he developed an intense interest in fires, and this was prevalent at the time of his hospitalization. He needed the fire to burn and to kill his sister in his hallucinations—yet in the next breath would profess to love her dearly.

In the hospital his hallucinatory and delusional restitution attempts pertained to incorporative and destructive tendencies toward his sister and mother. In his clearer periods he would state: "I'm afraid of killing my mother. I have ideas of wanting to kill her. Yes, I think of killing her, and these thoughts upset me so. That gives me bad feelings in my head. It makes me so upset when I am home. Doctor, you are supposed to take that out."

On the ward he seemed to be hallucinating almost constantly. While sitting next to the nurse whom he loved and hated most, he unzipped his overalls and began pulling at the nurse's skirt as though gathering up something. He then put his hands in his overalls as if pouring in what he had gathered. This went on for a short time, then he zipped up his overalls and sat there smiling. "I've got a Hollinger [name of the nurse] in there . . . that's what I've got in there."

George was hilariously elated for the rest of the day and sat off in a corner, communicating with the introjected beloved (Klein 1932).

It is obvious that this youngster in his childish way was making the same type of restitutive efforts to solve, albeit psychotically, his bisexual conflict as do adult schizophrenics.

This example of the bisexual conflict before puberty is far from rare. From a repertoire of such cases we select another one.

Clifford, age seven, was a patient of the Children's Service when he was six and a half, with a mixed type of childhood schizophrenia. For the first fourteen months of his life, his development seemed normal though he was never a cuddly baby and, in retrospect, seemed to have shown the characteristics of a case of early infantile autism during his second, third, and fourth years. At three and a half he became intensely jealous of his eight-month-old sister. His speech did not develop. He used sterotype phrasing, which he would perseverate in a sing-song voice, and spoke of himself exclusively in the third person. He became obsessed with mechanical and electrical equipment. At five restitutive symbiotic mechanisms became increasingly marked. Whereas up to then he had defended his secluded, autistic world, now he insisted on sharing his parents' bed and sought close bodily contact with both of them. His bisexual conflict manifested itself in a similar way as that described in the case of George. Clifford began to bite the nurses, suddenly and impulsively, for example, when he passed them in the hall. He said he "loved" the nurses, called them each carefully by name and sought their company for a type of ritualized conversation, consisting mostly of identifying them by name and telling his name, then naming other personnel on the ward. As his biting was discouraged, he began to dress in two handkerchiefs arranged as a skirt and a nurse's cap, and insisted, "Don't call me Clifford, call me Miss Clifford. I'm a nurse." He became anxious if this was not done, and for a period of time insisted on being called "Miss Clifford" or "Nurse Clifford."

This phase of behavior was introduced in the therapeutic sessions by a denial. "I don't want to be a girl. Girls wear dresses, boys wear pants. I don't want to be like my sister. Girls and boys are different." The above was repeated at home, but was quickly followed, as in the hospital, by the period of insistence upon wearing his younger sister's clothes and being called "Miss Clifford" also by his family.

THE FUNCTION OF AUTISM AS CONTRASTED WITH THAT OF THE MECHANISM OF SYMBIOTIC-PARASITIC FUSION IN CHILD PSYCHOSIS

Whereas in the symbiotic infantile psychosis panic reactions are most prominent, all observers emphasize, in contrast, the seemingly self-sufficient contentedness of the autistic child, if only he be left alone. Any approach, any change in the environment, in the social setting, is resented as an irritating intrusion. The autistic position is defended by catatoniclike temper tantrums (Geleerd 1945). Aggressive and destructive acts seem not to be aimed at the interfering person as a whole. The autistic child shoves away the "hand" that is in his way as he would a wooden block.

What is the nature, what is the function of this pseudo self-sufficiency of early infantile autism? It would seem that autism is the basic defense attitude of these infants, for whom the beacon of emotional orientation in the outer world—the mother as primary love object—is nonexistent. Early infantile autism develops, I believe, because the infantile personality, devoid of emotional ties to the person of the mother, is unable to cope with external stimuli and inner excitations, which threaten from both sides his very existence as an entity. Autism is therefore the mechanism by which such patients try to shut out, to hallucinate away (negative hallucination) the potential sources of sensory perception, particularly those which demand affective response. If we observe such psychotic children clinically, the most striking feature is their spectacular struggle against any demand of human (social) contact which might interfere with their hallucinatory delusional need to command a static, greatly constricted segment of their inanimate environment,[4] in which they behave like omnipotent magicians (Mahler, Ross, and De Fries 1949). It would seem that their capacity to master their inner feelings (proprioceptive excitation), their own thought processes, their own motility, their highly selective and restricted sensory awareness, all but overtax their undifferentiated ego. They cannot cope with stimulation from the external world. They cannot mediate between two sets of stimuli. In short, it seems as though these patients experience outer reality as an intolerable source of irritation, without specific or further qualification.

The mechanisms which are characteristic in the *symbiotic* infantile psychosis, on the other hand, are the introjective-projective mechanisms and their psychotic elaboration, the symptomatology

---

1. This observation was stressed by Dr. Lucie Jessner of Cambridge, Mass., in most helpful personal discussions.

of which we have described in a previous paper as Group II of "schizophrenia-like" clinical pictures in children (Mahler, Ross, and De Fries 1949). These mechanisms aim at a restoration of the symbiotic parasitic delusion of oneness with the mother and thus are the diametric opposites of the function of autism. As far as our research could ascertain up to date, the lack of separation of the representation of the self from the representation of nonself is clinically not discernible in the first two years of life (Jacobson 1953). Hence clinical evidence for symbiotic conflict of the order and unequivocality which points to autistic disturbance in the first two years of life cannot be expected. But it seems that the symbiotic psychosis candidates are characterized by an abnormally low tolerance for frustration, and later by a more or less evident lack of emotional separation or differentiation from the mother. Clinical symptoms manifest themselves between the ages of two and a half to five, with a peak of onset in the fourth year of life. These infants' reality ties depended mainly upon the early delusional fusion with the mother (unlike those of the autistic who had no reality ties to begin with). Reactions set in, as we described above, at those points of the physiological and psychological maturation process at which separateness from the mother must be perceived and faced. Figuratively speaking, it seems that from the third year onward the growing discrepancy between the rate of maturation of partial ego functions versus lag of developmental individuation causes the brittle ego of these children to break into fragments (Mahler 1947, 1949b). Agitated catatoniclike temper tantrums and panic-stricken behavior dominate the picture; these are followed by bizarrely distorted reality testing and hallucinatory attempts at restitution. The aim is restoration and perpetuation of the delusional omnipotence phase of the mother-infant fusion of earliest times—a period at which the mother was an ever-ready extension of the self, at the service and command of "His Majesty, the Baby." In their sterotyped speech productions one can discern the predominance of hallucinatory soliloqui with the introjected object, and their actions dramatize the same introjective reunion. These are the cases which demonstrate with obtrusive explicitness the mechanisms described by Melanie Klein (1932). The manifestations of love and aggression in these children's impulse-ridden behavior seem utterly confused. They crave body contact and seem to want to crawl into you—yet they often shriek at such body contacts or overt demonstrations of affection on the part of the adult, even though they themselves may have asked or insisted on being kissed, cuddled and "loved." On the other hand, their biting, kicking and squeezing the adult is the expression of their craving to incorporate, unite with, possess, devour and retain the "beloved." In other words, the restitutive mechanisms with which they wish to recapture the eluding reality are conspicuously aberrant and different from anything we observe in chronically aggressive, nonpsychotic children, or panic-stricken phobic cases— the two categories which might conceivably pose a differential diagnostic problem (Mahler 1947).

We cannot better illustrate this desperate attempt to perpetuate the symbiotic fusion when it conflicts with the struggle for separation and individuation, accompanied by the bisexual conflict than in the words and behavior of a patient.

Alma came to our attention on the ward at the age of fourteen.[5] Onset of her psychosis could be traced back to the age of four and a half. At that time she had a high temperature and was hospitalized for ten days because of measles complicated by pneumonia. Her inclination to "somatization" and to bodily symbolization occurred in what seemed to be infantile pregnancy fantasies. These were indicated by the fact that during the entire period of hospitalization of ten days she had no bowel movement. After her return home her abdomen protruded enormously, as verified by several observers. From then on Alma seemed quite different: weak, sick, whimpering and crying. During her first three days at home, she defecated constantly and her abdomen returned to normal size. Following this expulsion of feces, but not during it, she began to stutter. She became fussy about food, consistently refused all solids (warding off of oral sadistic fantasies?), and vomited frequently. She began school at the age of six but seemed to make no friends. At seven, according to her story, an older man made sexual advances to her. It is difficult to determine whether there had actually been an advance of a sexual nature or whether she had interpreted the episode in this way.

At ten, following a bad dream, Alma became very disturbed. Her

5. I owe this material to the cooperation of Dr. William H. Cox, Jr.

"nervousness" followed upon seeing the movie *Snow White and the Seven Dwarfs*. After this movie the patient had a dream from which she woke screaming and ran to her mother. It took a long time and much coaxing to persuade Alma to explain what was bothering her: *She heard a voice saying: "Strangle your mother, strangle your mother."* She therefore was afraid to sleep in her own room and insisted on sleeping with her father, thereby displacing her mother to another room. She was taken to a psychiatrist at this point.

Alma began to feel that her friends did not like her because something was wrong with *her face*. She felt it was too skinny, later she felt that it *looked much older* than her age (approximately the age of her mother). She has become overly solicitous about her mother's health, and also overargumentative. On the ward she was constantly looking into the mirror and said that the whole ward (or world?) was a mirror image of herself. She said: "All things are two substances, soul and sex; some people and some things are primarily 'sex' [mainly women], some people combine the sex and soul feelings together [mainly men]. The same feeling I have toward my mother, pertains to sex feeling." In a letter she said " . . . *Maybe then* [at ten] *I for the first time separated from my mother and I was afraid of reality and therefore didn't give it a chance.*[6] And I cut myself off and forgot soul feelings. Like maybe *when I saw* Snow White and the Seven Dwarfs, *somehow I was the witch and fed the girl the apple*— and I saw the prince and I saw soul and sex feelings which [feelings] in reality concern men.—*Maybe somehow I wanted to get my mother out of myself by strangulation and at the same time strangling or punishing myself* [for and by] *killing Snow White.*—All I know is after I said, 'Strangle your mother,' subconsciously *I equated my mother to the witch and sort of broke away from my mother.* I felt weird inside; strange, empty: an afraid weirdness. [Then] I was no more afraid of myself anymore for a few seconds. But *for a whole year I constantly threw up and always felt like dizzy.*[7] Maybe sub-

6. We know from the anamnesis that in fact the first real separation and prepsychotic reaction to facing reality apart from mother occurred when Alma was four and a half years old.

7. We again know from the anamnesis that this vomiting off and on and refusing solids (in warding off obviously oral-sadistic incorporative fantasies by ejection) began at four and a half.

consciously I was strangling myself [as the witch] or was it mother—or was it Snow White—or was it the mice that Ma killed[8]—but I imagine it was me.—I thought I would sleepwalk and kill her.[9] After a few seconds I didn't feel empty but different."

One could hardly ask for a more explicit description of the steps which introduced the gradual loss of reality, the psychotic break with reality, and the subsequent restitution mechanisms in this symbiotic psychosis. There is confusion between the self and the mother and a lack of direction between libidinal and aggressive tendencies. Both the mother and the self are confused and *fused* as the goal of unneutralized instinctual forces.

The introjected, persecuting mother makes Alma fear that she looks much older than she is; she has sex feelings toward the mother, has the impulse to strangle the mother—in herself and in the outside—and then she says either that she is her mother's mirror image or again that the world is her own mirror image. "It is as if I have to live with my reflection (like when I look in the mirror) [the mother in herself] and I have to face my reflection when I see people because they are my walking or live reflections." The fusion of all three representations—self, mother and world—is expressed in her own words: "What if I am the living reflection of my mother and when I look in the mirror it is a double exposure. And I see my reflection in others and it makes me miserable. . . . I go around in circles. There is no escape. I live in a world that has a plane surface, flat like my reflection in the mirror and the people I see in this world are the living reflection of myself and this sex-person that I see in the mirror isn't me. I refuse to accept that person."

The crux of the pathogenic struggle to give up the symbiotic-parasitic fusion with the parental image is clearly expressed, and the Kleinian mechanisms are strikingly illustrated by the patient when she says: "After I said, 'Strangle your mother,' subconsciously I equated my mother to the witch and sort of broke away from my

8. Alma was horror-stricken when her mother actually exterminated mice in their kitchen.

9. This was the rational reason Alma gave for sleeping with her father; to be protected from her dangerous impulse.

mother." "But for a whole year I *constantly threw up* and always felt like dizzy. Maybe subconsciously I was strangling myself [or the mother in herself] and felt guilty for stangling myself—or was it mother—or was it Snow White [whom the witch tried to kill]—or was it the mice that Ma killed—but I imagine it was me. After a few seconds I didn't feel empty, but I felt different."

This is but a brief excerpt of the wealth of material this young girl produced. Though these productions stem from a time when she was an adolescent, we cite them here because she was actually describing the genesis of her psychosis in retrospect (as verified by her mother, sister and father) and because with her queer talent for introspection she had described all the aspects and functions of the symbiotic-parasitic hallucinatory mechanisms of restitution.[10]

DIFFERENTIAL DIAGNOSTIC CONSIDERATIONS

I believe that the two types of infantile psychosis—the *autistic* versus the *symbiotic*—can in many cases be clearly differentiated in the beginning. Later the pictures tend to overlap. Differential diagnosis in retrospect may be attempted by reconstruction and appraisal of the earliest mother-infant relationship. The specific factor in differential diagnosis is the mother's role as reflected in the baby's nursing behavior during the process of individuation, during the period when the infant's body ego and representation of the self should emerge from the primal somatopsychic symbiotic stage and the fused representation (Jacobson 1953). As described above, the autistic baby behaves quite differently during the nursing period than either the normal infant or the symbiotic baby. We stated that the primarily symbiotic child often cannot be detected before awareness of separateness from the mother image throws these infants into a state of panicky separation anxiety. When we meet cases of child psychosis at a later stage, it seems that pure cases of autistic child psychosis as well as pure cases of symbiotic-parasitic psychosis are

10. They are identical with those in symbiotic cases like George's, Betty's, etc., whom we studied or analyzed respectively from the age of five to eleven (Mahler 1947).

rather rare, whereas mixed cases are frequent; by this time, symbiotic mechanisms have been superimposed on basic autistic structures and vice versa.

CLINICAL COURSE, TREATMENT AND OUTLOOK

We can make only a few tentative formulations on these most important points.

As somatic and physiological development takes its course, there is no conceivable human environment in which the autistic child could maintain his shell against the demands of the outside world. Indeed, the prerequisite of personality development, and the first requirement for treatment of the autistic child, is to lure him into contact with a human love object. At that point of development or of treatment, reactions which resemble parasitic-symbiotic mechanisms appear spontaneously or as an artefact of treatment.

On the other hand, children who begin with a symbiotic psychosis will use autism as a desperate means of warding off the fear of losing whatever minimal individual entity they may have succeeded in achieving, either through development or through treatment, which they then attempt to preserve by the opposite psychotic mechanism of autism.[11] Thus we often see children whose psychosis had primarily the characteristics of a symbiotic disturbance, but who then used autism in a desperate attempt to ward off the threatened regression into symbiotic fusion to preserve individual entity, separate from the mother or father.[12]

It is essential to differentiate diagnostically between basically autistic and symbiotic disturbances, because in each case therapy must follow different principles. It seems that in both types, as well as in the mixed type of early child psychosis, it is essential to keep in mind the extreme brittleness of the ego.[13]

11. Compare Anna Freud's beautiful paper, "Negativism and Emotional Surrender" (1951a).

12. *Ibid.*

13. The autistic group corresponds with Group I in our previous paper (1949). We deliberately have not dealt in this paper with our Group III of child psychosis (Mahler, Ross, and De Fries 1949), the clinical pictures of which in latency were recently described by Annemarie Weil (1953).

As we mentioned above, the *autistic* child is most *intolerant of direct human contact.* Hence he must be lured out of his autistic shell with all kinds of devices such as music, rhythmic activities and pleasurable stimulation of his sense organs. Such children must be gradually approached with the help of inanimate objects, always keeping in mind that gross bodily contact, touching, cuddling— which one might expect would reassure a deeply disturbed child—is of no avail and often a deterrent with these autistic children. Time and again we see that cases of the autistic type, if forced too rapidly into social contact and into facing the demands of the social environment, are thrown into a catatonic state and then into as fulminant a psychotic process as we see in some of the primarily symbiotic child psychoses.

In the *symbiotic type,* on the other hand, it is important to *let the child test reality* very *gradually at his own pace.* As he cautiously begins this testing of himself as a separate entity, he constantly needs to feel the support of an understanding adult, preferably the mother or the therapist as mother substitute. Such continual infusions of borrowed ego strength may have to be continued for a lifetime.[14] In other words, *separation as an individual entity can be promoted only very cautiously* in the case of the symbiotic psychotic child.

Prognosis as to the arrest of the process and as to consolidation of the ego is moderately favorable. It seems to depend on the right type, and the cautious, prolonged, and consistent nature of the therapy, which is a kind of substitution or infusion therapy. However, the outlook as to real cure is bleak. In cases of *symbiotic* infantile psychosis the development of individuation has been missed at a time when essential, basic faculties of the ego are usually acquired within the somatopsychic matrix of the primal mother-infant unit. In our experience, if and when differentiation in this matrix, highly specific for promoting sound individuation, is missed, the ego remains irreparably warped, narcissistically vulnerable, unstructured, or fragmented.

In the *autistic* type of infantile psychosis the deficiency is even more severe because the *specific matrix itself* was nonexistent, and

---

11. This opinion is shared by Paul Hoch who stresses the necessity of possible lifetime substitution therapy in certain cases of adult psychotics.

therefore the growth which it fosters could not take place. Establishment of contact and substitution therapy over a long period of time may sometimes give spurts of impressive and gratifying results. But they are usually followed by an insuperable plateau of arrested progress, which usually taxes the patience and frustrates the renewed hopes of the parents. Impatient reactions and pressures are then exercised and progress forced. But, as we said before, if the autistic type is forced too rapidly into social contact, and particularly if the newly formed symbiotic relationship causes frustration, the above described catastrophic reactions are the result, precisely the outcome which should be avoided. Therefore, if they cannot be avoided, it seems that such autistic infants are better off if allowed to remain in their autistic shell, even though in "a daze of restricted orientation" they may drift into a very limited degree of reality adjustment only. Diagnosis of their "original condition," of course, then usually escapes recognition; they are thrown into the category of the feeble-minded.

Any pressure in the direction of sudden separate functioning must be cautiously avoided in the *symbiotic* child. If the ego of the symbiotic type is overrated and expected to be able to cope with reality without continual ego infusion from the therapist, who substitutes for the mother, the panic reactions and acute hallucinations may cause regressions and withdrawal into stuporously autistic states or hebephrenic deterioration. Therefore simultaneous supportive treatment of the mother, if at all possible, seems to constitute the optimal and, perhaps, even the sine qua non approach to the problem.[15]

15. Compare also the opinion of Beata Rank and her co-workers (1950) as well as the works of Melitta Sperling (1951), Elkisch (1953), and others.

Chapter 8

ON EARLY INFANTILE PSYCHOSIS: THE SYMBIOTIC AND AUTISTIC SYNDROMES

[1965]

In private practice here and abroad and as a consultant to the Children's Service of the New York State Psychiatric Institute and Columbia University, I was brought face to face with the problem of children's cases that could not be fitted into the well-established nosological categories of primary behavior disorders, neurotic or conduct disorders, psychopathic character deviations or impulse disturbances; neither would they fit into the "wastebasket" categories of the organic, or brain-damaged group of amentia cases (Mahler 1947). At that time (in the late 1930s and even in the 1940s) Lauretta Bender's (1942, 1947) pioneering work in childhood schizophrenia was by no means accepted in the child psychiatric field, Bradley's (1945), Potter's (1933), and Despert's (1941) work notwithstanding.

It was in the early 1940s that Kanner's concept of "early infantile autism" (1943, 1944) rendered the idea of severe psychotic derangement in young children somewhat more acceptable to workers in the field. This acceptance of the existence of "early infantile autism" had one long-standing consequence, however: any clinical picture of childhood psychosis in which anything resembling autistic mechanisms was detected, and in which the psychotic break with reality occurred in a young child, was henceforth designated as "autism."

Seventeen years ago, I had already indicated that, among the sixteen child psychosis cases that I had by then thoroughly studied, cases where psychosis had begun before the age of ten years, a closer scrutiny of the case histories revealed disturbances that could be traced to two crucial periods of development (Mahler, Ross, and De Fries 1949). One was the period which Anna Freud (1952c) designated as that of the "need-satisfying object." This is the period which begins when a person in the environment, under the specific condition of the infant's need hunger, is perceived by the infant, transiently and dimly at first, later more distinctly, as being outside his orbit of the self, and is responded to by the child with the social emotion of "confident expectation," a phenomenon to the importance of which Therese Benedek (1938) had drawn attention. Normal "confident expectation" or "basic trust" (Erikson 1950) is derived from the fact that the rhythmically and predictably recurring experience of the accumulation of need tension, of "affect hunger" (Levy 1937), is just as predictably gratified and relieved by a "good" outside source. In this need-satisfying period of object relationship, which coincides with the phase of normal symbiosis, the mother still partakes in the omnipotent orbit of the mother-infant dual unity (*SPI*:6).

In the past histories of some of the sixteen psychotic children whom we studied, we could trace their disorders back to disturbances in the earliest rhythm of alternation between instinctual need tension (expressed in affectomotor discharge phenomena) and the states of saturation expressed in the infant's quiescence and sleep. In the anamneses of those children we often, though not always, found that, during their infancy, they had not passed beyond (or after an imperceptible and short progress, had relapsed into) the earliest infantile mode of perceiving the proprioceptive and enteroceptive increase of physiological tension as diffuse organismic distress.[1] Those children seem to have been unable, as infants, to recognize or to learn from experience that, whereas physiological tension originated within their own body, the "confidently expected" relief from instinctual tension, that is, gratification of needs, came from somewhere outside of the body! They could not develop the ability to wait,

---

1. For example, very early intractable sleep disturbances were reported in several cases, from as early as eight months, and earlier.

one of the first reliable signs of a functioning rudimentary ego. Hence, the response of these infants to instinctual hunger tension remained immediate, violent, and diffuse random activity, reminiscent of affective panic; and if this tension was not immediately responded to (the random activity being the only available undifferentiated cue), then retraction of affective contact, that is, regression, took place, culminating in a few cases in apathetic withdrawal. The tendency to diffuse, random activity is reminiscent both of the affectomotor storm-rage reactions of early infancy and the clinical picture of catatonic agitation, whereas the reaction of apathy was in turn reminiscent of the terminal states of psychoses (Mahler, Ross, and De Fries 1949).

The second important period of the manifest onset of childhood psychosis seemed to take place later in infancy, at a time when the symbiotic, need-satisfying relationship with the mother should be gradually becoming more mutual and consolidated. This is the time when the mental representation of the mother, the infant's memory traces of her, should be in the process of becoming gradually and slowly representations of the whole object and the way be paved to object constancy (Hartmann 1939), whence the infant's functioning indicates that he is capable of maintaining the mother's mental representation even in her absence for increasingly longer periods of time.

The mental representation of the object is built through identificatory and differentiation processes during the separation-individuation phase. The existence of the established mental representation of the object makes it possible for the toddler to experiment with separation and return (i.e., reunion with the mother) (*SPI*:6, *SPII*:2).

Maturation of the mental apparatuses, of which the maturation of the sensorimotor apparatus may serve as the paradigm, brings with it an increasing awareness of separateness from the mother. *Pari passu* there is an increasing sense of emotional dependence upon the mother arising out of the feeling of helplessness and of the threat of object loss. The predicament of the individuating infant is complicated by the fact that he has to cope with an expanding reality, in the midst of the age-specific psychosexual conflicts. These new requirements seem, in some constitutionally or experientially vulnerable toddlers, to cause undifferentiated, often agitated panic tantrums instead of eliciting signal anxiety. These states of panic seem to be the immediate trigger for psychotic regression or, we might say, for psychotic fragmentation of the rudimentary ego structure. The clinical picture is either dominated by abysmal panic or else it is characterized by the well-known secondary restitutive mechanisms (Mahler, Furer, and Settlage 1959).

Let me say at this point that there are two important areas of agreement between the psychoanalytic theory of child psychosis and that of the academic schools. I fully agree, for example, with Lauretta Bender's thesis that the different groups of clinical pictures of childhood schizophrenia depend upon the stage of maturity of the central nervous system at which the psychosis becomes manifest. I believe that psychosis, in adults as well as in children, consists of, or implies, a functional failure of the controlling, steering, integrating part of the central nervous system—in other words, the "ego." In adolescent and adult schizophrenics, the schizophrenic process acts upon a mental apparatus in which the three essential, structurally differentiated components of the personality—the ego, the superego, and the id—have been fully developed. But in child psychoses the organization of each of these structures is still in a state of flux. Thus, the essential differences between the syndrome of the psychotic child and that of the adult schizophrenic would seem to be due to the degree of structural differentiation.

The second area of agreement between analysts and the academic school of childhood schizophrenia is that we too fully believe that childhood psychosis seems to afflict only constitutionally vulnerable infants, or else very, very young ones, whose rudimentary ego was subjected during the first weeks or months of life to unusually severe, accumulated traumata.

Our differences, I believe, are in the realm of emphasis. We believe that the lack of, or loss of, the ability to utilize the symbiotic (need-satisfying) object is the core deficiency, which impairs the ego's integrating, synthesizing, and organizing functions. We believe that all other disturbances are accessory to this absence of the human beacon of orientation in the world of reality and in the inner world.

Therefore, we have come to regard the psychotic small child as only half an individual, one whose condition can be optimally studied only through as complete as possible a restoration of the original symbiotic mother-child dual unit. Only in this way can we find out to what extent he can be helped to individuate.

You may protest that this sort of restoration is, in the first place, very seldom possible; and that, even if it were possible, it would not always be, in the practical sense, the best therapeutic method. However, our hypothesis dictates that the natural history, the dynamics, the pathogenesis be reconstructed, to begin with, by our trying our utmost to reconstitute the mother-child symbiosis of the original dual unit, on the grounds that its alienation or interruption was the primary cause for the psychotic fragmentation of the ego.

In contrast to this kind of reconstructive or regenerative approach, the academic schools, which look upon the child as the carrier of the disease, place their emphasis on dealing with him therapeutically as a separate individual entity, within the limits of what is constitutionally given, and attempting to substitute as far as possible for that which is irreversibly lost.

THEORETICAL CONSIDERATIONS

In the human young, the instinct for self-preservation has atrophied and become unreliable, so that, as Freud (1923) said, the ego has to take over the role of adaptation to reality which the id cannot fulfill. But the neonate appears to be an immature, almost purely biological organism, with instinctual responses to stimuli, not on a cortical but essentially on a reflex and thalamic level and with no ego to speak of. He has at his disposal (since cortical inhibition is still undeveloped) only somatic defense mechanisms, which consist of overflow and discharge reactions. The neonate's and the very young baby's mental apparatus is thus not adequate to organize inner and outer stimuli for survival; instead, it is the psychobiological rapport between the nursing mother and the baby that complements the infant's undifferentiated ego (*SPI*:7, Benedek 1959).

Empathy on the part of the mother is normally the human

substitute for those instincts on which the animal can rely for its survival. In a quasi-closed system or unit, the mother executes vitally important ministrations, without which the human young would in fact be unable to survive. During the postnatal period, the intra-uterine, parasite-host relationship has to be replaced by the infant's being enveloped, as it were, in the extrauterine matrix of the mother's nursing care, a kind of social symbiosis. Even this primitive sym-biosis must develop as a somewhat more differentiated phase than the neonate's and the infant's postneonatal state.

I think that we may profitably describe the very first weeks of extrauterine life as the stage of "normal autism" of the infant (SPI:9, Mahler, Furer, and Settlage 1959). In this "normal autistic" phase, from birth until about the second month of life (a period which Hartmann, Kris, and Loewenstein [1946] speak of as the "undifferen-tiated" phase), the infant makes no discernible distinction between inner and outer reality, nor does he seem to recognize any distinction between himself and the inanimate surroundings. As he gradually moves into the symbiotic phase, the infant becomes dimly aware that what relieves his instinctual hunger tension comes from the outside world, whereas the painful accumulation of tension stems from within him. However, this recognition requires that there take place, during the symbiotic phase, some rudimentary ego differentiation. In the intrapsychic organization of the infant, the boundaries of his self and of the mother are still more or less confluent and fused; the distinction between them is dependent on the degree of affect hunger, when this distinction fleetingly exists, and its alternation with satisfaction, whence the boundaries are fused again (Lewin 1950).

We can observe how, from the second half of the first year on, the young infant gradually begins to differentiate from the mother-infant symbiotic dual unit; he separates his own self (and his mental representation) from that of the mother. While the consolidation of the symbiotic phase is by and large achieved within the first year of life, it is from the second half of this first year that it is overlapped by the separation-individuation process, which culminates during the second year of life in gradual disengagement from the symbiosis (SPII:2).

In the normal autistic phase, as well as in the symbiotic phase, the mother complements the more or less deficient innate stimulus barrier, performing the vitally important ego functions that the infant's primitive ego cannot execute and serving as a buffer against excess stimulation. In the phase of individuation and disengagement, on the other hand, the mother's role should be that of supportive encouragement for the toddler's gradual attainment of ego autonomy. Some mothers function excellently throughout the symbiotic phase; they are able to respond with empathy and skill to the cues that the infant gives. There are mothers who help the toddler gradually to disengage and individuate; but there are also mothers who cannot bear the child's steps toward disengagement, and who thus impede his individuation (*SPII*:1).

It is undeniable that, in the anamnesis of early child psychosis cases, we often find an accumulation of severe frustrations and traumata within the symbiotic milieu; for example, a debilitating emotional unavailability on the part of the mother because she has a depression. We also find, at the opposite pole, an interference with the infant's gratification-frustration experiences, a stifling of his budding ego, by a smothering disregard of his need to experience gratification and frustration at his own pace. This then results in an interference with individuation which carries over into the second and third years of life and even beyond. But we have found in our study just as many cases of infantile psychosis in which the mother belonged to Winnicott's group of ordinary, devoted mothers, and we could reconstruct in some cases such extreme, seemingly intrinsic vulnerability on the part of the child which even the most favorable environmental situations could not conceivably have counteracted, thus preventing infantile psychosis.

Of relevance here is the genetic principle, as drawn from embryology—namely, the experiment by Stockard, in which he demonstrated that a pinprick administered to the developing chick embryo results in major anatomical deformities, whereas the same physical trauma applied to the hatched chick has inconsequential effects. "The organ which missed its time of ascendancy is not only doomed as an entity, but it endangers at the same time the whole hierarchy of organs" (quoted by Starr 1954). This principle is also applicable, in the psychobiological field, to the ego and its functions. Interruption of the timetable of maturation and development of the ego is the more detrimental to the total personality, the earlier in life it occurs.

The psychopathology of infantile psychosis clearly attests to the significance of "missing the time of ascendancy," with regard to certain functions of the ego, of object relationship, and other areas of psychic maturation.

Let me repeat my main thesis: I believe that from the genetic, dynamic, and structural points of view, the paramount—that which appears to be the cardinal—difficulty is the inability of the psychotic infant to use the external maternal ego for structuralization of his own, rapidly maturing and, therefore, most vulnerable, rudimentary ego. The designation of early psychotic pictures as "symbiotic-psychotic syndrome" rests on this hypothesis. The term "infantile symbiotic-psychotic syndrome" calls attention to the decisive fact that the survival of the human young depends on the sociobiological symbiosis with the mother organism, in the sense previously elaborated.

Disturbances of the symbiotic phase may go unrecognized, so that the psychotic picture emerges at the age when separation-individuation should begin and proceed. In these cases, delusional symbiotic restitutive mechanisms and panic prevail. On the other hand, if defenses are already built up during the symbiotic phase, against apperception or recognition of a living outside object world, then retreat into secondary autism dominates the clinical picture.

In every case of infantile psychosis that has been subjected to prolonged observation and treatment, we have found the basic mechanisms, the psychotic defenses, to be delusional autistic modes of adjustment. The essential aim of the latter is restoration of the omnipotent oneness with the symbiotic mother, although along with this aim goes a panicky fear of fusion and of dissolution of the self. Syndromes may show a prevalence of one or the other, but our research bears out the hypothesis that the autistic picture is a secondary formation.

CASE ILLUSTRATIONS

The following are two child psychosis cases; both of these children suffered from the sequelae of the failure of the mother-infant symbiosis. Neither could use the mother as their beacon of orientation, as their external ego (Spitz 1957). In one case (that of two-and-a-half-year-old Violet) secondary autism dominated the clinical picture, whereas in the other case (that of three-and-a-half-year-old Benny) delusional symbiotic mechanisms prevailed.

Violet's parents were both very young, both of them, in fact, rather infantile, when she was born. The mother, who had grown up friendless and alone in the house of her brutally sadistic grandmother, felt profoundly abandoned by both parents. In addition to the grandmother, there had been a crippled maternal uncle; he had died shortly after Violet's parents had married. The uncle's death had caused Mrs. V. recurrent nightmares in which he would emerge from his coffin, neither alive nor dead, and fold up upon himself like a fetus. In struggling to distract herself from these dreams, it had occurred to Mrs. V. that a child might completely preoccupy her; it would be something all her own!

In relating this fantasy, Mrs. V.'s immediate association was that her father had given her a doll when she was three years old. She had kept this doll all her life; she still had it in a trunk. The little girl born to this twenty-year-old mother obviously represented in her emotional economy another, this time an animated, living, doll.

Seven weeks after Violet was born, Mrs. V. became deeply depressed; this coincided with the death of her father. From that time on, the mother's relationship to the baby changed abruptly. According to her own statement, her care of Violet was limited to breast feeding her, the closeness of which she felt was her sole reason for hanging onto life itself. In between, the "live doll" was carted away; she was never played with, talked to, or smiled at; no interest of any sort was shown in her. There was thus an alternation of extremes—on the one hand, the very intense relationship of the breast feeding; on the other, the mother's complete withdrawal between feedings.

Mrs. V. was unable to gratify Violet's overall symbiotic needs except in this incongruent, in fact contradictory, way. Such a compartmentalized pattern, with its sharply contrasting feeling tones, not even a fully structuralized ego—let alone the rudimentary ego of an infant—could possibly have synthesized and integrated. Whether the infant's constitutional "sending power" was normal or underdeveloped we do not know, but it certainly went unheeded, and by one year of age it had petered out. During the first nine months, the infant cried a great deal, expressing her need tension quite vociferously. Mrs. V. frequently responded to this with rage, at times even with physically aggressive acts. We do not know how far this baby was able to find solace in her own, fitfully libidinized body through autoerotic means such as sucking, stroking herself, etc. We do know, however, that at eight or nine months of age Violet made an attempt to smear her feces, and that when her mother discovered this, she flew into a violent rage and beat up the infant, with the result that Violet allegedly never smeared again. At least during the first months, Violet seems to have engaged the mother with her eyes during feeding, and smiled at her; she vocalized at around eight or nine months. All these signs of "social contact-seeking" stopped or slowly disappeared by the age of fifteen months. Although there were no events such as might have provided evidence of a massive regression, at about one year of age something seems to have gone wrong. Violet did not respond to people, did not "smile much," did not appear to have fun, etc. The parents were told by the pediatrician when Violet was fifteen months old that there was something "strange."

The description of Violet's daytime routine at the time of intake, at two years seven months, indicated the same kind of almost bizarre handling that must have prevailed during the first year of the child's life. Violet's parents were both musicians, and for many hours she was "locked out" while the parents practiced their instruments, even though Violet protested and usually had a temper tantrum. "If the mother had time, she might take time to bribe Violet in various ways. But the chances were that she would put Violet in the hall and leave her there to bang her head on the floor and thrash her arms and legs about while the mother resumed her practicing. She believed that Violet would stop when she heard her mother starting to play, and realize that she just wasn't going to get anywhere with her tantrums."

When Violet made her first appearance with us, she was mute; she had an absolutely blank and unanimated facial expression, and she focused on nothing and nobody. She had no verbal language. The child's movements, large and small alike, seemed to be well coordinated; she moved with that well-known elflike grace that some psychotic girl patients display. Her straight blond hair was frequently unkempt. While her features were delicate and pixielike, they were congealed, as it were, into a flat and spiritless expression. She showed no response to people and acted as though she did not hear their voices. Psychological testing (at twenty-three months) placed Violet in a superior classification on the performance scale; her neurological examination was completely negative; EEG was mildly and diffusely abnormal.

The chief complaints of the mother were the child's destructiveness and unmanageability and her sleep and feeding disturbance. She was concerned that Violet was not toilet trained, that she threw frequent temper tantrums, and that she did not speak.

From the time she was able to crawl, upon being left alone, Violet would tear books and chew music records and strew these around until the room was a shambles. This usually happened when the parents were practicing and Violet, with great skill, was able to get hold of those scores and records. (Mrs. V. felt that it had been natural for her to leave Violet so much alone, because she herself had always been so much alone.)

The description of Mrs. V.'s interaction with Violet, which we observed when she brought Violet to us for diagnosis at intake, is noteworthy. Mrs. V. appeared to be a somewhat tense, slender woman in her early twenties, who smiled a sphinxlike, enigmatic smile. She appeared to be easily irritated in her relations with the child and generally quite tentative in her contacts with her. She would frequently offer a half-formed direction to the child, but at the first sign of withdrawal on the child's part (a typical reaction), the mother would also withdraw. The mother was observed through many a long session during which she did not utter a single word to the child.

During intake, while the mother and the psychiatrist were talking in the playroom for about fifty-five minutes, the child occupied herself with wandering about the room, examining and momentarily playing with small toys, the phonograph, and the light she reached by climbing on a chair. On one occasion she went exploring down the hall; she had to be recovered by the psychiatrist, because the mother made no effort to follow her out of the room. During the time of intake observation, the child did not attempt to engage the mother's attention and only occasionally approached the doctor. When she did, she avoided eye engagement; instead, she would glance at the doctor very briefly, and then turn her eyes away.

The only communication involving sound between mother and child, the only situation that elicited smiles from the child in relation to the mother, pivoted around the piano. In fact, the child displayed phenomenal musical gifts, an unusual ear, and an incredible ability to reproduce on the piano almost any music she heard, even if she heard it only in passing. If her father, in practicing, failed to produce music precisely as she had repeatedly heard it on a record by a great master, she would have a temper tantrum.

In Violet's case we have a schizoid mother who is warding off her own murderous impulses by detachment and isolation.

In Benny's case, we meet, by contrast, an intrusive, smothering, managerial, overwhelmingly affectionate and physically over-stimulating mother, who pushed her son to individuate at a rapid pace, and without really giving him the chance to disengage himself gradually from what was a mutually parasitic symbiosis.

Benny, on the occasion of his first visits to the Center, was essentially dragged or carried into the building and into the room. He exhibited extreme distress and diffuse panic. He clung to and pulled at his mother, but as soon as the latter actively attempted to soothe him by taking him into her arms, he would try violently to extricate himself, pushing against her and arching backwards.

When he was first seen by us, he was in what one would have to describe as an acute catatonic state. He clung to his mother, emitting shrieks of distress, alternately arching his body into an extreme opisthotonus or melting into her body. When standing alone, he was up on his toes, with an extreme tension in all his muscles, to the point where one could not help believing that this was very painful. On the other hand, he showed some degree of waxy flexibility, and could be directed up the stairs by the tip of one's finger.

The impression the child provided was that of a classical symbiotic-psychotic syndrome in a three-and-a-half-year-old. Benny's speech was mostly in fragments, which the mother related to TV commercials that he had heard many months before. However, at intake we immediately had the impression that there were occasionally brief but directed verbal communications. He said "hello" when he was introduced to the doctor and made small appropriate remarks from time to time.

A great deal of the child's energy seemed to be directed toward eluding the mother, who was astoundingly ever-present. He did occasionally follow her directions with some pleasure, even though the mother was often physically and directly overwhelming, kneeling over him, blotting out the sky from him, tickling him. The mother's entire array of comforting behavior was displayed; she talked to Benny, even lied to him, almost incessantly, and at the level of the most primitive reality, "causes and consequences." For example, if she wanted to keep him in the room, she would tell him that the door was broken or jammed; when she wanted to distract him from play, she said that his fingers would get stuck. She could be observed constantly hovering over Benny, "teaching" him, offering endless directions to his play.

In spite of careful consideration, during Benny's and his mother's lengthy treatment, the mother could not come up with any evidence of deviation during the first year of his life: he had been an attractive and responsive infant.[2] In his second year, too, the mother was pleased with him, thinking this firstborn son of hers to be a gifted child (the correction, she hoped, for her own denigrated self-image). At this time, the child performed, to the amazement of everyone, such feats as reading the totals on the cash register and reciting memorized songs and rhymes that he had heard both from his mother and on TV.

When he was sixteen months old, he became very anxious; this was at the beginning of toilet training. During the next half year, there was a fairly rapid development of the symbiotic-psychotic clinical picture. He developed severe tantrums and a very severe anxiety upon being separated from his parents, even for the shortest time. He alternately clung to the mother and pushed her away,

2. Scrutiny of recently viewed "home movie pictures" shows Benny, at eight months of age, looking without focus upon the outside world, his facial expression indicative of some disturbance.

gradually developing a continuous state of extreme distress that lasted throughout the day and night. He slept only little. He would implore the mother with gestures to help, moaning pitifully; but as soon as the mother took him into her arms, he would ward her off, arching his back in a stiff opisthotonus. There was a very apparent avoidance of meaningful interchange with any human being through facial expression or bodily contact.

During treatment, this boy made considerable advance in the direction of awareness of, and communicative involvement with, other human beings, including the beginnings of speech. However, with each new step in development, in individuation, there was a regression to the state of acute panic, expressed in alternate clinging and pushing away such as we saw at first. It should be mentioned that, as time went on, despite the panic, the extent of withdrawal from human contact in these states seemed to decrease.

In conclusion, I wish to state that the core of child psychosis must be sought in one or the other of the described distortions of the symbiotic phase. In the first case, what lay at the heart of the psychotic disturbance was the marked emotional unavailability of the mother, which alternated with a purely physical extreme closeness during the breast-feeding situations, and particularly with the destructiveness of the mother's unpredictable rage attacks. The contrasting experiences drove the child to the autistic warding off of any human contact and the deanimation of the world of reality. Constitutional factors could not, in this case, be evaluated with any degree of accuracy.

In the second case, it was, by contrast, the mother's ever-presence that created an unendurable instrusion upon and interference with the structuralization of the budding ego, which constitutionally and perhaps predispositionally may have been very vulnerable. This made it impossible for the infant to experience the normal alternation of the gratification-frustration sequences at his own pace; it also made the process of individuation in the separation-individuation period one which was beset with abysmal panic.

In both instances, we can see that it was primarily in the severe distortions of the normal symbiosis that the child psychosis had its roots.

Chapter 9

AUTISM AND SYMBIOSIS: TWO EXTREME
DISTURBANCES OF IDENTITY

[1958]

My hypothesis of infantile psychoses is based upon two of Freud's fundamental concepts. It is a quasi-sociobiological proposition. Freud (1923b) emphasized that whereas the animal has an instinctual faculty for sensing danger in the outside world which enables it to take appropriate action to cope with such danger, this faculty has atrophied in the human being. In the human being the ego has to take over the reality testing which the id neglects. The predicament of the human young is immensely increased by still another biological circumstance—namely, by the fact that he is born at an earlier, less matured stage of physical development than any other mammal. These two interrelated circumstances, namely (i) the atrophy of the instinct of self-preservation, and (ii) the immaturity of apparatuses at birth, result in the human infant's absolute dependence for his very survival on the nursing care of a mother or a mother substitute for a long period. Long after the child has been born, a species-characteristic social symbiosis between the infant and mother is necessary. I shall try to demonstrate that the syndromes of early infantile psychoses, both the autistic as well as the symbiotic type, represent fixations at, or regressions to, the first two developmental stages of "undifferentiation" within this early mother-child unity. Within that twilight stage of early life which Freud designated as primary narcissism, the infant shows hardly any sign of perceiving anything beyond his own body. He seems to live in a world of inner stimuli. The first weeks of extrauterine life are characterized by what (according to Ferenczi) we call the stage of hallucinatory wish-fulfillment. Whereas the (coenesthetic) enteroceptive system functions from birth, the perceptual conscious system, the sensorium, is not yet cathected. This lack of peripheral sensory cathexis only gradually gives way to perception, particularly to distance perception, of the outside world. However, most babies are born with appropriate signal equipment for dealing with instinctual tensions when they mount beyond a tolerable degree. Their affectomotor reactions serve automatically to summon and use the mother as external executive ego (Spitz). Furthermore, as early as the first day of extrauterine life the full term neonate displays a discriminatory grasping reflex (Stirnimann 1947) which proves that he has a significant innate endowment for distinguishing in a sensorimotor way between the living part object and lifeless matter. This primal ability to discriminate between animate and inanimate was given the name *Urunterscheidung: Protodiakrisis,* by von Monakow (Stirnimann 1947).

The presymbiotic, normal-autistic phase of the mother-infant unity gives way to the symbiotic phase proper from about the age of three months on. During his wakeful hungry periods of the day the three-four-month-old baby seems to perceive, temporarily at least, and, in a Gestalt kind of perception, that small part of external reality which is represented by the mother's breast, face, and hands, the Gestalt of her ministrations as such. This occurs in the matrix of the oral gratification-frustration sequences of the normal nursing situation. This phase of dim awareness of the "need-satisfying object" marks the beginning of the *phase of symbiosis* in which the infant behaves and functions as though he and his mother were an omnipotent system (a dual unity) within one common boundary (a symbiotic membrane as it were). The symbiotic phase is followed by the so-called separation-individuation phase proper. This occurs parallel with the maturation and consolidation of such autonomous ego functions as locomotion, and the beginning of language (*SPI*:6).

Two conditions are requisite for structuralization of the ego and neutralization of drives in order to achieve individuation, that is to say, a sense of individual entity and identity: (i) the enteroceptive-proprioceptive stimuli must not be so persistent and so intense as to prevent formation of structure; (ii) in the absence of an "inner organizer" in the human infant (Spitz) the symbiotic partner must be able to serve as a buffer against inner and outer stimuli, gradually organizing them for the infant and orienting it to inner versus outer world, i.e., to boundary formation and sensory perception. Freud (1923) emphasized, "Perceptions may be said to have the same significance for the ego as instincts have for the id." Hartmann has pointed out that formation of structure and neutralization of drives is a circular process: structure is formed by perceptual turning toward the outside world, and *vice versa*. If the two aforementioned conditions are not met, the ego's perceptual faculty cannot gain ascendancy nor can the ego's integrative and synthetic function develop (Hartmann 1953, Hartmann, Kris, and Loewenstein 1946).

Hermann's (1934) and Bak's (1939) theories of schizophrenia indicate that predisposition to psychosis has its origin in those early physiological distress situations which are connected with or ensue from psychophysiological incompatibility of the mother-infant unit in the first weeks of life in which these *overflow assimilatory* processes take place. There are situations in early infancy in which enteroproprioceptive overstimulation due to illness, or an adverse maternal (symbiotic) milieu generate great quantities of unneutralized explosive and, therefore, disorganizing aggressive drive energy. These are the situations in which neutralization or countercathexis cannot be effected by the usual contact perceptual libidinizing process of the mother's nursing care (Hoffer 1950b). In certain cases the severity of the physiological upheaval not only impairs the perceptual activity of the sensorium and thus formation of structure (ego), but even the faculty of primal discrimination (protodiakrisis) between living and inanimate may be lost.

Such catastrophic shifts and reactions seem to be the pathogenic agents in *early infantile autism*. The pivotal disturbance lies in these children's inability to perceive the Gestalt of the mother and the Gestalt of her vital functioning on their behalf. There seems no perceptual awareness of an inside versus an outside world, no awareness of the child's own self as distinct from the *inanimate environment.*[1]

From our sociobiological point of view these infants remain fixated or regress to the autistic phase of extrauterine life or (as far as protodiakrisis is concerned) to an even more archaic fetal stage of functioning. Among the clinical findings bearing out the above-described dynamics are the grossly inadequate peripheral pain-sensitivity in these children and also the signs pointing to the insufficiency of the peripheral blood circulation. Concurrent with this cathectic deficiency of the sensorium is a lack of hierarchic stratification of zonal libidinization and sequence. This is evident from the relative *paucity of autoerotic activities* on the one hand, and a facility for libidinal positions substituting for each other. Instead of autoerotic activities these children show autoaggressive habits such as head-knocking, self-biting, or other self-hurting activities. Auto-aggressive activities in a quasi-restitutive attempt serve to sharpen the awareness of the body-self boundaries, often at the expense, or at the actual sacrifice of parts of the body image (Szasz 1957). As a consequence of this lack of cathexis of the *Pcpt.-Cs. system,* these children are completely impervious to their mother's voice and commands, nor do they seem to see you; they look through you. It is an open question whether this turning a deaf ear toward mother and, consequently, toward the outside world is inborn or an acquired defense. Their inability to use the symbiotic partner makes it necessary for these children to find substitute adaptive mechanisms for survival, and these substitutive formations represent the symtomatology of early infantile autism (Kanner 1942, 1949).

The symbiotic psychotic syndrome (*SPI:7*) represents fixation at or regression to the *second undifferentiated stage* of the mother-child unity, which is the stage of delusional omnipotent symbiotic fusion with the need-satisfying object.

Primary autism gradually becomes manifest as sequelae of the autistic isolation become more and more apparent with the maturational growth of the organism. But the symbiotic psychotic picture in contrast develops, more often than not, with crises of catastrophic

---

1. Compare Buytendijk as quoted by Werner (1948).

and panic reactions marking its course. Unlike the persistent imperviousness of the autistic cases, the anamnesis of these symbiotic psychotics show unequivocal signs of a defective stimulus barrier, an insufficiency of the protective courtercathexis of the *Pcpt.-Cs.* system with hypersensitivity, labile homeostasis, increased vulnerability of the ego, and impairment of many functions, but particularly the repressive defensive function of the ego (Jacobson 1957a, (*SPI*: 6, 11). The slightest additional trauma causes the rudimentary brittle ego structure to fragment. One of the characteristics of the symbiotic psychotic ego structure, in contradistinction to that of the autistic one, is its great incohesive *interpermeability with the id*. The lack of distinction between the primary and secondary process and the dominance of the pleasure principle persist. Inner and outer reality are fused because of the incohesive boundary formation of the self: hence, the original common symbiotic boundary of self and object world, of the child and mother, is maintained beyond the symbiotic age, and the ego cannot perform those developmental tasks which would result in further self-differentiation and separation from the mother. In consequence, these children do not attain the separation-individuation phase which is the first level of the normal child's subjective, but all-important, sense of individual entity and identity. Very little is known in psychoanalytic (and other) literature about this all-important cohesive cathectic state which gives us our sense of identity (Mahler 1958b). Those who work with psychotic children are impressed by the most pervasive feature of this disorder, namely, a partial or complete loss of personal identity, which seems to usher in alienation and withdrawal from reality.

THE SENSE OF SELF-IDENTITY

The sense of individual identity is mediated by our bodily sensations. Its core is the body image which consists of a fairly stabilized predominantly libidinal cathexis of the body in its central and peripheral parts (Greenacre 1953). "The infant's body is both internal and external at the same time. By virtue of this characteristic, it stands out for him from the rest of the world and thereby enables him to work out the distinction between self and non-self. (Hartmann 1950; see also Hartmann, Kris, and Loewenstein 1946). Proprioceptive inner stimuli, as well as contact perceptions, deep pressure sensitivity and thermal interchange, in addition to kinesthetic experiences (equilibrium) in the nursing situation contribute much more importantly and immediately to the core of our feeling of identity, to our body image, than the later maturing distance-perceptive visual and auditory images. The latter contribute primarily and most importantly to the recognition of and distinction from the object world. Integration of our bodily feelings, and unconscious phantasies about the body self, especially its contents, with visual, auditory, and kinesthetic data about it are a relatively late acquisition of the ego. It coincides with the first level of integration of the sense of identity which is dependent on separation-individuation and which is characterized by a negativistic phase (A. Freud 1951a).

The maturational spurt which takes place in the second year puts the (normal) toddler in the position of a relatively advanced physical autonomy. Locomotion is one of the autonomous ego functions whose maturation may become the most conspicuous paradigm of discrepancy between the rate of maturational and the developmental growth of the personality (Hartmann, Kris, and Loewenstein 1946).[2] Locomotion enables the child to separate, physically to move away from the mother, when emotionally he may be quite unprepared to do so. The two-year-old child very soon experiences his separateness in many other ways. He enjoys his independence and exercises mastery with great tenacity, and thus large quantities of libido and aggression are utilized by the ego. On the other hand there are junior toddlers who show adverse reactions and increased clinging to the mother in reaction to their own autonomy. The awareness of separate functioning may elicit intense anxiety in these vulnerable toddlers, who then try desperately to deny the fact of separateness, on the one hand, and struggle against reengulfment by increased opposition to the adults.

2. According to Hartmann, Kris, and Loewenstein (1946, p. 18) *maturation* indicates the processes of growth that occur relatively independent of environmental influences; development indicates the processes of growth in which environment and maturation interact more closely.

Experimental and academic psychologists also found the phase of individuation in which the child develops "self-awareness" an uneasy period in his life. Wallon and his pupil, Zazzo, have studied the young child's recognition of his own image in three different situations: in the mirror, on photos, and in films. It was found that recognition of the mirror image does not occur until two years and two or three months.[3] A few weeks before this occurs the observers "noticed a kind of disorganization, as if a sudden state of awareness of self had caused an affective upset." (Zazzo 1953). Up to the end of the third year the child displays a certain fearfulness and at the same time a certain pleasure in looking at himself in the mirror. At about two years and ten months the image has become familiar and no longer causes uneasiness. It is at the same time, that is, two years and ten months to three years of age, that the personal pronoun "I" begins to be used without hesitation and grammatically.

The normal negativistic phase of the toddler is the accompanying behavioral reaction of this process of individuation, of disengagement from the mother-child symbiosis. The fear of reengulfment threatens a recently and barely started individual differentiation which must be defended. The less satisfactory or the more parasitic the symbiotic phase has been, the more prominent and exaggerated will be this negativistic reaction (A. Freud 1951a, Loewald 1951, SPI:6). An ego which is unable to function separately from the symbiotic partner tries to reentrench itself in the delusional phantasy of oneness with the omnipotent mother, by coercing her into functioning as an extension of the self. This device, of course, usually fails to halt the process of alienation from reality (a reality still represented almost exclusively by the mother).

The separation-individuation phase is vulnerable in any child's life. If the struggle is lost, as in symbiotic psychosis, fragmentation of his ego has as its consequence a complete breakdown of integrative functions on all levels. To begin with, proprioceptive perception may be mistaken for and confused with sensory perception: inner intentions are attributed to outside factors, biodynamics are taken for

3. There seem, however, to be some exceptions to the rule of timing of this self-identity-recognition. Such an exception (premature recognition) was observed by me in the case of a monozygotic twin (Mahler, and Silberpfennig 1938).

mechanical dynamics (Mahler, Ross, and De Fries 1949). The ego regression seems to be aimed in particular at dedifferentiation of function and contents because the fragmented ego cannot cope with complexities. Dedifferentiation seems to be the adaptive mechanism serving survival under these circumstances with secondary autistic mechanisms. If this process is complete, the clinical picture may show superficial resemblance to primary autism. Let me give a clinical example.

George was the firstborn of his parents. Immediately after his birth, the father left for the Navy. Among many interesting data, I mention only that mother and infant saw practically no one but each other and that the mother treated the child as though he were a vegetative appendage of her own self, e.g., there was hardly any verbal communication between mother and baby. When the child was approximately two years old the father returned, but he was always morose and uninterested in the boy. In his third year of life George's behavior clearly demonstrated an overgrowth of unchecked and unmitigated (unconscious) aggressive phantasies. There was evidence of his utter misunderstanding of the affective meaning of social situations, in terms of projection of his unneutralized aggression. For example, he would cry like an infant of eight months when greeted by an unfamiliar person with a friendly hello. If friends or relatives patted him on the shoulder or head, he became terrified, stated that they hit him, and seemed frightened that they would harm him. The momentum of his pent-up aggression broke through the patient's hitherto mute behavior. At the age two and a half to three, George's mutism abruptly changed to flighty and panic-stricken language of the primary process variety which his mother aptly described and called "talking tantrums." When frustrated, but also without apparent cause, he would pace around the room, talking angrily to himself about something which seemed entirely unintelligible and irrelevant to his environment. During the second half of his third year, in the separation-individuation phase of George's development, the mother again became pregnant. George began to have night terrors. When he was past three, his baby sister was born and George became *acutely* disturbed. During the last months of his mother's pregnancy he developed an absorbing, exclusive interest in examining his inanimate environment by touching objects. Regression to contact-perceptual as well as olfactory and gustatory reality testing is often found in infantile psychosis. George became conspicuous during his mother's pregnancy by his strange compulsive interest in barrels, beer barrels in particular (they lived near a brewery). He would stop and touch each barrel and examine it with care. Following this preoccupation with barrels he became fascinated by pipes of all sorts, which, again, he would have to touch, size up, stroke, etc., commenting on their size, shape, or other characteristics. After a few months he developed a similar preoccupation with electrical appliances; he would endlessly pretend to be putting a plug into a socket. Still later George developed an intense interest in fires, and this was predominant at the time of his hospitalization at six and a half years of age.

Two aspects of this frantic reality testing in the wake of the symbiotic psychotic process are characteristic and deserve discussion. First, we can see the slipping away of the *living* object world (through withdrawal of the libidinal cathexis) so that an estrangement in terms of *deanimation* and dedifferentiation takes place. With the decathexis of the living object world, the child's *own body*, the body feelings deriving directly from instinctual processes not sifted by the ego gain ascendancy. These feelings usurp the place of the "not-me" object world. The body and the feelings it conveys are the only remaining objects of the patient's ego! The second aspect to be discussed is the alienation from the child's own body, the fragmentation of the body image, the parts of which are cathected with grossly aggressivized energy. This second aspect of the symbiotic-psychotic break hangs together or is the counterpart of the delibidinization of the object world. It becomes manifest as the psychotic elaboration of the bisexual conflict which in George's case coincided with the sister's birth (and his phallic phase). The second level of integration of the sense of identify is the resolution of the bisexual identification. *Psychosexual maturation is also biologically predetermined* and thus proceeds even though object relationship and reality-testing may not. It seems that the phallic phase brings with it a most consequential maturational event, massive concentration of libido in the sexual parts of the body image. This process occurs regardless of what environmental influences there are. Normally, it inevitably causes important shifts of cathexis in terms of body image representations emerging via pregenital libidinal phases, and bisexual identifications to firm establishment of sexual identity. This second phase of integration of the body image and feeling of identity seems to be dependent on a number of important conditions: (i) on the successful integration of pregenital phases of development; (ii) on the successful identification with the parental figure of the same sex in which both parents' emotional attitude toward the child's sexual identity is of the utmost importance; and (iii) the ability of the ego to organize the memories, ideas, and feelings about the self into a hierarchically stratified, firmly cathected organization of self-representations.

The dissociation of the constituents of the feeling of identity is ushered in by the loss of the innate human faculty of discrimination between the animate and the inanimate, the living and the dead. This primal discrimination, this "protodiakrisis" (Monakow) seems to depend on and consists of impressions of warmth, resiliency, turgor, deep tactile sensations between two living higher organisms at contact with one another.

George demonstrated this utter confusion of animate and inanimate. For example, he was panic-stricken when he had to pass a certain picket fence for fear that the holes might swallow him; he also demonstrated confusion of anything moving. He became frantic about and later obsessed with the workings of electrical appliances (which obviously symbolized his body and particularly his genital.) The symbolic oral connotation of the fence holes, the barrel bellies; the anal meaning of George's interest in the shapes of the pipes and the plumbing, etc.; and the phallic meaning of the machines, are quite obvious. My emphasis, however, is on the pathognomonic significance of the animation of the inanimate and deanimation of the living environment in the wake of the psychotic process. When gradual transition from primary to secondary identification with the love object has failed, it seems that all the libido is suddenly withdrawn from the object world.

The clinical manifestations must be regarded as restitution attempts. Shortly after the baby sister came, George wanted to wear her clothes, and often also his mother's dresses. This was not like a normal child's make-believe play, for these psychotic children believe that they *become* the mother or the sister by wearing their clothes (Mahler, Ross, and De Fries 1949). He spoke to everybody of his sister and again and again of his pet kitten: "I have a cat at home. It's a girl cat. I like my cat. I am a girl cat."

George's parasitic-symbiosis was suddenly terminated by several factors: (i) the father's reappearance and hostility; (ii) soon afterward, the mother's pregnancy; (iii) the birth of a female sibling; and (iv) the father's preference for, as well as the mother's preoccupation with, the baby sister. George was suddenly faced, in a hostile oedipal atmosphere, with separateness in the functional-maturational sense, without being emotionally at all prepared to give up the delusion of omnipotent fusion with the mother. We may assume that neither were his self-boundaries cathected with neutralized energy, nor was his body image differentiated beyond confused bisexual self representations and object representation. George seemed to have tried frantically to adopt countercathectic devices against fragmentation of his brittle ego. He tried to counteract the threatening loss of the libidinal object world by attempting to recapture it in a concrete sense through the contact-perceptive faculties of his ego. George compulsively and feverishly tried to finger, "to feel" things around him; he obviously tried to distinguish between, to compare, beer barrels and his pregnant mother's body. After his baby sister's birth, George compared, in this tactile way, concrete symbols of male and female anatomy, and at the same time perhaps endeavored to distinguish the semi-animate and inanimate shapes and phenomena of oral and anal experiences.

The bisexual problem augmented to a spectacular degree this boy's struggle to regain his symbiotic completeness with the "lost mother." Castration fear and envy of the intimate relationship of the girl-baby and the mother seemed to drive George into intense body hallucinations which were characterized by psychotically destructive contents.

George's outstanding hallucination during hospitalization was of seeing a fire destroying his little sister. At first George used to verbalize during these fire hallucinations, and hence we knew how to read his agitated behavior when it betrayed these visions.

It seemed that his hallucinatory and delusional restitution attempts consisted of incorporative and destructive tendencies toward his sister and mother. In his clearer periods he would state: "I'm afraid of killing my mother. I have ideas of wanting to kill her. Yes, I think of killing her, and these thoughts upset me so. That gives me bad feelings in my head. It makes me so upset when I am home. Doctor, you are supposed to take that out."

Defusion of instincts seems to result in uneven aggressivization of bodily part images, and a confusion of object representations with the introjects. The fragments of the self-images are secondarily recathected although with grossly instinctualized energy. The result is the frequently found body delusions and hallucinations observable in the schizophrenic child. After withdrawal from the object world, he recreates in his own internal reality both the subject and the object, the mother and himself. He may alternately take the outside object or parts of his own body, an eroticized hand or the aggressivized skin of his arm, or an inanimate object as symbol for the introject. He may show outward rage and destruction or all kinds of self-mutilating and self-destructive tendencies. That George's hallucinations served restitution as well, the following example will illustrate: While sitting next to the nurse whom George loved and also hated most, he appeared to hallucinate the big fire. During the conflagration George unzipped his overalls and began pulling at the nurse's skirt as though gathering up the ashes. He then put his hands in his overalls as if pouring in what he had gathered. This went on for a short time, then he zipped up his overalls and sat there smiling. "I've got a Hollinger [name of the nurse] in there . . . that's what I've got in there." George was hilariously elated for the rest of the day and sat away in a corner, communicating with the introjected beloved (Klein 1932, Klein et al. 1952).

By this behavior and the resulting affect we saw that George introjected the loved object and by so doing succeeded in restoring his former symbiotic unity with mother.

SUMMARY

Research in child schizophrenia points to:

1. An inborn or very early acquired basic defect of the ego, *(a)* one of the manifestations of which in autistic children is the inability of perceptual discrimination of animate and inanimate, and of the mother as a living being in particular; *(b)* whereas in the symbiotic psychotic child the most important manifestation of this basic defect is the insufficiency of the stimulus barrier (which prevents the mother from acting as an efficient buffer against overstimulation from without).

2. In consequence of these defects, the mother is either not perceived at all (as in autism) or remains undifferentiated from the self (symbiotic syndrome). Hence, all relations to the object world, to the child's own body as well as the concepts of the self, are altered.

3. Apart from the basic defect, additional problems are created by virtue of the fact that maturation proceeds while development lags.

4. One of the most momentous maturational thrusts occurs in the phallic phase. The concentration of psychic energy in the sexual organs (and in the child's own body) leads to further depletion of the already precarious object cathexis. This phase resembles in many respects the picture of pre- or pseudo psychosis in puberty (in which grave, subjectively registered disturbance of the sense of identity is so conspicuous), of which it seems to be the forerunner.

5. In order to survive the child has to develop several restitutive devices, which I have tried to illustrate in one such case.

Chapter 10

PERCEPTUAL DEDIFFERENTIATION AND PSYCHOTIC OBJECT RELATIONSHIPS

[1960]

When we speak of "object relationship in psychotics" or of "psychotic object relationships" we must redefine and vastly broaden the concept of "object relationship" as the term was originally used in psychoanalysis. In the original, Freudian sense, object relationship meant a person's endowing another human being with object libido. In this sense object relationship is the most reliable single factor by which we determine mental health on the one hand and therapeutic potential on the other. In contradistinction to object relationship, we used to speak of relationships of a narcissistic nature.

Object relationship develops on the basis of differentiation from the normal mother-infant dual unity, which may be designated as the phase of symbiosis (SPI:7, Starr 1954).

The phases of the development of object relationship were described by a number of psychoanalytic authors. To mention only a few: by Anna Freud (1958), who distinguishes the earlier phase of the "need-satisfying object" from the later phase, in which object-libidinal cathexis of the mother—as a whole person—becomes independent of satisfaction of instinctual needs, highly specific, and attains mutuality and consolidation; and by Hartmann (1952), who speaks of object constancy.

Development of object relationship is paralleled by differentiation of an object as well as a self (Jacobson 1954). Differentiation of the body image, in particular, conveys to the child a sense of separateness and individual identity (Mahler 1958b, Greenacre 1958). This separation from the object occurs through processes of libidinization and *partial* identification. Bak (1939), Greenacre (1953), Hoffer (1950a), and others contributed to our understanding of the libidinization processes which seem to be the basis for perceptual activity of the ego and formation of structure. I have described and emphasized in earlier papers (Mahler, Ross, and De Fries 1949, *SPI*:9) what appears to me to be a *first* and important step towards perceptual activity and eventual perceptual-emotional integrative capacity of the ego, namely, the progression of the libidinal cathexis from the internal organs, the viscera in particular, towards the periphery, the "rind" of the body-self. Freud (1923) stated: "Perception may be said to have the same significance for the ego as instincts have for the id." Libidinal cathexis of the body and the human love object paves the way to that kind of fully developed object relationship which is the attribute of the mature ego and which moves parallel with the attainment of genital primacy, as Freud pointed out.

It is obvious that if we speak of "psychotic object relationships", we abandon such stringent definitions. We must broaden and enlarge the concept of "object" as well as of "relationship." In the broadest sense, then, we may speak of anything as an object which, in a field of interreaction, physiologically or otherwise impinges upon the organism *in utero* or in extrauterine life, as its environment. This broadened concept of object versus subject is necessary, and may prove invaluable in research into earliest ontogenetic development, as well as for deciphering some of the enigmas of psychosis. We must learn from modern ethology as well as from those workers who, to my mind, correctly emphasize that in earliest development physiology rather than psychology shows us the way.

Recent research into physiological interreactions between fetus and mother and neonate and mother, such as that of Greene (1958), elucidates some of the vascular-respiratory rhythmic interreactions of the mother-fetus and mother-neonate dual unit. According to Greene's observations and hypothesis, the key configuration or

Gestalt which causes the subject to become eventually aware of (to perceive) the object is this compatible rhythmicity. It renders the perceptual experience predictable. It would seem that early incompatibilities may contribute to early failure of libidinization processes. This may be one of the factors at the root of regression to psychotic levels of object relationships in Winnicott's sense. In his paper "Transitional Objects and Transitional Phenomena" (1953b), Winnicott described how optimal use of transitional, *inanimate* objects facilitated autonomy of the ego, whereas too rigid adherence to, or substitution of, transitional objects in lieu of human relationships may be the first and reliable sign of later pathology.

The phenomenon which more or less overtly *is* common to all psychotics, is the blurring, if not complete failure, of distinction, of affective discrimination of the social, the human object world from the inanimate environment. In some cases we find lack of or very tenuous emotional contact, phenomena of estrangement, complaints of derealization only. In cases of acute severe psychotic breakdown we find deanimation of the human object world with concomitant animation of the inanimate environment. Between these two groups of cathectic derangements there seem to exist fluent transitions. (Compare, e.g. [Greenacre 1953, 1959], fetishism.)

The following passage from Mme Sechehaye's patient Renee's autobiography (Sechehaye 1959) graphically describes the subjective experience connected with the last-mentioned group of animation-dehumanization processes: "I was [as] if frozen. I saw . . . each thing separate . . . detached from the others, cold, implacable, *inhuman* by dint of being without life. These people—became void . . . Mama I perceived a statue, a figure of ice which smiled at me. And this smile, showing her white teeth, frightened me." Renee goes on to say: "'Things' began to take on life, suddenly the 'thing' sprang up . . . the stone jar . . . I looked away, my eyes met a chair . . . a table . . . they were *alive* too,—'things' have become more real than people." In other words, as in Schreber's *Weltuntergang* experience (Freud 1911), or as in the case of my young patient George whom I described in 1957b, one could reconstruct this acute, step-by-step failure of the perceptual integrative capacity of the ego, which is eventually relegated to becoming the passive victim of the defused, rapidly deneutralized instinctual forces. The ego tries to ward off the onslaught of the two sets of stimuli from without and from within by a number of psychotic mechanisms, described in earlier papers. The outstanding mechanisms are massive denial, displacement, condensation, and *dedifferentiation*. Complex stimuli, particularly those demanding social emotional response, are massively denied, autistically hallucinated away, so that ego regression may not halt before a *level* of perceptual dedifferentiation at which primal discrimination between living and inanimate ("protodiakrisis" of Monakow) is lost. I have described (Mahler 1958a) how seven-year-old George gradually lost this perceptual faculty of his ego at the sudden loss of the symbiotic possession of his mother. I described his bizarre preoccupations, his feverishly seeking to find beer barrels near the brewery where they lived, in order to touch and feel their surface. He attempted to recapture, to mend with this primitive tactile perceptual experience the broken tie with his pregnant mother's body. In his case, as in those of some other psychotic patients, the steps of this dedifferentiation demonstrably contain the elements of dehumanization, devitalization of the human living object world, including the patient's own body feelings, and relative animation, quasi-humanization of the inanimate environment. The phase in which his world appears populated with hallucinatory-delusional projections of preterhuman introjected objects is only one (better known, because conspicuous) phase in this regression of the psychotic (cf. Bychowski 1956a, 1956b).

It would seem that the uncanny, unpredictable acts of destruction, of cold, seemingly unemotional, yet calculated violence are based upon this fateful regression, this psychotic defence mechanism of the ego, which, because of its *perceptual* capacity disintegrated, becomes reduced to that degree of passivity vis-a-vis the instinctual drives which, according to David Rapaport (1958), characterizes the ego in earliest infancy. In this regressed state the impulse is experienced as a compelling command which continually threatens the disintegrating ego from within. This ego experiences outside stimuli, acceptable only if they are simple, soothing, and predictable, and do not require active and complicated emotional response. The more complex, variable, and unpredictable sensory stimuli are, the more threatening they become. Stimuli reaching the rapidly fragmenting ego from the living object world are much more complex, and seem to be much more dangerous. They seem to conjure up the demoniacal inner impulses (personified often as tormenting introjects). The psychotic child, as well as the adult, is often tormented by murderous impulses which are triggered by stimuli coming from residual human "love objects."

Eight-year-old George, upon returning from his weekend visits at home, would imploringly say to me: "I'm afraid of killing my mother. I have ideas of killing her, and these thoughts upset me so! That gives me bad feelings in my head. It makes me so upset when I am home. Doctor, you are supposed to take that out" (*SPI*:9).

Ten-year-old Alma's psychotic alienation from reality could be traced to the age of four and a half, when (suffering with measles complicated by pneumonia) she was hospitalized and thereby separated from her mother. She did not become acutely psychotic before the age of ten, however, after seeing the film *Snow White and the Seven Dwarfs*. She heard a voice saying: "Strangle your mother! Strangle your mother!" At fourteen, in the hospital, she wrote to her doctor: "Maybe then . . . when I saw *Snow White and the Seven Dwarfs* somehow I was the witch and fed the girl the apple. Maybe, somehow, I wanted to get my mother out of myself by strangulation and at the same time strangling and punishing myself, killing Snow White. All I know is after I, after the voice said 'Strangle your mother' . . . I felt weirdness. Then I was not afraid of myself any more. But for a whole year I constantly threw up . . . maybe subconsciously I was strangling myself, or was it the witch or was it mother or was it Snow White or was it the mice that Ma killed . . . I imagine it was me. After a few seconds I felt different."[1] From then on, Alma acted and behaved in a mechanical, robotlike fashion interspersed with episodes of catatonic agitation.

Whereas Alma's own description could be cited to demonstrate the devitalization, deanimation struggle against all elements of the social living object world, including her own self, I should like to cite briefly the cases of six-year-old Barry and seven-year-old Betty, to

---

1. I owe this material to William Cox, Jr., M.D., of New York.

illustrate the compensatory or restitutive *animation, machineization* of the inanimate object world. Barry, who had an I.Q. of 170 or more, had to be hospitalized at six years of age, when with clever purposefulness he went about applying a drill to the temple of one of his classmates in order to look into his head to see if the little boy had any brains. Barry appeared a strangely detached, brilliant little boy—whose mother had suffered postpartum psychosis—and intermittently had episodes of (probably schizophrenic) depression. During these episodes she would keep Barry in the double bed beside her in a semi-darkened room. These episodes occurred in Barry's second year of life. Whenever the little boy whimpered or fussed, his mother, in order to keep him occupied, would throw various picture books to him. Barry's father had great hopes and ambitions for the little son; he drew and taught the alphabet to him at about the same time. At two and a half the toddler shocked and surprised the adults by citing cautionary sentences he had read in magazines. He read and understood big words in the dictionary and talked with the vocabulary of an adult. On admission, this intellectually so superior and very precocious boy acted with peculiar lethargy, had no emotional contact, and spoke a private language. He seemed to live in a world which he called the "Underground land" which was populated by animated quasi-personified symbols. In this world people communicated by sign and gesture language. For example, they indicated maturity by lowering their eyelashes; they indicated emotions by changing the color of their skins, and so on. Barry would talk to you only about his underground people, of whom he was the master; and his only display of emotion manifested itself when one tried to pull him away from the land of the underground people. (He later on, in an unemotional tone of voice, parroted what he must have heard his father say, namely, that his mother had no love for him, and that was the reason, Barry said, that he preferred and loved the underworld people so much.) In other words, Barry was somehow aware that his substitution of the human object world for these self-created creatures was due to the failure of his primary love relationship. Barry annihilated the real people, by drawing all the libido from their representations and substituting for them delusional creations.

In rare cases, the steps taken by the ego regressively to counteract the murderous impulses can be reconstructed after years of analytic work. The analytic treatment of Betty, a seven-year-old child, had been preceded by so-called release therapy with a noted child psychiatrist, who had succeeded, when Betty was four years old, in luring her out of her mutism which she had maintained from the age of three years on. At the end of the second year of analytic treatment, Betty started spontaneously to enact and demonstrate in a peculiarly emotionless way the release therapy sessions of five and a half years before. She set "the stage" which was set for her by her previous psychiatrist in order to express and "abreact" her hostile feelings and impulses. Betty, in the typical way of the psychotic child, had not repressed but remembered minute details of how she wanted to bite off her brother's penis, push him in the river.[2] After reenacting all this, Betty paused, and then, in the same recitative voice, remarked: "And isn't it sad for a little girl to do all that to her own brother?" Still, to a child, like Betty, the difference between life and death—that is to say, rendering things inanimate which had been alive—does not have the same emotional meaning as for normal people. Betty attributed to the dolls of my doll collection all the emotions she thought their features displayed. These were constant and predictable features, whereas the emotions of living people she tried to, but could not, decipher. This was a child who wanted desperately to identify with people by mimicking them, by learning their emotions. For weeks she would greet me by asking: "Do I look sad today? Please say I look happy. . . ." Somehow she expected that my saying she looked happy would impart to her the feelings of happiness. Betty struggled against any unsolicited activity on the part of people in her environment. In her analytic sessions, she would fly into a rage whenever I tried to deviate from my role of a puppet whose strings Betty pulled. Betty had concretized and believed in the transfer of emotions and thoughts.

This concretization was characteristic of a particular adolescent, Teddy, who also believed I knew his thoughts, and whose idea of transfer of emotions and of strength were expressed in his delusional system. He had the idea and fear of losing body substance, of being

2. Noteworthy also was Betty's failure to repress affect-laden situations of the past, similar to the case of Stanley (Mahler, Furer, and Settlage 1959).

drained by his father and grandfather, with whom his body, he believed, formed a kind of communicating system of tubes. At night the other, the father-grandfather part of the system drained him of the "body juices of youth." Survival depended on who was more successful in draining more life fluid from the other, he or the father and grandfather part. He invented an elaborate heart machine which he could switch on and connect with his body's circulatory system so that he would never die. This much for Teddy's deanimation and concretization defense. Betty's self-boundaries and identity were equally blurred, her self became fused with whomsoever she was with. She expected, and believed, for example, that I concretely took part in her thoughts, intentions and feelings—that therefore I could give them and take them away. She expected the same of her mother. Around Easter, Betty had come home from the park bringing two twigs which she arranged crosswise and then asked her mother what she thought this was. Her mother answered: "I guess it is a cross." Whereupon Betty began to whip her mother furiously, crying all the while that her mother deliberately hurt Jesus's feelings, that she ought to have acknowledged it was *the* Cross to which He was nailed and which, according to Betty, her mother knew. I took this up in Betty's analysis, and it turned out that there had occurred a number of psychotic vicissitudes to the sadomasochistic fantasies of the child. She employed in particular massive denial, condensation, and displacement. The crucified Savior's likenesses, which Betty had seen in church, and their miniature replicas on sale, she endowed with animation (life). There was (self-) identification with Jesus, and a condensation of the cruel persecution of and martyrdom suffered by Him, as well as her own suffering attributed to her mother's "meanness." Condensed sado-masochistic impulses were acted out in the above-described concrete way (*SPI*:12, Bettelheim 1959).

Betty's rage and panic reactions, for which she was brought to analytic treatment, concerned inanimate objects with which she was incessantly and at first lovingly preoccupied. As time went on, they became alive and persecuted her. She had first accused her brother of robbing her Japanese garden arrangement, then the contents of her beloved jewel box. At a later stage she had delusions and frank hallucinations about these things coming towards her at night. Her most persistent persecutor became the animated waste paper basket. It may be of interest that this psychotic idea is still present with Betty now that she is in her twenties and has succeeded in encapsulating and somewhat distancing (isolating herself from) the psychotic areas of her personality. (From adolescence on she had been in analysis with a colleague.)

Only object relationship with the human love object, which involves partial identification with the object, as well as cathexis of the object with neutralized libidinal energy, promotes emotional development and structure formation. Only libido which is neutralized by human "objectpassage" becomes deinstinctualized enough to be available to the ego.

In this short contribution on psychotic object relationships, I have described and brought a few short clinical illustrations of the mechanism of dehumanization and reanimation, to which the disintegrating ego regresses in quest of adaptation, when its perceptual integrative capacity fails; an ego which has become the passive victim of the deneutralized, defused drives, particularly of the unmitigated destructive impulses. Elkisch and I (*SPI*:12) have described psychotic mechanisms which we felt were infantile precursors of the influencing machine described by Tausk in 1919. We described such a case, Stanley, in whom similar dedifferentiation and quasi-equation of animate versus inanimate was at work. Dedifferentiation, in Stanley's case, was based upon massive denial of percepts, of stimuli coming from the *outside world*. In the wake of this kind of negative hallucinatory psychotic denial, inner percepts, saturated with aggression, gain ascendancy. These inner excitations cannot be denied; they force themselves into the sensorium. In order to cope with these proprioceptive-enteroceptive stimuli the psychotic ego tries to dedifferentiate, to deanimate them. Emotions are equated with motion via perception of motor innervations and are also equated, it appears, with mechanical movements. These inner sensations of one's own body and other life-phenomena are projected and confused with machine phenomena. The ego's split into an intentional part and an experiencing part is frequently clearly discernible. The body image seems thus mechanically put together in a mosaiclike way, by fragments of a machinelike self image. As the psychotic child—like the normal one—sees the world in his own image, in the psychotic child's reality all objects take on the same machinelike, preterhuman quality that his own body image has. Betty at first identified her own body-self with the Japanese garden and, via the jewel box, with the waste paper basket. At the next stage she projected her own deanimated aggression-saturated self-image onto these objects and felt persecuted by these animated objects.

In summary, I should like to point out the lasting validity of what Freud (1911b) regarded as the essential criterion for psychotic break with reality: namely, the slipping away of the libidinal *human* object world. We can only rarely observe but can often reconstruct the prepsychotic struggle, the desperate efforts of clinging, of holding on to the human object world. Psychotic object relationships whether with human beings or otherwise are restitution attempts of a rudimentary or fragmented ego, which serve the purpose of survival, as no organism can live in a vacuum and no human being can live in an objectless state (Rochlin 1953, 1959; Rollman-Branch 1960; Winnicott 1953b).

Chapter 11

SOME OBSERVATIONS ON DISTURBANCES OF THE
EGO IN A CASE OF INFANTILE PSYCHOSIS

[1953]

Parents of psychotic children frequently stress the fabulous memory these youngsters have. Closer examination of this phenomenon in severely disturbed children reveals that this seemingly positive ability actually expresses grave pathology of the ego in the most crucial and important mechanism of defense: *repression*. The elements of this defect, in turn, can be traced to peculiarities in the areas of perception and affects; the interaction and connection of both are essential for personality development, and the sine qua non for the evolution of a structured ego.

Stanley, six years old,[1] struck everybody who met him with his memory for small details of certain affect-laden conditions or situations of his past. Some extraneous or tangential quality of a detail of a subsequent experience would remind Stanley of the past situation and elicit in him a sweepingly diffuse total reaction. Through a seemingly slight similarity, he was reminded of the past and became

1. The observations communicated in this paper were carried out during the first year of treatment.

In collaboration with Paula Elkisch, Ph.D.

completely overwhelmed by the affect which the past experience once had evoked.

Innumerable examples of this child's failure in selective forgetting came to the fore in the course of treatment. However, in this brief communication, we confine ourselves to the description of only a small segment of his behavior indicative of his ego's inability to recall selectively and to react specifically to certain perceptual and affective stimuli.

Ever since the time when Stanley had been read to, his mother used to read to him a book called *When You Were A Baby*, which made him cry uncontrollably. His reaction to this story never changed; at the age of six he still cried bitterly while listening to the story, yet he often insisted upon hearing it. However, not only this book elicited that sweeping total emotional reaction: it was transferred to any other story about babies which seemed to cause recall of the same total memory and affectomotor response. On several occasions, when his kindergarten teacher read a story to her group in which a baby was mentioned, Stanley burst into uncontrollable crying. He cried so hard and became so upset that his teacher found it necessary to telephone Stanley's mother to ask her to come and console him or take him home.

In his book, *When You Were A Baby*, which originally made him cry every time it was read to him, there were two pictures on two pages opposite one another. One picture showed "the Baby" in his playpen, of which one could see the bars only; the opposite picture showed "Panda" sitting in a cage, of which one also could see only the bars. The baby cries, it has his toys thrown out of the playpen and cannot retrieve them; Panda, on the opposite page, has a bowl of food sitting beside him. For anybody, the two pictures suggest certain similarities, besides the dissimilarities, between the Baby's and Panda's situation. Both Baby and Panda are behind bars. This similarity is also expressed in the text of the book which reads: "And Mama thought: 'That baby looks like the fat Panda at the Zoo sitting in his cage.'" But the interesting and unusual thing was what this little patient did with the situational similarity. He completely discarded, it seemed, each or both of the obvious motivations for the baby's crying. According to our observation in the treatment situation, whenever Stanley has come in contact with either a baby doll or a baby picture he has called it "Panda." From the situational similarity Stanley equated: Baby and Panda. Baby and Panda were together in that book; therefore, they always belonged together. The image of one elicited the other; the two "concepts" *became fused and quasi interchangeable.* Stanley seemed unable to separate or differentiate the two parts of the composite image once perceived. The two "personalities" of the picture book, whose image at one time happened to appear "syncretically" (Werner 1948) became engrams, forever connected in his memory. Furthermore, there was evidence in the material for the assumption that for Stanley the *perception and the affect,* "Baby and crying," had become *irreversibly connected* (Piaget 1952). The crying baby in the book sat opposite the noncrying Panda who had a bowl of food beside him. Stanley would ever so often feed a crying baby which he detected in another book. One would have assumed that Stanley's diligent bottle-and-spoon feeding of the "crying baby" was motivated by his wish to console the "crying baby"—and himself in identification with it. This was not so. Neither his reactions, nor his answers to questioning, bore out the slightest causality to this effect. On the contrary, as we will elaborate later, the feeding of the "crying baby" by Stanley was acting out a need for completion of restitution from a syncretically formed traumatic affective memory. (We will see, in particular, that crying and feeding by mother belonged inseparably, irreversibly—but not causally—together.)

During our observations of this patient, we had proof that with Stanley not only the psychic representations of Baby and Panda, but of the three figures of Baby, Panda, and Mother were blurred, undifferentiated from each other, and intermingled with the representation of his own self. Not only were Baby, Panda, Mother, and he himself, easily fused and confused with one another, but so were certain emotional (affective) qualities which had been connected with those four syncretically coincident images at the time when the conglomeration of concepts had originally occurred, very likely in the second half of the first year of his life. Clues for such an assumption were reconstructed from the following material and data.

Stanley, at times, became quite absorbed in a children's book which he found at Dr. Elkisch's, *Fun With Faces*. In this book there was a picture of a baby's face whose expression could be changed by pulling a little tag attached to the bottom of the face and then pushing the tag up. In other words, this tag worked like a "switch"[2] with which one could "turn on" one physiognomic expression and "turn it off" for another. One of the baby's expressions was "crying," the other was "not crying." He "turned on" one expression and "turned it off" for the other. That is, he switched the baby depicted as "crying" to the picture of the baby depicted as "not crying" and vice versa. He called the baby "Panda." When Panda, the baby, did not cry, Stanley said: "Now she[3] is happy!"[4] and he would insist that the mother substitute should "say she is happy." Only when Dr. Elkisch said, "Now she is happy" was Stanley satisfied for some moments.

It seems important to interpolate here some data about this boy's general behavior during the treatment. Every time he was "switching" the baby's expression "on and off" he displayed paroxysms of excitement. That is, he threw up his stiffened and flexed arms, strained and tightened his arm muscles rhythmically in this position for some time, while twisting his head downward and to the left side. His face was bizarrely distorted with wide open mouth and protruding tongue. Grimacing in this way, Stanley jumped up and down like a rubber ball so that his whole motor behavior impressed the observer as the "performance" of a mechanical toy that had been wound up, rather than that of a human being.

This type of behavior (catatoniclike excitement) was, in contrast to another type of behavior with which it alternated. While the patient exhibited the above-described catatonically excited behavior, his activity was concomitantly confined to one single pursuit, for example, "switching the faces" of the baby pictures. It was impossi-

2. The significance of the switch, mechanical devices and "the machine" in particular, will be elaborated on in chapter 12. Compare also Elkisch (1952).

3. Dolls, "octopuses," Pandas, etc., were girls to Stanley. For example, he always spoke about the "octopus girl."

4. Actually, the "not crying" baby on that picture did not look "happy" at all. It looked sullen in terms of our perception and interpretation of emotional facial expressions.

ble to distract the child from this sterotyped pursuit or to "lure" him into any other for a long while. However, at times he would behave in a diametrically opposite way from the beginning of some treatment sessions, or, all of a sudden would "fall" from the autistically stereotyped behavior into complete listlessness. Then all focus seemed lost; he would not play or "want to do" anything. Instead, he would fumble, as if in a dazed state, with whatever might be at hand. For example, he would finger some toys which lay around, drop them and move lethargically back and forth from one place to another, without any aim or goal. At those times, he seemed to be a quasi part of the environment, a "particle" of the surroundings, in a state of cohesion with it and undifferentiated from it. Volkelt attributes this state to the animal, about which he explains that its "perceptions exist only in so far as they are part of a wider totality of action in which object and inner experience exist as a syncretic indivisible unity" (Werner 1948).

According to our observation, it was in this state of semistupor that, all of a sudden, he would touch the arm of the mother substitute and with this excitation, which was at first very slight, would "switch himself on," as it seemed, into an intense and diffuse affective state. Such was the case with body contact, as well as with a trigger engram. For example, the word "baby" spoken or read to him from story books seemed to be such a trigger engram. It seemed as though the patient *very deliberately* sought such a sweeping excitation, via the trigger stimulus, as if to defend himself against his apathetic state, as if to ward off the danger of symbiotic fusion through which his entity and identity would become dissolved in the matrix of the environment. It appeared as if the child had switched himself into excited crying or catatoniclike motor paroxysms as well, to gain momentum, as it were, like an engine, to counteract symbiotic dissolution of the boundaries of his "self." Although he could not stop once he had "turned on" these paroxysms of jumping, cramping, and twisting, he nevertheless sought the diffuse overcathexis of his ego, the increased body sensations, because they seemed to enable him to achieve some kind of self-identity. (cf. Eissler 1953, Mahler 1952, 1953a.) We believe that his aim was delimitation of his self from his mother and from the environment by deliberately cathecting his ego from without (like touching the therapist) and generating excitement from within. He used a mechanism which, though much less differentiated, to be sure, yet reminds one of the grown-up patient of K. R. Eissler (1953). This patient would use the mechanism of "feeling dead" to be able to engender emotions from within, "pump up" a pretended emotion which in the patient's estimation fitted the social situation.

The fascination which the two baby pictures in the book *Fun With Faces* had for Stanley corresponded to his quest for rather primitive and undifferentiated mechanisms of restitution (defense of psychotic children) with simple, learnable patterns, which he could imitate and "switch on." By these patterns he endeavored to orient and adapt himself in the disconcerting diversity of a highly structured social reality for which his unstructured and fragmented ego had neither the modulation capacity of affects, nor the prerequisite of selective perception, selective forgetting (repression), and selective recall. Psychotic child patients often seem to realize that they cannot respond adequately to affective stimuli in reality and, therefore, try to "learn" emotions or emotional reactions as, for instance, one might learn a habit. So Stanley showed evidence that he desperately persevered to learn gestures, to "study" emotions mechanically and physiognomically,[5] as it were, to substitute for his ego's inability to react to real experiences specifically, and in a modulated way, as well as to selectively recall them. With his own baby book he behaved like a traumatic neurotic who tries to overcome a trauma, bit by bit, by endless repetitions. Through treatment he seemed to have progressed in such a way that he began to master the overwhelming affect which hitherto inundated his own self, by making the "baby face" (in the second picture book) cry, instead of crying uncontrollably himself. In other words, he was enabled to relegate his need to cry to some other subject (or image) with whom he actively and even playfully identified. This was borne out by the fact that he accompanied the baby's "crying" physiognomic expression in the picture with the appropriate crying sounds of his own intonation. Is this not

5. Compare Kris's (1933) interpretation of the case of the sculptor Messerschmidt.

an attempt at restitution, and a successful one, with which Stanley expressed satisfaction by his paroxysmal ecstatic jumping and elation?

On the other hand, we should emphasize the fact that when the "crying baby" was fed by Stanley (mother) "it" never would stop crying as a consequence of being fed. This made us aware of the fact that the nature of the ego defect and the restitution attempts with which we are dealing are even more complex. Would one not assume that the "crying baby" being fed by his mother (personified by Stanley) would stop crying? Instead, for Stanley, being fed and crying had to continue, to go on simultaneously. In trying to understand this, some references to the child's early history seem relevant.

As a baby, Stanley suffered from an inguinal hernia. Allegedly, from the age of six months on he had suffered intense pain which came on suddenly while the child was "happily" and quietly playing. "All of a sudden Stanley would break into violent crying." The abrupt violent pain attacks were not only distressing to Stanley's mother and father, but the parents dreaded these attacks because of the possibility that the violent crying in turn might cause incarceration of the hernia. The parents were deeply worried lest the crying would necessitate an emergency operation. Hence, upon the doctor's advice, and their own dread of the consequence of crying and pressing, they went about to prevent the child from crying, at all cost. Thus, Stanley's need to cry was utterly frustrated. At the same time, and all along, Stanley was a feeding problem. He vomited a great deal and often would refuse to eat, but being fed by his mother while he was crying seemed to have merged in his memory into "one experience"; being fed and crying remained perceptively, as well as affectively, synchronized in his memory, so that one might speak of "syncretic engram conglomeration."

Stanley continued to insist that the "crying" baby in the book *Fun With Faces,* had to be fed while crying. Stanley himself fed the "crying" baby as though he wished actively to do to the baby what he had passively endured when he was a baby—being fed while in pain and crying. Now, when he played out his desire to feed the crying baby, which he did with diligence, glee, and amidst paroxysms of excitement, it was not in order to console the baby, as one would expect, but in order to overcome, it seemed, the other part of two simultaneously perceived traumatic experiences which he suffered in utter passivity in his babyhood. As they happened to him together, both experiences, pain-crying and feeding, remained connected and condensed in his memory. Therefore, he seemed compelled, as it were, to overcome the trauma of the total situation, pain-crying plus being fed, synchronically, *and not by the laws of causality.* In this reaction we could observe a specific disturbance in thinking and feeling, resulting in the failure of the selective repressive function of the ego.

This is only one of many examples which demonstrates that this little patient could not connect situations which for normal people obviously belong together in terms of cause and effect, according to the secondary process. In Stanley, the mechanisms of the primary process—condensation, substitution, displacement, synchronicity, etc.—were never supplanted by the secondary process. Two simultaneously experienced emotions remained irreversible and inseparable. Hence, when he wanted to cope with one—being overwhelmed by crying when the trigger engram "Baby" was touched—the same trigger seemed to call for restitution attempts for the simultaneously experienced displeasure of his early feeding situation.

Stanley's perceptive and affective disturbance which we have illustrated in one small segment, taken from the wealth of material we gained in studying his case, resulted in a severe defect of the thinking process. This defect arrested him at the most primitive level of reality testing. He could not make the connection between two operations in such a way as to *conclude* that satisfying a need (being fed) might result in satisfaction, in cessation of pain, and render affectomotor discharge (crying) superfluous. Thus, he was partially arrested in the development of primitive reversibility within action (Piaget), a level at which babies who grow to the stage of so-called confident expectation (T. Benedek) seem to be able to grasp. He could not differentiate between two operations which occurred synchronically, for example, pain-crying and being fed, as being different activities per se, with different connotations. Such conclusions imply the ability to abstract and the ability to connect cause and effect. But Stanley was unable to grasp perceptions in their sequence and relatedness to one another. He could not integrate perceptions into reversible thought operations (Piaget 1952).

The material presented in this paper has shown that the so-called "fabulous memory" of psychotic children pertains to their remembering minute details of affect-laden past events. This phenomenon is based on the above-described proclivity of such patients to regress to much earlier ego states of their infancy (Federn 1952) and recall undifferentiated affective-perceptual engram conglomerates, which seem to be stored, unchanged, in the patient's mind. We have described the mechanism of syncretic memory storage, which might also be called "pseudo repression" because its content is not really decathected and no countercathexis seems to be established. According to Freud (1915), "the different mechanisms of repression have at least this one thing in common: a withdrawal of the cathexis of energy."

Clinical observation of Stanley, who showed autistic and symbiotic mechanisms,[6] revealed that at the age of six and a half he still was unable to combine, to blend, and to organize perceptions and affective reactions according to his age-level, because he had not repressed selectively and could not recall in a differentiated way experiences of his past life. The boy's perceptive and affective reactions were primary-process reproductions of early infantile syncretic engram conglomerates, which appeared to be irreversible (Piaget 1952) and irrepressible. To these early ego states he readily regressed because they were not decathected. (Cf. Federn 1952.)

The pathogenesis of this ego defect, which amounted to a grave disability of learning, had at its root hereditary-constitutional and early predispositional somatic and environmental causative factors. As to hereditary-constitutional factors, there were circular and schizoid personalities in the ascendancy of this child. As to early predispositional factors: as early as in 1915 Freud, in his paper on "Repression," pointed out that a painfully destructive stimulus (for example, organ pain) may acquire "far-reaching similarity to an instinct. . . . The aim of this pseudo instinct, however, is simply the

6. For the distinction of these mechanisms, see Mahler (*SPI*: 7, 1953a).

cessation of the change in the organ and of the unpleasure accompanying it." Freud went on to say, "Let us take the case in which an instinctual stimulus such as hunger remains unsatisfied" ... (or pain in an organ remains unattenuated) "it keeps up a constant tension of need. *Nothing in the nature of a repression seems, in this case to come remotely into question.*[7] Thus repression certainly does not arise in cases where the tension produced by lack of satisfaction of an instinctual impulse is raised to an unbearable degree."[8] There were many traumata and a state of "silent traumata" in Stanley's earliest life which we cannot describe in this brief paper, but which increased beyond the threshold of repressibility, it seems, great segments of his inner and outer perceptions. We may assume that, concomitantly, this infant's tolerance to pain and unpleasure was diminished and his anxiety predisposition enhanced (Greenacre 1941, Hoffer 1952). "The infant's traumatized body, as such, does not easily provide the amount of body-ego experiences for which the growing and recovering self longs" (Hoffer 1952). It seems that if there are too great and chronic states of organismic distress, progress toward me-experience and object love, as well as reality testing, are impaired. The conditions under which Stanley grew up in his first four years of life[9] seemed to render me-experience and object experience vague. Added to inherent constitutional proclivities was the early environmental condition that Stanley's mother was very much involved with her own father and mother at crucial periods of the infant's life. She seems to have been somewhat detached, or at least torn between her role as a mother and as a daughter. Though she functioned for Stanley as his "external ego" (*SP*I:7, Mahler 1953a, Spitz 1953),

7. Our italics.

8. Compare A. Freud (1952b).

9. At the age of three several traumatic changes occurred in Stanley's life: (1) the family had to move from the familiar household which they shared with the maternal grandparents, because (2) the grandfather became acutely psychotic (agitated depression), and (3) the maternal great-grandmother to whom the maternal grandmother was morbidly attached died. Both the maternal grandmother and Stanley's mother reacted with depression. It was at the same time that Stanley's maternal uncle became so alarmed about Stanley's behavior that he called the parents's attention to the fact that Stanley seemed to be completely withdrawn and apparently was living in a world of his own.

Stanley apparently did not experience her ministrations as real and efficient rescue from the traumatic situations which suffused his "rudimentary ego" (Greenacre 1952). Thus, through diffuse oversensitivities, plus painful traumatic conditions in the second half of his first year (Greenacre 1952), overdetermined by "silent traumas" (Hoffer 1952), and adverse environmental influences at the age of "normal separation," Stanley seemed to have become arrested, fixated, as it were, at the primary symbiotic stage of mother-child relationship, so that he was not able to establish his individual identity separate from the mother's self.

Another characteristic deficiency of the patient's ego ensued: a defect in the faculty of abstraction. There did not seem to exist any clear-cut differentiation between the actual object and the mental representation of it.[10]

It seemed that Stanley perceived outside sensory stimuli like very young babies do: in a physiognomic way. He kept in his mind two or more syncretically perceived objects fused with the subjective, affective state in which he had once perceived them with the accretion of most unessential and irrelevant details. In normal repression, different objects, although perceived simultaneously, are handled as separate entities and may be disconnected from each other and from the affect with which they had been accompanied. In Stanley's case, a trigger stimulus caused total recall of the stored syncretic engram.

In this brief communication, we have tried to show the sources and the function of Stanley's "fabulous memory," which was in fact an inexpedient substitute mechanism for the lack of the ego's ability to execute repression.

10. For example, one day during his thereapeutic hour, Stanley looked through the baby book of his infancy. On some of the picture pages the mother is absent. He became very anxious, saying, "Where is the Mommy? Where is the Mommy?" While frantically turning the pages he "found" the mother, yet he could not really quiet down until he ran out of the room to his mother who was waiting for him in another room.

Chapter 12

ON INFANTILE PRECURSORS OF THE
"INFLUENCING MACHINE" (TAUSK)

[1959]

In normal development the infant endows his own body (especially the periphery of it) as well as the mother's with libidinal
cathexis. This process begins, according to Bak (1939), as a kind of
overflow phenomenon and is paralleled by the differentiation of the
body ego in which the mouth and oral cavity, aided by the hand and
eventually the eyes, lead the way (Hoffer 1949, Spitz 1955). The infant
reaches the height of normal body narcissism during the symbiotic
phase which begins in the second month. This phase of mother-child
unity gives way to the separation-individuation phase which overlaps the symbiotic phase and replaces it (from the age of four to five
months on). During the symbiotic phase, exclusive body narcissism
declines and gradually gives way to secondary narcissism. The body
is taken as object of this secondary narcissism with the well-known
focal concentration on the libidinal zones. This object finding of the
own body in turn seems a prerequisite for rendering the outside
object fit for identification by projective and introjective identification mechanisms. Identification through partial introjection enables the infant to separate gradually, leaving the mother outside the

Paula Elkisch, Ph.D. in collaboration with Margaret Mahler, M.D.

hitherto "omnipotent common orbit." Hoffer (1950b) postulates a psychological stage from about three to four months onward, in which primary narcissism has already been modified, though the world of objects need not yet have taken a definite shape. As far as the aggressive drive is concerned, aggression must be deflected from the body in the course of the above-described development. There are protective systems which safeguard the infant's body from the oral-sadistic pressures which potentially endanger his body integrity (Hoffer 1950a). Among these protective systems against self-destructive pressures in the phase of oral sadism, the pain barrier is frequently cited. This, however, is unreliable in early infancy. This pain barrier must be reinforced and supplemented by progressive libidinization of the body surface, which seems to be greatly promoted by the bodily care of the mother (*SPI*: 7). Adequate libidinization of the body for the development of the body image within the mother-infant relationship has been particularly emphasized (Hoffer 1950b). Deflection of aggression from the infant's own body and concomitant secondary narcissistic cathexis of his body in its central and peripheral parts seem to be other prerequisites for the partial introjective and projective mechanisms which lead via normal identification to separation from the mother.

It seems that contact-perceptual and kinesthetic experiences are essential for the development of the body image in its central and peripheral parts (Greenacre 1953) as well as for the formation of a concept of the self (Jacobson 1954), whereas distance perceptions seem to facilitate separation from the mother's body and demarcation of the own body image from the environment. We assume that formation of structure (ego) (Hartmann, Kris, and Loewenstein 1946) is dependent upon both of these processes—upon the contact- and distance-perceptual experiences. Progressive libidinization of the rind of the body ego (the *Pcpt.-Cs.* system) and ego development involve a circular process. In this circular process the mothering partner is an indispensable catalyst. We know from the work of Greenacre (1953), in particular, about the vicissitudes of the mother-infant relationship and distortion of the body image in the fetishist. Greenacre has shown that in the prefetishist child increase of visual overstimulation at the expense of tactile experiences has caused distortions. In some of our cases the opposite seems to have occurred. The mothers in these cases would walk or pace back and forth holding the baby tightly clutched in their arms with the intent to keep him quiet or, preferably, somnolent. Hence the crucial disproportion concerned overstimulation of contact and kinesthetic perceptions, with frustration, even almost total elimination of distance-perceptual (particularly visual) experiences. This kind of "mothering" predominated in one of our (previously briefly described) cases, that of Steve (Mahler, Ross, and De Fries 1949).

Steve's mother, a psychotic woman who was desperate over having a boy child for fear he would become a ne'er-do-well like her brother, could not stand the baby's wakeful state. She thought that if the baby would just sleep all the time the chances for his vegetative thriving would be better. Hence she would walk up and down with Steve clutched in her arms, until: "My arms were numb and I did not know where I ended and the baby began." No wonder that, when we met Steve at the age of eight, his main symptom was a complete lack of identity, uncertainty, and perplexity about his body image, particularly its boundaries. He would walk up to each and everyone, asking the question: "Are these my hands, are those your hands? Can these hands kill? I am many people!" Steve sought another mode of compensation through histrionics and addiction to television and movies, mirroring all the actors. That is to say, he tried to compensate for the deficit concerning the visual part of his bodyimage demarcation by his voyeurism and by attempts at mirroring identification (Elkisch 1957).

The anxiously coercive mechanical mothering which kept this infant in such close bodily contact with the mother in infancy prevailed throughout Steve's childhood. Distance-perceptual, visual and auditory orientation experimentation toward exploration of the world beyond the mother-infant symbiotic unit in Steve's case (as also in the case about which we shall report in some detail) was thwarted. The mother discouraged any sign of individual automony of the toddler. Increased autoerotic manifestations, the increased need for which was created by the mother's overstimulation through tight and prolonged bodily closeness, were met with scathing impatience and punitive hostility. A symbiotic parasitism with hypochondriacal self-observation was nurtured and progress from primary to secondary identification was thus impaired.

From the point of view of the separation-individuation process, what occurred in this case, as in similar cases, was that during the symbiotic phase there was no choice or possibility for experimentation which ordinarily prepares the infant for gradual separation, gradual and partial identification with the object (mother). Hence in some cases in which during the symbiotic phase experimentation with separation fails to pave the way to gradual separation-individuation, separation panic becomes so great that partial introjection, gradual identification with the mother does not abolish the fear of annihilation (cf. *SPI*: 6). Total introjection is employed to counteract separation panic with the symptomatology of psychosis following this fateful occurrence.

When the mother is totally introjected, this very defense mechanism removes her as the beacon of reality orientation in the outside world (*SPI*: 9). The entire cathexis is drawn into the central parts of the body image, so that the peripheral parts of the body (the *Pcpt.-Cs.* system) are proportionately depleted of libidinal cathexis. The mechanism of total introjection thus creates a regressed situation similar to that of primary identification. Object choice and object finding remain in the realm of the own self, with impairment of perceptual awareness of the nonself. The result is loss of the ego's ability to integrate external and internal stimuli. In other words: If the human partner as the beacon of orientation in external reality is missing (because totally introjected and bare of object libido), the ego loses its perceptual integrative capacity. Ego development thus is seriously impeded. Freud (1915) emphasized: "Perceptions may be said to have the same significance for the ego as instincts have for the id." Hartmann (1939) has pointed out that structure is formed by perceptual turning toward the outside world and vice versa. Freud (1911b), in the Schreber case, described complete withdrawal of libido from the object world as the experience of *Weltuntergang*. The ego-regressive process in psychotic children akin to this *Weltuntergang* experiences can be studied in symbiotic psychosis, as was described in earlier papers.

In this paper we should like to describe some of the psychotic defense mechanisms of the ego which appear to be precursors of the phenomena of the "influencing machine" described by Tausk (1919). We postulate that where there is a breakdown of the perceptual integrative capacity of the ego, external perceptions are massively denied, as Edith Jacobson (1957a) has described in some of her borderline cases. In fact, repression seems to take place to that stage of reality testing which, we surmise, dominates the pleasure ego of the small infant: the stage of negative hallucination. However, *massive denial cannot cope with those endogenous stimuli which are continually generated by physiological processes in the organism itself* and which are very close to the instinctual drives not neutralized by the ego. There is no escape from the enteroceptive and proprioceptive excitations. *These excitations gain predominance and force themselves continually into the sensorium.* Whereas the external object world has been lost by delibidinization and thus has become deanimated, the endogenous excitations *which have a predominantly aggressive momentum gain ascendancy. These stimuli undergo concretization and quasi animation and replace the lost outside object world.* They determine the psychotic child's concept of the self and constitute or seem to make up his body image. *The delibidinized, quasi-animated forces are thence projected onto the external world.* Delibidinization serves as a defensive function to the fragmented ego of the psychotic child. The fragmented ego cannot cope with changeability and complexities. It cannot integrate and it cannot synthesize. Living objects are much more changeable, vulnerable, and unpredictable than inanimate objects; biodynamics are much more complex, subject to infinite modulations, and therefore much less predictable than are machines with mechanical dynamics. The internal psychotic reality dominated by the aggression-saturated proprioceptive-enteroceptive bodily sensations seems to be experienced as if the body were powered by more or less demoniacal, ego-alien mechanical forces (the introjects), and whatever object libido is available is in turn vested in inanimate objects and/or quasi-animate machineries.

Seven-year-old Stanley was in psychoanalytic treatment for severe ego disturbances. At the age of six months Stanley had suffered from an inguinal hernia. The pain came on suddenly while he was happily and quietly playing. "All of a sudden Stanley would break into violent crying." Throughout many months the child suffered those sudden attacks of intense visceral pains. The child and his parents lived in the maternal grandparents' house and the mother was forced to prevent violent crying by whatever means, partly because the pediatrician was afraid of possible incarceration of the hernia and partly because the grandfather had to remain undisturbed because of a beginning mental illness. Hence the infant was carried back and forth by the mother so that his expressions of pain and rage were muted—a circumstance which was very similar to Steve's case. In addition, in Stanley's case, however, at the height of the symbiotic phase there were those pain attacks which disrupted formation of a normal body image. Stanley had no opportunity to deflect aggression, to eject pain and discomfort, the "bad experiences," into the world beyond the body-self boundaries. His own body-self's representation became populated by painful and bad introjected objects. The early traumatic visceral sensations have disrupted the continuum of the libidinization process; the child regressed to primary identification. This could be reconstructed. After having uttered a few words in the second half of the first year, Stanley stopped talking. As far as we could ascertain, he used his mother as an extension of himself, an inanimate or semi-animate tool as it were, not as a love object. From the age of three, Stanley would lie limp on the floor, stare into space, never play; and though he clung tenaciously to his mother, this clinging differed conspicuously from that of a fairly normal, though overly dependent, small child. We recognize this clinical picture as that of primary symbiotic psychosis in which the mother became fused with the self again and belongs within the orbit of the symbiotic system. It was interesting to see how Stanley's mother was oblivious of the gross pathology, denied its existence as long as possible. Such behavior is fairly typical of the mothers of symbiotic children. A maternal uncle was the one who drew the mother's attention to the fact of Stanley's bizarre peculiarities. When finally the child was old enough to enter school, of course, pathology could not be denied any more.

Ever since we met Stanley and even before that time, he displayed a special "interest" in mechanical things.[1] For instance, in the city where he lived, there was an advertisement for beer, representing a mechanical robot riding a bicycle. This robot was in constant motion twenty-four hours a day. Ever so often Stanley asked his parents to take him to the place where he could see "the man on the bike." His wish was usually granted and he often talked about his trips to "the man on the bike." Sometimes Stanley would move his legs as though he were riding a bike himself. He would also "wheel" his arms around in a seemingly unmotivated robotlike fashion. This mechanical robotlike behavior also occurred independently of his trips to "the man on the bike" and of his talking about them. One day he came from one of these visits directly to his analytic hour and, overcome by ecstatic joyousness, expressed in paroxysmal movements, shouted: "He was off today, he was off—this is my luckiest day." The man who "stopped," the man who was "off" or "on" has become one of Stanley's endlessly repetitious topics ever since that day. It is noteworthy that we had learned from his mother that Stanley, at the age of five, was given a tricycle on which he would sit but never pedal.

The "on" and "off" topic was also expressed in other ways: for hours and hours of his treatment Stanley would draw wheels that "spin," or "stop spinning." He drew the wheels in such a way that each wheel had a man or a boy in the center; he also drew several "switches" which he pretended to turn "on and off." He would turn his wheels "on" by spinning his crayon in circling motion, and pressing it on the paper around and around with such violence that each crayon would be broken into bits. Again and again he would say, "It will stop soon," indicating his intention to stop crayoning, an intention as if dictated by an alien, isolated split-off part of his ego. And when he stopped crayoning, he would say, "Now *it*

1. We know that even normal children are interested in machines, an interest which seems to be fundamentally connected with their phallicity. On the occasion of an extensive study of drawings of normal school children, Elkisch (1952) pointed to the significance of the boys' projection of their body feelings onto the machine. In the art productions of twenty-two latency boys, there were only two whose subject matter did not include predominantly mechanical devices.

stopped." He seemed obsessed with what he was doing, overly excited—an excitement that he apparently "turned on" within himself (Eissler 1953). In this state he could not be approached. If one asked him a question or tried to reason with him, for instance, saying that it was not the wheel that stopped "by itself," but that it was *he* who had stopped the wheel, by stopping crayoning, he would behave as if he did not hear and would withdraw from contact. This confusion of the relation of the active subject and the passive object, the projection of his own intention onto a split-off part of his ego, was remarkable.

Stanley's obsession with "the man on the bike" became interwoven with another obsession about another machinelike object. In the treatment room there was a wall telephone which buzzed when someone pushed the button downstairs in order to get into the house. The noise of the buzzer, at a certain point of treatment, became the most startling, frightening, and fascinating experience to Stanley. Since that time he would enter the office with his ears covered by his hands, a most anxious look on his face, and would rush into the farthest corner, remaining there throughout the hour. If by chance he would come near the telephone, he would look at it with fright and fascination, always covering his ears. From any topic being talked about, he inadvertently would arrive at asking the sterotyped question: "What will the wall telephone do today when the time is up?" When the therapist said, "It will ring," Stanley answered: "It will not ring." When the therapist further said: "What do you think will happen—because Benny will come and he will push the button downstairs, just as you did," Stanley would say, "It will not ring." As Stanley remained so frightened, perplexed, and confused about the wall telephone, he was taken downstairs with all the doors left open so that he could both push the button downstairs and hear the simultaneous buzzing upstairs. Also someone else was asked to push the button for us while Stanley and his analyst "waited" for the buzzing upstairs. During this waiting period the boy looked at the wall telephone with apprehensive anticipation and when it rang he remarked, "It was not so loud today, because *it knew* we were waiting for it to buzz."

This last remark indicates rather clearly the extent to which this patient projected his own tense anticipation onto the lifeless machinery's mechanical response. The machine "knew that we were waiting . . . "—the implication being not simply that an animation of the wall telephone would occur as could be expected in the case of a normal small child, but the real belief of a seven-year-old that the machine functions in a human way, that the machine took his waiting into consideration and therefore deliberately did not ring so loudly. We can see further his complete confusion of the categories of time, space, cause and effect, besides the confusion of modalities concerning phenomena of life versus machine phenomena (Elkisch 1956; Mahler, Ross, and De Fries 1949; SPI:9). Although the demonstrations of the function of cause and effect, as described above, were repeated innumerable times, Stanley could not bring into causal connection the button being pressed downstairs and the buzzer being affected by the electrical current upstairs. In fact, he remained as anxious, confused, and startled as before.

This behavior is reminiscent of that stage of early ego development which Piaget (1923) described in the young child who cannot conceive of causal relationships unless cause and effect were in his "immediate perceptive field." In fact, there is a normal developmental stage—at the height of animism—in which the toddler to a greater or lesser degree for a longer or shorter period of time is startled and frightened by such sounds or other mechanical occurrences, the source of which is not immediately perceivable. There is also a time when normal toddlers are afraid of buzzers, vacuum cleaners, an ironing board coming down from the wall, or other such mechanical devices.

In order to help Stanley overcome his anxiety and also for us to learn more about his ego's functioning, a simple electrical instrument was constructed, a board on which a button and a buzzer were installed close to each other, so that both the affecting and the affected thing, or "cause and effect," were in his immediate perceptual field. However, for Stanley, this device had no explanatory meaning whatsoever. He brought "*his* wall telephone," as he called the device, with him when he came to his hour, and he played with it the whole time. His play consisted in the following: the board telephone had an electrical cord which had to be plugged into a socket; only then did the bell on the board ring by pressing the button. Stanley plugged the cord into the socket and then took the plug out, back and forth, which to him meant nothing else but switching something "on" and "off." When his wall telephone was "on," then Stanley could push the button and the buzzer would buzz. This activity was intensely pursued and accompanied by orgastic jumping, and it was alternated with the performance for which the machinery was originally devised, namely, the pushing of the button with the result of buzzing. Yet to him these two activities—the plugging and unplugging on the one hand, and the pressing of the button and buzzing, on the other—seemed entirely disconnected from each other. Moreover, his "wall telephone" became just another machine to Stanley, a machine which permitted him to time and exert his own power: thus it did not arouse his anxiety. It is noteworthy that Stanley soon lost complete interest in his own gadget, but he continued to react to the wall telephone in the office with unaltered fright and panic.

Stanley felt both fascination and fright at the surprising machineries. He displayed the same fascination and surprise at these machineries as he exhibited when he felt an inner impulse or intention. "It will stop soon." He treated his own impulses and reacted to them with the same emotional tone of passive experience as to an outside person, or outside force, as we saw him react to the machines: "*it* stopped"—meaning the wheel he was drawing. We can clearly see here the splitting of his ego into an isolated intentional part and a passive experiencing part. We can also see the equation of the inner impulse and the outside phenomena of machines.

Shortly after his "lucky" experience with the bicycling man "unable to move," Stanley became obsessed with switching lights on and off. For weeks he would arrive at the office, not paying any attention to anything or anybody, nor taking off his coat and cap, but rush in wild excitement from one room to the other turning the lights on and off, an activity which seemed the most primitive realization of his own magic omnipotence, as we see in so many psychotic children. Stanley would turn the light on and then look at the bulb as though he had seen a light for the first time in his life; and then he would turn it off and look at the light-being-off with the same perplexed amazement. He would shout, "Now it is off," and give a smile to the therapist or hug her, jumping in great excitement. There were thirty-one switches all counted of which none was left unturned. His activity of switching on and off always found its climax in manipulating the light in the refrigerator, one of his greatest fascinations, as this was the place for food, in fact, as he verbalized it: "Spoiled baby food."

Very many of the machines with which Stanley was so obsessed and which he demanded to explore again and again seemed related to Stanley's desperate perplexities concerning his body image; they were quite conspicuously related to intense oral and anal preoccupations. For instance, when he was in a food market, he would not rest until his mother took him to one of the big freezers, which he "investigated." The "man on the bike" advertised beer, a fact which incited the boy to bring forth a flood of nonsense words, klang associations, all related to "beer," as, for instance, Esslinger-Beer, Beerlinger, Linger-Beer, Smear-Linger, Linger-Smear. About the wall telephone, Stanley would remark: "It will come down from the wall and take a bite out of you." His intense fear of the elevator, which he also developed, was related to the fact that he might fall into the small gap between the elevator and the floor—a passive oral fantasy of being swallowed up, which he verbally related to man-holes in the street, anxiously avoiding them, to the flushing of the toilet, and elaborate fantasies about his food going down the sewer.

Stanley's anxieties and panic reactions had always had a diffuse character. In this respect, too, he was a typical representative of similar cases of infantile psychosis. Their anxiety was more reminiscent of the organismic distress—the annihilation panic of the infant, or else of the separation anxiety of the toddler—than of castration anxiety. His entire body being suffused with primitive aggression, the fear of exploding and disintegrating into bits seemed his basic fear. Moreover, Stanley's essential fixation occurred at the oral-sadistic level and most of these cases regress to that stage.

Freud (1938) postulated that in cases of splitting of the ego "by the help of regression to an oral phase, it [castration anxiety] assumed

the form of a fear of being eaten by his father." Freud reminded us of
the myth of Kronos, who swallowed his children. In Stanley's case
there was the typical fear of being swallowed, engulfed as it were—
engulfed primarily by the mother who was perceived in his own
image, deanimated, as if she had lost her human nature.[2]

The other fear encountered in older psychotic children in pre-
adolescence and adolescence is the fear of losing body substance, of
being drained of the "body juices of youth," as one of our schizophrenic adolescents put it. Teddy was preoccupied with the delusion
that father, grandfather, and he himself were a communicating
system of glass tubes which competed at draining the life fluid from
each other during the night. Survival would depend, so Teddy
believed, on who was more successful in draining more from the
other's life fluid at night. On the other hand, he would invent a heart
machine which he could switch on, connect within his body's
circulatory system so that he would never have to die.

Returning to Stanley: Stanley's most persistent delusional obsession concerned string beans going down the sewer. He had eaten
unusually long string beans at a meal in school. Since that incident,
Stanley asked every day his infinitely repetitious questions about the
string beans: where they had gone, where they were now, what they
looked like now, what the sewer will do to them, and so on. Three
months after this occurrence, Stanley would still talk about it: "The
string beans I ate in Miss A.'s class—they have gone down the sewer.
Why should I worry about them? This is silly, I know, for it is long
ago and they give me strength, they make my muscles strong and
only the waste goes away. What color do they have? I guess they have
taken on the color of my body—going down like that in the sewer.
They must have the color of my b.m.—I shouldn't worry about
them." These and similar verbalizations indicated Stanley's intense
hypochondriacal fears and perplexities; his complete confusion
between inside drives and outside powers, between inten-

2. In his paper on "The Delay of the Machine Age" (1933), Hanns Sachs
commented: "Animistic man vitalized the inanimate world with such narcissism as
he could find no other use for, the schizophrenic transforms his own body into
something alien and inanimate (first, through 'feelings of alienation,' in a further
stage of regression into the 'influencing machine')" (p. 127).

tional and passive experiences, *particulary affectomotor and motor phenomena.*[3]

Ever since the pain attacks in his first year of life Stanley had been a feeding problem. He voiced unusually frequent complaints concerning his stomach. Gas pains and the urge to vomit, particularly at times of physical illness, became very frightening experiences to him—so much so that for periods after such illnesses when he had recovered sufficiently to be permitted to eat anything he wanted, he would refuse to eat. In a previous paper (*SPI*:11) we described how Stanley's fabulous memory was symptomatic of his ego's failure of repression. Considering the facts that Stanley was unable to forget certain affect-laden situations of his past, and that he, as many of these children, seemed to have had an uncanny *somatopsychic memory*, may it not be assumed that the sensations or urges arising in his gastrointestinal tract, like the gas pains, abdominal distress, or vomiting, have been reminiscent to him of the sudden attacks in his babyhood? We are reminded of Tausk's reference (1919) to the case of Staudemeyer: "Every single peristaltic motion coming to his awareness is attributed to the activity of special demons allegedly located in his intestines." It would seem that because of the ego's fragmentation, the enteroceptive stirrings of the viscera and the hunger sensations of the oral cavity, the sensations experienced at defecation—the feeling of nausea, the urge to vomit—all these sensations and experiences remain unintegrated.

In his classical paper Tausk (1919) suggested that the end product, the "influencing machine" of his adult patient, Miss N. "must have forerunners in that developmental stage in which the child's own body is the goal of object finding." In the case of Stanley, this very time of life was a time of intense pain and distress. In conjunction

---

3. In his discussion remarks, Dr. M. Schur emphasized that Stanley's case illustrated Rapaport's conception of passivity (1958), namely, that the transition from passivity to activity is an essential step to structure formation and ego autonomy. At first there is no activity vis-a-vis the drives. It is only with gradual development of structure that activity and with it all the inhibitory functions vis-a-vis the drives come into being. States of regression result in return to more or less complete passivity. This is clearly shown in Stanley's case in whom the "complete" passivity toward the drives was so obvious, and who in a very frantic and primitive way tried to turn the drive on and off.

with the described visceral pain attacks and the distortions of the early mother-infant symbiosis, Stanley's body ego was not sufficiently cathected with secondary narcissistic libido. The mother image remained fused or was regressively totally fused. The necessity of separate functioning in Stanley's case triggered a psychotic break with reality. When maturational growth confronted the child with the fact of separateness, the obligatory panic reactions with agitation which ensue in such cases at this crossroad were denied or perhaps clinically unnoticeable by the symbiotic mother. Libido was withdrawn and stored in an undifferentiated form—in the inside of the body. Alienation, that is, delibidinization and aggressivization of the body ego in its peripheral parts could be seen in Stanley's manifest behavior: the peculiar mechanization of his own functions and movements, his own machinelike quality was striking.

Indeed, the endlessly repetitious preoccupation with the quasi-animated machines, so obviously identified with the dehumanized, devitalized representations of his oral, anal, and phallic functions, the split-up ego-alien introjects, expressed this child's struggle for finding a self-identity and some orientation and integration of internal versus external reality.[4]

In several other cases this utter bewilderment concerning boundaries and identity was spectacular and dramatic. For example, we have witnessed psychotic children's behavior at defecation which was a major crisis. They behaved as if the cyballum was a dangerous ego-alien introject, a painful object inside, but more dangerous even when passing the sphincter into the outside world.

We may describe how Stanley's body was treated by him as a machine: Stanley appeared to be unable to express his emotions and affects other than in the most primitive and extreme forms. He had no capacity for modulation. If he displayed any emotion at all, they represented extreme affects, panic or else orgastic ecstasy (SPI:11). At other times he showed complete apathy or even a catatoniclike stupor. These two crudely extreme forms of affective behavior sometimes alternated within one treatment hour, sometimes even several times back and forth; therefore it seemed to the observer as though the

----

4. This phase of Stanley's treatment was described by Elkisch (1956).

boy were switching himself, as it were, from one mode of behavior into the other. Once he had switched himself "on," it often seemed as if the motion were generated from within him, as from an engine—an engine gaining momentum and running so powerfully that the child had no way of stopping it. Moreover, the emotions which Stanley seemed to turn "on" and "off," like one of the switches, were created by him in a most peculiar and rather "unemotional" way. The child, evidently knowing that certain emotional expressions were expected of him by his environment, and, in his attempt at adaptation, trying to comply with these expectations, at times gave the impression that he made himself "learn" emotions. Here is an example: on several occasions during his hour, all of a sudden, the boy would get up and, without the slightest provocation or detectable connection with what had gone on before, would go from one place to another, take things which were within his reach, throw them on the floor and try to destroy them. He would look up smilingly and somewhat proudly say: "Today I want to be naughty." Even though such behavior could strike you as "aggressive," actually the boy would convince you of real aggressiveness no more than would a very poor actor. Another peculiar, artificial manipulation to satisfy, as it appeared, his affectively depleted sensory self-image: he begged his father to spank him! We have seen and have described other cases in which the child resorted to bizarre modes to obtain greater libidinal and aggressive cathexis of the "rind of the ego" in order to obtain bodily self-demarcation. Stanley's father cooperated in a playful way, spanking the boy, but certainly not hurting him. But while he was, so to speak, "spanking" the child, Stanley started to cry. He cried and cried and his parents found it most difficult to stop him. The engine in him had gained momentum and had to be stopped by an outside operator. These "scenes" had to be repeated frequently.

Stanley's attempts at some kind of homeostasis and adaptation to reality expressed themselves in numerous other ways, all of which were mechanical or machinelike. The learning of emotions and the displaying of the learned emotions had an equivalent in the intellectual field. There they appeared to be less peculiar and less surprising than in the realm of affects. His way of communicating altogether had a quality of parroting. The child would pretend to read without being able to read, running through the books which had been read to him, and which, through listening, he had learned by heart. He would use phrases which he had picked up from others, mostly from the adults in his environment, and he would use those phrases with the same tone of voice, sometimes even accompanied by the kind of mannerisms, gesture or posture or facial expression that the adult might have exhibited while speaking. With some exceptions, these phrases which Stanley parroted were not entirely inappropriate to the situations in which Stanley would use them, so that his parroting speech and mannerisms actually constituted a bridge, a link between him and reality.

Stanley's intellectual learning in a narrower sense, however, did not afford him such a link with reality. There his "methods," because of their mechanical, mosaiclike quality, lacked the essential human features of learning by trial and error, by transfer and abstraction. As described in our previous paper, Stanley commanded a fabulous memory, but this memory at close examination turned out to be a storage of disconnected engrams, unorganized as to the qualities of essential or unessential. "The most minute details of certain affect-laden situations of the past were preserved and some extraneous or tangential quality of a detail of a subsequent experience reminding him of a past situation would elicit in him a sweepingly diffuse total reaction."

Here again, the child reacted as though a switch had been turned on in him and the memory machine was set in motion. So when Stanley parroted someone in speech and mannerism, it seemed as though the content of the past conversation could not be divorced from certain qualities peculiar to that conversation or situation, or person, who might have talked or read to him. "Two or more things, images, or concepts, affect and perception at one time experienced together, became engram-conglomerates, syncretically and therefore forever connected with each other in his memory" (SPI: 11). The most essential defense mechanism for normal development, that of repression, has failed in Stanley's case.

SUMMARY

We found that the infantile precursors of the "influencing machine" are based upon: (i) delibidinization of the body image (especially its boundaries); (ii) total introjection of the mother and withdrawal of libido from her and the rest of the object world.

The result was a narcissistic state, in which the ego was fragmented and the self-boundaries blurred, fused with the mother's.

The most essential failure of the fragmented ego pertains to the overall mechanisms of integration and synthesis of inside with outside stimuli. There is failure of repression *as well*.

Replacing these defense mechanisms dedifferentiation was used.

Dedifferentiation is based upon massive denial of percepts—in the wake of which aggression-saturated inner percepts gain ascendancy. These inner stimuli or percepts undergo deanimation and machinization.

The psychotic child—like the normal one—sees the world in his own image. Thus all objects in the psychotic child's reality take on the same machinelike, semi-animate, preterhuman quality as his own body image.

The main difference between the adult and the child psychotic seems to be that in the adult the hallucinated (projected) outside machine influences the self, whereas in the child psychotic the influencing quality still manifestly pertains to his own self-representation and is then projected (secondarily) to the outer world.

OBSERVATIONS ON RESEARCH REGARDING THE "SYMBIOTIC SYNDROME" OF INFANTILE PSYCHOSIS

[1960]

Our previous work has resulted in the hypotheses that children pass through a *normal-autistic* a *symbiotic,* and a *separation-individuation* phase of development. We postulate that in the normal autistic phase, the infant has not yet become aware of anything beyond his own body. In the symbiotic phase, the infant seems to become vaguely aware of need-satisfaction from the outside, but the mother is still a part of his own self-representation: the infant's mental image is fused with that of his mother. In the third phase, the infant gradually becomes aware of his separateness; first, the separateness of his body, then gradually the identity of his self. He subsequently establishes the boundaries of his self. We have postulated in previous papers that the primarily autistic-psychotic child has never developed beyond the autistic phase, whereas the symbiotic-psychotic child has regressed from the challenge of separate functioning at the onset or during the separation-individuation phase into a symbiotic-parasitic, panic-ridden state. As states of panic are unbearable for any organism, the child's very survival requires further defensive regression. We therefore find that many, if

In collaboration with Manuel Furer, M.D.

not all, primarily symbiotic children secondarily resort to autistic mechanisms.

Our first therapeutic endeavor in both types of infantile psychosis is to engage the child in a "corrective symbiotic experience."[1] This most essential step requires a long period of time to achieve and to consolidate, and a still longer interval elapses before the higher levels of personality development, beginning with the separation-individuation phase, are attained.

To achieve this goal we had at our disposal, and at first could not help but use, the existing methods of approach to the treatment of psychotic children within conventional institutions, all of which routinely entail exposure of the preschool psychotic child to group situations. Our experience with these facilities convinced us that premature efforts to expose such children to group situations which interfered with or diluted the corrective symbiotic experience by subjecting them to any kind of social situations, even in the most carefully planned therapeutic nursery, were harmful. Not only was progress impeded but in many instances there were detrimental traumatic effects.

One boy, for example, who was referred for private treatment at the age of four and a half as a case of infantile psychosis, promptly developed a symbiotic attachment to the therapist. This child, S., was given a thorough preliminary examination as an inpatient in an academic center. During the psychological testing it was readily observed that he responded best to bodily affection. In fact, in the course of treatment his need for bodily contact, which he could provide for himself either only very passively or very violently, was continually in evidence. Before referral the psychologist noted: "It may be of interest that S.'s highest level of success occurred when he was being caressed by patting or stroking on the head and shoulders; he was given this demonstration of affection because he seemed to be

---

1. "Corrective" is not used by us to indicate a manipulative kind of intervention. By promoting the reexperiencing of early stages of development, the child should be enabled to reach a higher level of object relationship. We arrived at calling this approach "corrective symbiotic experience" by comparing it with Dr. Augusta Alpert's research on "corrective object relationship," conducted at the Child Development Center.

entirely impervious to vocal expressions of praise and encouragement." His selective awareness of emotional situations was demonstrated by his correctly noting in a picture of the test that a child depicted with his mother was crying.

S. responded rather unspecifically but very well to any exclusive relationship with an adult. In fact he loved to have two or more adults concentrate on him simultaneously. However, he clearly showed anger or proneness to tantrums if the adults excluded him by talking with each other. When his mother talked on the telephone, he would deliberately take apart one of his toys and yell, "Fix it, fix it!" He was fascinated by his baby cousin and imitated the baby talk, thus showing us the way he wanted to be treated.

This child's mother was, unfortunately, a very rigid and proper lady who, though loving her child very much in her own way and consciously ready to make any sacrifice for him, could not provide the warmth he needed. The child's father had abandoned them on S.'s first birthday. The mother could not tolerate her child's bizarre behavior, particularly in public. She talked with him almost exclusively on a rather adult level, despite her awareness that what she said had very limited meaning for him. She could not give him any tender physical affection. She was probably not capable of it. Gravely deficient in adequate self-esteem herself, the child was for her a conspicuous proof of her worthlessness and social inacceptability.

After a few months of treatment it became apparent that four hours weekly therapy in the office was not adequate for the child or the mother. The concentrated, partly symbiotic-parasitic, partly autistic atmosphere of an exclusive living arrangement of mother and child in a small furnished room needed to be counterbalanced; furthermore, the mother felt keenly that some more formal learning situation with other children should be provided for her child. We succeeded in having S. accepted in a small nursery school. He behaved there as we had expected; not as a participant in the group but as a tangential appendage. Even this was possible only because his mother remained passively by and the school staff was most patient and helpfully understanding. He did not profit either socially or intellectually during the months he was patiently tolerated there, despite the fact that in the therapeutic relationship he made definite progress.

At the end of the school year the teacher's report stated: "S. does not participate in most of the activities of the class. He seldom talks to children or adults, but frequently communicates by sound and action rather than words. When he does talk, and this is when *one* teacher has time to be with him, he shows particular interest in trains and book illustrations, etc."

S. grew especially tall for his age and as it was impossible to keep him in the nursery, he was transferred to a kindergarten when he was five and a half years old. In kindergarten his panic and tantrums instantly recurred. He had catastrophic reactions to the situation, especially as his mother was not permitted to remain with him. She was asked within a few days to withdraw him. This failure upset her more than all the other signs and proofs which should have made her aware of the gravity of the child's mental illness.

A few weeks later special tutoring was provided for S. Again, in this exclusive one-to-one relationship he made progress in a characteristic, peculiarly unspecific symbiotic experience, just as he had in the therapeutic relationship. With the help of the tutor and of the therapist, his tendency to autistic withdrawal diminished. His courage to test reality increased, as did his vocabulary and his perception of the outside world. For the first time in his life this child displayed fondness for such soft, transitional objects as pillows and toy animals. These now served—as they had not before—to allay his anxieties and tensions. He surrounded himself with these transitional objects, particularly at night, and relived early stages of babyhood in a more normal way.

Again we made the mistake of enrolling him in a group, this time in our pilot project, in what we thought was a particularly sheltered learning situation in a special therapeutic nursery group. S. was bewildered but made, we thought, an initial adaptation because he shared the teacher with only one other child. His distress soon became apparent when a few more children joined the group. We were still inclined to attribute a rapid regression in his speech and in other areas of his functioning to measles he had contracted near the end of the school year. But when after a fairly good summer at the seashore he rejoined the group, his ego threatened rapidly to disintegrate. In uncontrollable panic and rage he violently attacked his mother and teachers. His speech became unintelligible, and he seemed to hallucinate.

This much of S.'s case is presented to demonstrate that in all situations this child desperately craved and violently demanded exclusive symbiotic possession of an adult. He repeatedly retreated after severe tantrums into lethargic states of hallucinatory withdrawal whenever he could not be given the exclusive attention of an adult to the extent that his fragmented ego craved and needed.

The last of numerous similar experiences which led us to abandon the therapeutic nursery design for psychotic preschool children was the case of a four-year-old psychotic child who had been placed in a smoothly organized group of five disturbed but not psychotic children with two teachers. When P. arrived at the therapeutic nursery school, she appeared to be a serenely beautiful child. She quickly became extremely restless, sought constantly to find her mother, and then roamed through the building, followed by the teacher who had to leave the other children and go after her. The teacher learned that by rocking her and other devices she could induce P. to remain in the room with the other children, to whom the child paid absolutely no attention. In her relationship to the adult, for P. there were only two alternatives: either in a phase of autistic withdrawal she used the teacher as an extension of her own body in order to control the environment with this exeecutive external ego, or there was a clinging, burrowing type of behavior during which the teacher had to focus her attention completely on P. lest she have a panic-tantrum. It became apparent that to keep the child at this higher level of relationship, the teacher had to abandon her duties to the other children. The child's behavior demanded an exclusive relationship with the teacher; any demand for the teacher's attention by the group was increasingly deleterious to her.

For a while we continued to believe that the deleterious effect of the group on P. was due primarily to the fact that she was a case of early infantile autism, particularly vulnerable as she began to attain a symbiotic relationship. When we saw the process occurring with still another, a symbiotic-psychotic child, we realized that a revised research had to be designed for all cases of infantile psychosis. Our hypotheses about psychosis had already indicated this from a theoretical point of view.

That there was a conflict in P.'s mind about her growing attachment to the teacher and her relationship to her mother was apparent, for example, whenever she was hurt. She would run to and from the door leading to her mother, and then back to the teacher until finally she rubbed the injured part against the teacher's body. What was most amazing was that as the child's conflict mounted and she ran to seek her mother, the mother was increasingly difficult to find in the building. The mother was, in fact, almost consciously trying to avoid her child as the child became more demanding and expressive. These changes in P. made the mother so anxious that she became angry with the child's therapist.

From this case we recognized another important factor in revising therapy and research. The revised design would not involve the child with other children in a group situation before he is ready for it. The two cases described and many others like them made it clear that to provide the psychotic child's need for protection within the corrective symbiotic experience must be the basis for treatment. The child's development from autistic withdrawal toward primitive, unspecific clinging to the therapist as well as to the mother gave us another significant clue for the revision of our research design. We had repeatedly observed that the presence of the mother within the therapeutic situation was not only very well tolerated but that it was a sign of progress when a mother was sought by her psychotic child. The mother's presence proved, furthermore, to be most helpful to our understanding of the child's "signal communications" throughout treatment. In our experience, even though the mothers were not able to fulfill these children's needs, they understood their own child's nonverbal communications to a surprising degree.

It was evident that these considerations were not only of theoretical importance but that they indicated the direction which must be taken for the immediate treatment and for optimal future planning for the psychotic child's mental health. We evolved from this a method of research in which the mother, the child, and the worker are present in the room during the sessions, which extend from two to three hours, the mother and worker collaborating in the re-habilitation of the psychotic child.

The advantages of this design are manifold. Our initial under-standing of the child comes not only through observations but also through information and explanations given by the mother. By this method there can be mutual exchanges of information and under-standing between the child's therapist, the supervising psychiatrist, and the mother, as the child's behavior is being observed by all three. The mother is first gratified by our interest, and then heartened by the feeling she gradually acquires that someone believes her child can be helped. There also appears to be a great sense of relief produced by the understanding, initially intellectual, which the mother gains. She may, and often does use it defensively, but it gives her the feeling that some possible control can be exerted over what previously had been to her a desperate, hopeless, and uncontrollable problem.

The information the mother gives us enables the therapist to institute those procedures which seem to foster the development of the need-satisfying symbiotic relationship between the child and the worker. In the beginning, for example, a signal type of communica-tion has to be fostered between the child and the worker, which can later be used by the worker in a corrective manner.

A four-year-old boy, M., frequently rolled a toy car to and fro. The mother explained to us that this indicated he had to urinate. We had discovered from our observations that he also meant by this action that there was something wrong with the car; that it was broken. We learned, moreover, that this activity, which we took as a signal of his bodily need, occurred after many hours of withholding his urine, to the point where he was in pain and probably afraid that he could no longer withhold. We then understood these signals to mean that he was afraid of being overwhelmed by these inner bodily stimuli. Our therapeutic procedure was to respond to this signal as a mother would to an infant, that is, as an auxiliary ego which we hope the child can add to his own ego, thereby overcoming otherwise over-whelming anxieties. Instead, therefore, of interpreting the displace-ment and anxiety, the therapist tells the boy that he will feel very good when he goes to the toilet and that she will help him. She takes him with her to the toilet, encouraging him to urinate, and expressing her pleasure and admiration when he does. In this way we believe we have begun to liberate the child from the feeling of being the passive victim of bodily discomforts and discharges, and with this help he may proceed to independently active functioning.

In general the new design allows for the development of a more and more specific relationship with the therapist without interference from other children. The development of the child's relationship to the worker, which always brings with it changes in the relationship with the mother, can be observed directly, and the frequently occurring defeatist attitudes of the family counteracted. With the emergence from autism, and the achievement of a higher level of behavior, the patience of these children's families is often greatly taxed. The endlessly repetitive banging of doors, throwing of objects, switching off and on of lights often generate uncontrollable hostility within the family, and sometimes lead to ill-considered placement of the child away from home.

After M. became better able to comply when he was encouraged to urinate, he began to spit in an uncontrollable way. He first spat at his therapist, and soon at his mother. His mother reprimanded him for it, and he withdrew into his autistic shell. We had learned that the child's disturbance of urinary functioning had occurred as a consequence of the mother's disgust at finding that he urinated into the bathtub instead of the toilet. Had the spitting happened at home as an extension of the child's behavior in the therapeutic situation, this mother might well have reacted, as had P.'s mother, with hostility. But M.'s mother had been made a member of the "therapeutic alliance," and the simple explanation she was given of the beneficial value of M.'s transient regressive behavior made sense to her. She had, in fact, previously reported in the course of the therapy that M. had begun at home to invite her to exchange babbling and cooing sounds with him. The mother spontaneously expressed her opinion that he seemed belatedly to be permitting himself indulgences of babyhood which—in contrast to his brothers—he had missed completely. Observing the way the therapist handled the situation gave the mother a security of feeling, a way of understanding, a model for helping her child.

Such experiences with the example and help of the child's therapist, the supervising psychiatrist, and the social worker become assimilated in time if the mother herself is capable of learning and of providing the additional and essential corrective symbiotic experience for the child. Why the spitting developed in the case of M. could be directly explained to the boy's mother by the worker, by the psychiatrist, and subsequently more fully gone into by the social worker. Whatever deeper fears and defenses might be involved in her reaction, the mother's immediate response to the child—and this is always partly dictated by unconscious forces—is opposed by her conscious determination, aided by her understanding and the example given to her by the team. This kind of therapeutic help for the mother of the psychotic child is consistent with our theory that the treatment of the child must extend over many years of the child's life and that his development must be reexperienced and relived, not only with the therapist but with the primary love object. The mother, therefore, must be trained to assume and maintain the corrective symbiotic experience developed by the therapist. This emotional-intellectual learning is stabilized by the mother's individual sessions with the supervising psychiatrist and the social worker.

In this method we believe we have evolved a mother-child-therapist unit, supervised by a male child psychiatrist, which can result in the development of the personality instead of in fixation at the stage of the psychosis. It is interesting and disquieting that it took us so many years to arrive at these inevitable conclusions and to apply their logical requirements in therapeutic research. They were inherent from the start in our theoretical hypotheses of autistic and symbiotic psychosis. Gradually, tardily, and retrospectively we came to these conclusions from clinical data which abundantly demonstrated that failures ensued whenever the corrective symbiotic relationship was threatened by disruption—as it too frequently was when we adhered to traditional methods.

The crucial therapeutic problem in psychosis remains the same. The psychotic child must be kept from retreating into the autistic defensive position. He must be enticed into and be encouraged to relive a more fully gratifying—albeit still regressive—exclusively symbiotic-parasitic relationship with a substitute mother. This relationship is made liberally available to the child for whom it becomes a buffer in the process of dissolution of the vicious cycle of the distorted relationship with the mother. Gradually and cautiously the child is then helped to develop some autonomous substitutes for the pathological primitive regressive demands exacted from the pathologically defensive and ambivalent mother. In this manner the child is led to discover the boundaries of his self, and to experience a sense of himself as a separate entity in his environment.

In the treatment of primarily symbiotic or primarily autistic children, a contradiction sometimes confuses workers in the field. Although these infants seem insatiable in their need for the passively available symbiotic partner, their symbiotic claim is at first not at all specific. Several adults are well tolerated and often simultaneously enjoyed. But at first, and for a long time, they are utterly intolerant of any type of group relationship involving other children, even the most carefully devised ones. Only the most important symbiotic partner who seals herself off as completely as possible with the child can form for him that insulating layer against the give-and-take aspects of social group situations for which he has no capacity or tolerance during the period described. Only after a prolonged period of corrective symbiotic experience should the psychotic child be given carefully graduated dosages of rhythmic play—preferably to the accompaniment of soothing music—in which the symbiotic partner is right at the side of the child. In the course of the therapeutic research, we carefully watch the preferences of these children as they slowly evolve interest and reach out for association with the other children treated at the Center. They show us unmistakably when they are ready for such social learning, and also how much of it they can take.

Chapter 14

LONGITUDINAL STUDY OF THE TREATMENT OF A PSYCHOTIC CHILD WITH THE TRIPARTITE DESIGN

[1976]

DR. MAHLER: As Dr. Pao read the title of this presentation it occurred to me that it is somewhat of a misnomer. We neither had the means nor the foresight to film this case in a planned systematic fashion. The scant samples of a few filmed, more or less representative sessions of the therapeutic action research, as Ernst Kris would have called it, were just recently put together. In the beginning of Violet's treatment, silent films were made of a few random sessions. Sections of these were put together for the purpose of demonstrating the clinical syndrome of secondary autism in comparison with the case of a little boy who displayed a typical symbiotic psychosis. Later on, when occasional sessions with Violet were filmed, narrative was superimposed. The film from the beginning of the patient's treatment to the tenth year of her life (the latter filmed with sound track) has been shown by Dr. Furer and particularly by Mrs. Bergman to a few groups of professional people. The urgent requests of several psychoanalyst colleagues prompted us to bring Mrs. Bergman's remarkable work up to date. Hence, the last section that you will see showing Violet at fifteen and one-half years was only recently filmed and will be shown for the first time here and now.

Illustrated with Film

Film begins with an introduction by Dr. Furer

This film will illustrate the tripartite treatment of symbiotic child psychoses in which child, mother, and therapist work together. Treatment sessions occur four times a week, and last two and one-half hours. First, the therapist carefully lures the child from her autistic withdrawal into a symbiotic form of attachment to the therapist. Then she brings the mother and child together into a corrective symbiotic experience. Later, mother participates with therapist and child in helping to interpret the child's feelings and conflicts and to clarify and reconstruct present and past reality. Eventually mother is not present in all sessions, but she must be available.

Other important aspects of the treatment design developed at Masters Children's Center by Dr. Margaret Mahler and myself are not shown in the film. The child psychiatrist discusses the child with the therapist once a week; the mother talks to the psychiatrist about herself and her child and their life together. Together they observe the child and therapist through a one-way screen, sharing their understanding of the child. The understanding thus gained is shared by the psychiatrist with the therapist. Mother discusses with the social worker each week her own personal life and problems. Finally, there is a weekly conference at which all professional staff members, therapists, supervising psychiatrists, and social workers discuss each of the children under treatment in turn.

Usually the treatment of two preschool-age psychotic children is as much as one therapist can undertake. These children develop a symbiotic psychosis because there has been a disturbance in the development of their object relations, in the separation-individuation process, and in maturation toward greater independence. Panicky anxiety in response to awareness of separateness and helplessness results in regression to pathological forms of the autistic and symbiotic phases of early development. In the autistic phase the infant is not yet aware of a comforting, buffering, external mother or, as Dr. Mahler calls her, "a beacon of orientation." The result, as you will see, is a child who deanimates her world, withdrawing from human interactions. The symbiotic psychotic child regresses to what

Dr. Mahler calls a "mother-child omnipotent dual unity" in which mother and self are not yet differentiated. The continuing anxiety of reengulfment often results in a further regression to secondary autism. That is what happened to Violet, whom we will see in this film.

Originally, Dr. Mahler and I started working with three children, including one in individual treatment with Dr. Mahler who emerged from autism to symbiotic attachment to her. Soon he regressed dramatically to an acute, excited, catatoniclike state. At first we thought this was a reaction to an infectious illness but finally we concluded that he had panicked at having to share possible symbiotic partners, the teachers, with other children.

In 1959, Dr. Mahler and I obtained a National Institutes of Mental Health grant to study the natural history of symbiotic child psychosis through a therapeutic action project. We set up a conventional treatment program with a new group of six preschool-age children who were either symbiotic or secondarily autistic. Dr. Mahler and I supervised the two teachers. This time five of the children, although severely disturbed, were not psychotic. The study concentrated on the sixth child who was secondarily autistic.

The group in time was divided into five nonpsychotic children with one teacher, and one psychotic child with the other. This little girl led the way for the final development of our treatment approach. She emerged from her autistic shell to develop a symbiotic relationship with the teacher and to become more involved with her mother. This advance disturbed the autistic balance between mother and child; the child, no longer respecting the mutual distance between herself and her mother, would take the teacher's hand, dragging her along as she searched for mother in the building. She became more bizarre, appearing sicker. Unprepared for these changes, mother was frightened and resentful and hid from the child at home and at Masters. When the child found her mother in a closet at Masters and when the mother tried to leave the building, the child had a tantrum resembling the catatonic spell of the boy.

This overwhelming confirmation of our understanding of child psychosis led to the tripartite treatment in which the therapist lures the child out of his autistic shell and becomes a bridge between mother and child to establish a symbiotic dual unity between them. After this is lived in for some time, subsequent stages in treatment which can be likened to the normal separation-individuation process can then take place. From this, the child as an individual entity can emerge.

This film shows Violet who, when she enters treatment at three, is dominated by autistic coping mechanisms. There has been a pervasive dedifferentiation. She no longer discriminates between herself and the external world, between animate and inanimate. She treats people like inanimate objects. When we see her again at five years old she is the symbiotic phase of her treatment. You will see her at ten years old—and again at fifteen, when she still requires treatment but is no longer psychotic.

Picture appears on the film—The film is silent

Dr. Furer continues: At two years nine months, Violet is elfinlike and graceful, but relates only to inanimate objects. She is an autistic child. Violet avoids all eye contact with her therapist who subtly tries to engage her in play. In keeping with the tripartite treatment design, the mother is in the therapy room. Violet accepts objects from the therapist but does not acknowledge her presence. Slowly, Violet begins to be able to use body contact with Miriam, her therapist, as long as she can avoid facing her. Violet uses Miriam's arm, but only as a tool to get what she cannot reach. Dr. Mahler and Violet's mother observe and discuss the therapy session. As Miriam lures the child from autism, she acts as a bridge between Violet and her mother. Violet has an uncanny ability to play the piano which she treats as her exclusive love object, for which Furer (1964) used the term "psychotic fetish." When she is taken away from the piano, she has an unconsolable panic tantrum. Later, when she returns to the piano, she explores it, reassuring herself of the love object's existence. She explores the insides of the piano the way a normal infant might explore the body. Violet explored the piano with great intensity over many years of treatment.

Film is stopped—Informal discussion

DR. MAHLER: Violet's parents were both very young and rather infantile when she was born. The mother, who had grown up friendless in her rather cruel grandmother's house, felt profoundly abandoned by both her parents. The little girl Violet represented for her twenty-year-old mother an animated living doll. Several weeks after Violet was born, Mrs. V. became deeply depressed. This coincided with the death of her father. During the first nine months the infant cried a great deal. During the first months, at least, Violet is said to have engaged her mother with her eyes during breast feeding and to have smiled at her. She vocalized at around eight or nine months, but at one year, Violet did not respond to people.

Violet's parents are both pianists; for many hours she was locked out of the room where they practiced even though Violet protested and usually had a temper tantrum. Mother thought that Violet would stop when she heard her start to play and when she realized that she just wasn't going to get anywhere with her tantrums. The parents could not bear to have their practicing interfered with and they resorted to locking Violet in her room as soon as she was able to crawl. In her room Violet would have severe temper tantrums, kicking with her feet against the closed door. Thus, the piano came to be both loved and hated. It created a lifeline of sound between her world of isolation and the world of her parents, and at the same time it seemed the cause of her isolation.

At intake, the only communication between mother and child—the only situation that elicited smiles from the infant—involved the piano. In fact, the child displayed phenomenal musical gifts, an unusual ear, and an incredible ability to reproduce on the piano almost any music she heard. The piano, in other words, became Violet's psychotic fetish, as Furer calls these transitional objectlike attachments of the psychotic child. Early in her therapy Violet explored the insides of the piano in a way that made one feel the piano represented the mother's body. It was through music that Violet expressed her first dawning awareness of people outside herself. At certain times her playing would be tender and ecstatic; at other times she would bang at the piano mercilessly, or just jump on it and make terrible sounds. Years later she still expressed her anger by banging or jumping on the piano. Besides her muteness, one of the symptoms that prompted the parents to seek professional consultation was the child's very early and skillful attempts to destroy the parents' music, tearing the sheets into shreds and attacking their pianos whenever she had a chance. Whereas the film sections do not do justice to the positive aspects of Violet's fabulous musical gift since we had no proper sound-recording equipment, one can observe Violet's hands, which are those of a real pianist. Also, it can be seen that her libido, as well as her aggression, revolves around the piano.

Silent film resumes

Dr. Furer comments: Nine months later Violet was able to engage in a greater variety of play with Mrs. Anni Bergman, her new therapist. There now exists a silent recognition of the therapist's presence. Violet is able to reproduce any music once she has heard it. She takes all of her precious possessions to the piano. Violet is now almost four years old and she uses music to communicate, as she still does not talk. She chooses her music to convey her moods or a recent event. Violet and her mother attend therapy sessions four times a week. Violet's memory enables her to reproduce the signs she sees on the subway on the long ride to her sessions. There are moments of pleasurable contact with her mother. While in her autistic withdrawal and not interfered with she appears serene; now that a symbiotic relationship with the therapist and her mother is established, her facial expression appears bizarre. This is a distinct improvement since it indicates the beginning of an emotional relationship which is painful to her. At four and one-half Violet has a temper tantrum when her mother leaves the room and now *only her mother* can soothe her. Violet also allows her mother to take care of her.

Film is stopped—Informal discussion

DR. MAHLER: The next filming was done with sound track. It will show Violet at five and one-half years of age at the height of what we regard as the symbiotic psychosis syndrome. She was not brought by her mother. That week Mrs. V. was protectively hospitalized at her own request since Violet's acting out was at its height and had become more trying than the mother could bear. In the film we will see that Mrs. Bergman, by Violet's sixth year, had succeeded in helping the child invest both aggression and libido in their relationship. The musical interaction has reached the duet stage, which corresponds, I think, to what Spitz has described as happening between the very young baby who has reached the *stage of dialogue* with the mother. I believe that I ought to emphasize that, in addition to the bridge function of the therapist in the treatment design mentioned by Dr. Furer, the buffering function of the therapist is very important as well. She lends herself as the main target of the child's psychotic aggression. The patient realizes in time that her violent aggression cannot destroy the therapist as a love object: she cannot destroy their relationship. One is reminded of that which we learned from Winnicott (1969) about "the use of the object."

Film resumes with sound track

   Dr. Furer: Violet at five and one-half is now at the height of her symbiotic psychosis as seen in her bland facial expression and her bizarre gestures. At this session she is particularly distressed because her mother is ill. Violet is also disturbed by the intrusion of the photographer into her intimate relationship with her therapist, Mrs. Anni Bergman. At this stage, Violet still does not relate to people in general, even though she does have as intense a tie to her therapist as she has developed to her mother.

> *(Violet is brought by the maid. She and Anni Bergman move to the piano.)*

AB: Violet still has quite a cold.
       (Violet and AB both have recorders.) One for you, one for me. You can blow. What shall we play? All right, go ahead, go ahead. You play it. You start. *(Violet then plays the piano instead of the recorder.)* Too fast. That's too fast.

You play this *(on the piano)* and I'll play it on the recorder.

Dr. Furer comments: Violet becomes aware of the photographer. She becomes aware that love and hate can be invested in the same object. She shows her anger and her feelings in the way she treats the piano.

AB:	Which one shall we play, Violet?
	(AB and Violet are at the table, writing.)
	One, two. . . .
Violet:	Tooo, tooo.
AB:	Violet likes two. One-two. One-two. Violet-Anni.
Violet:	Tooo, tooo.

Dr. Furer comments: At the age of five and one-half Violet still does not talk.

> *(Violet leaves the table and reaches, that is, points to a container of milk on a shelf.)*

AB:	Is that what you're looking for? The milk? The milk for Violet? The milk? Milk with bubbles. Good?
	(Violet sips milk through a straw.)
	(Violet now goes back to the piano where she explores it.)

Dr. Furer comments: A second piano had to be provided because Violet's aggressive exploration destroyed the first one.

AB comments: It has become a sort of a game to jump on the piano and wait for me to play with her and to take her off the piano. Taking her off the piano has been very pleasurable and she has relaxed in my arms.

AB:	You can sit up here. I think that will be okay.
	(Violet is perched on piano.)
	There goes, my girl, there you go. I've got you, I've got you up there. I got you. You know, we are still together.

AB comments: She really felt like a normal child in my arms at times. Today she remains stiff and quickly wriggles out of my arms.

(Violet turns pages of sheet music.)

AB: Here, let's start together. Here, which song should I play, Violet? Which one should I play for you? Shall I play "I Love Little Pussy?" This one?

Violet: Nnn . . . .

AB: I think you can sit up here the way you usually sit, Violet. I think that will be all right. Did you hurt yourself? Show me which one *(which song)*. All right. *(They play.)* Good . . . Sit here. Shall we do that one again?

AB comments: Our contact, tenuous at best, on this day was constantly disrupted by Violet's awareness of the photographer.

(Violet goes off, AB follows her.)

AB: Violet, uh, uh. No, sweetie, you have to go back. We have to go back to our room. I know it.
(AB leads her back to the piano. Violet plays a medley of tunes.)

AB: And now, instead of saying "I'm mixed up," Violet mixes up the songs.

AB comments: No matter how hard I tried, or perhaps because I tried so hard to get her to perform for the film, Violet would not play with her usual facility.

(AB sings as Violet plays.)

AB: Violet isn't mixing up the songs anymore. Which is this one? *(Sings)* "Sing a song . . . " *(as Violet plays)*. You still have to mix it up just a little.

AB comments: By playing a bit from *The Magic Flute* Violet is recalling our theater visit and is communicating to me her awareness that I am different today.

AB: I think this is what you heard when we went to the theater together. That's what you were just playing, *The Magic Flute*. That was also a strange place *(strange situation).*

AB comments: Instead of trying to understand her I am concerned with her behavior, as I was at the theater.

AB: Don't mix it up. Play it nicely. Do it again and I'll play it on the recorder.
             (At the piano Violet hurts herself.)
             You hurt yourself when you banged the piano. Poor Violet hurt herself.
             (Violet has temper tantrum on floor.)
             Let's see where you hurt yourself. I'm so sorry. It's so hard for you today.

AB comments: Although she continues to have tantrums Violet can also direct her anger at a person. Here she's attacking me while appealing to me to get rid of the camera.

             (As Violet complains loudly, AB talks to her.)

AB: . . . want them to go away. I'll have to hold you. I'm afraid you're going to fall off otherwise.
             (Before her departure, Violet uses the few words that she utters when she expresses her wish to feel better: "Happy Girl.")
AB: There you go, little girl.
Violet: Happy girl.
AB: Happy girl? Happy girl? You weren't such a happy girl today.

Dr. Furer comments: Violet would appear to have a better prognosis than many of the children we deal with because she has come a long way and has established emotional relationships to people. She is in a stage where she is moving and while she is moving we have high hopes. However, sometimes they reach a kind of plateau within these relations and can't get off.

Film is stopped—Informal discussion

DR. MAHLER: We will now see Violet at ten years of age. There is no doubt that she is gravely psychotic, observable in her primary process ideation, in her emotional outbursts, in her behavior, and in her speech. I must confess that when Violet was past six years of age and still did not speak, I gave this case up in my mind. This was for two reasons: (1) my own experience with the treatment of many psychotic children, none of whom were mute beyond five years of age; and (2) the statistics of such experts as Kanner and Eisenberg about mute children beyond five years of age.

From 1964 on, Dr. Furer's and my hitherto shared research projects were by mutual agreement divided up, so that I devoted my time almost exclusively to the Separation-Individuation Project of Normal Children and Their Average Mothers, whereas Dr. Furer carried on the Child Psychosis Project. The latter in 1965 became a New York Mental Health Clinic servicing the community for a while. Thus, it was solely due to Mrs. Bergman's never faltering faith in her own ability to help, and her absolutely unselfish devotion to her patient that prompted her, with Dr. Furer's encouragement, with practically no help from us, to continue Violet's treatment.

Film resumes with sound track

AB comments: Dr. Mahler and Dr. Furer came visiting to chat with Violet. She began to talk at eight years of age. Now at ten her speech is strange and difficult to understand.

Violet: (*Mutters to Dr. Mahler.*)
  I didn't see you for a long time.
Dr. M: For a *very* long time, indeed.
Mother: (*To Dr. Mahler.*)

We went home in your car—she remembers that—she remembers riding with you in your car.

Dr. M: *(To Violet.)*
Really?

Violet: Yes.

Dr. M: That was really long ago—you have quite a good memory. *(Violet reverts to communication by gestures; she puts her hand at her shoulder height, then to the top of her head.)* What is this, Violet? *(meaning her gestures)*.
Oh, you want to tell me how much you grew!

Violet: Don't get funny. Don't get funny.
(Dr. Furer, meanwhile, sits down at a table and plays with Violet. They arrange many toy people and toy animals in a circle. Violet loudly but unintelligibly speaks, of which one can discern only—) Everything is crowded. Everything is much too crowded. Too many people. Too many—

Dr. M: Many people and many animals!
(Violet gesticulates to Dr. Mahler that her comments are most unwelcome. She, as a third person, is an intruder, and is violently warded off by Violet. Dr. Mahler, however, deliberately sticks to the topic and says—)
It is very crowded, do you like it crowded?

Violet: *No!* I don't like it crowded.

Dr. M: I don't like it crowded either.

Violet: *(Chants)* No, crowded, crowded—

Film is stopped—Informal discussion

DR. MAHLER: In the next long film sequence Mrs. Bergman comments that one month before summer vacation Violet wrote a letter which was intended to show what kind of a letter she wished to receive at camp from her parents. It demonstrates how she, by then, was able to express emotions, especially her modulated feelings about separation. Underneath the wished-for text of the letter you will also see a drawing of the overcrowded "West Side Highway." The drawing depicts a conspicuous traffic jam. This traffic phobia remained one of Violet's psychotic preoccupations at ten years and beyond.

As soon as Violet was able to talk in sentences and to use symbolic play, puppet shows were inaugurated through which the child's state of mind, her most recent anxieties, her defenses, and her preoccupations, as well as the state and flavor of her relationships, could be rather accurately discerned by Mrs. Bergman. Through these puppet shows, the mother again takes part in the therapy sessions. She is very helpful in that she can supply the "day residue," so to speak, of Violet's phobias and preoccupations, and, along with the therapist, make her mood and her play better understandable to the patient. We cannot take the time to give more explanations. The full strength of the child's strong symbiotic tie to the mother escapes demonstration. You have to take our word for it.

There is only one more feature I want to emphasize. You will see that Violet's violence is expressed much more readily toward the "other-than-mother" than toward her mother. When Mrs. Bergman continues to confront Violet with her most recent anxieties, Violet fleetingly kisses the therapist on the mouth to shut her up; but as this libidinal maneuver does not work, she violently continues trying to shut her up by shouting "West Side Highway, West Side Highway" and by putting her finger over Mrs. Bergman's mouth! During the puppet show the mother is more mildly admonished when she is commanded by Violet: Jean Anne (mother's name), give that back to me (meaning the puppet). And later on Violet says: "Let me decide." It would seem to me that Violet tames her aggression toward mother considerably. Also, later in the session, when mother reads a story to Violet, you will observe the serenity of this libidinal interaction between Violet and her mother. The child's face and voice express outright enchantment. It is a truly affectionate interchange. At the end of the story mother asks: "Is that a good story?" and Violet very softly says: "Yes." Mother asks again: "Should we take it home?" and Violet gently murmers: "Yes."

Film resumes with commentary by Dr. Furer

At the beginning of the projection of this part of the film, Anni

Bergman also comments on the letter Violet has written to herself before summer vacation. Under the text there is her drawing of the "West Side Highway," so crowded that one car runs on top of another in the traffic jam. After the letter scene, there begins the puppet play which was inaugurated at that stage of Violet's treatment.

(AB and Violet are at the puppet stage.)

AB:	Here's a bed for daddy.
Violet:	We don't need beds. We don't need beds.
AB:	And one for Violet.
Violet:	We don't need beds.

AB comments: Violet, for the past five years, has been able to use symbolic play to deal with anxieties about past and present events.

AB:	We have to find out what makes you so scared that you can only say (think about) "West Side Highway" instead of other things.
Mother:	*(To Violet.)* What's the elf (puppet) doing?
Violet:	He says "West Side Highway."

AB comments: Her mother participates again in all therapy sessions.

Violet:	*(As mother takes a puppet.)* Hey, Jean Anne (Mother's name), give that back to me! *(Chants unintelligibly.)*
Mother:	*(As a puppet she does not heed Violet but says to her:)* The mother gets up and she says: Hey, I think it's time for breakfast this morning. We've got someplace to go. Is that what I said this morning to you, Violet?
Violet:	*(Chants unintelligibly.)*

AB comments: At the moment mother becomes too intrusive. Violet asserts herself and says:

Violet: Jean Anne, you better let *me* decide. You let me decide.
AB: *(To Violet.)*
             You know, mommy told me something about yesterday.
             Something else that you wished to talk about. You remem-
             ber? What you and mother talked about last night? She
             said something came in the mail and you looked at it and
             you liked it and you didn't like it. . . .
Violet: What?
AB: Remember it? I talked to mommy yesterday on the tele-
             phone about when you were going to come here. She told
             me yesterday that you wished to talk about something,
             some letter that came about camp.
Violet: I don't like camp.
AB: That you were a little worried about it because you don't
             really know it yet . . . *(meaning the new camp).*

AB comments: For Violet, cars and crowded highways are the
latest in a series of consuming preoccupations. These serve as a
defense against realities that frighten her.

> *(Violet wants to drown out Anni Bergman's comments*
> *and shouts "West Side Highway," etc. She kisses Anni's*
> *mouth to shut her up and finally puts her hand violently*
> *on Mrs. Bergman's mouth. This cannot be clearly seen.)*

Violet: I only want to talk about the West Side Highway. West
             Side Highway—
             (Abruptly impersonating a puppet, Violet starts to whis-
             per.)
             Sh . . . Sh . . . Don't talk too loudly.
             (As puppet directed to another puppet.)
             You shit . . .
             (As mother puppet.)
             Don't say shit.
             Shit.
Mother: Say: Shucks.
Violet: Shit, shit is bad. I don't know how to say shucks.

Mother: *(As puppet remonstrating to Violet's puppet.)*
             Oh, yes you do! *(Meaning you know how to say shucks.)*
Violet: *(Shouts again.)* West Side Highway, West Side Highway!
AB: You know, yesterday we found out something about you.
             You keep saying West Side Highway when you are scared
             about something. Yesterday—
Mother: You were thinking about camp.
AB: Right, and you thought about Mrs. Auerbach (directress of
             former camp).
Violet: *(Screams.)*
AB: You were scared that Mrs. Auerbach did not like you
             anymore and that's what makes you shout West Side
             Highway.
Violet: She do like me!
AB: She does like you. Yes. So, you do not have to be scared
             anymore. So I wonder what you are scared about this
             morning that makes you shout.
Violet: I don't want to talk about *that* now.
Mother: Why not? Maybe you won't be scared then.
Violet: West Side Highway, West Side Highway!
AB: Then you won't have to say West Side Highway anymore.

AB comments: Later in the session Violet's mother reads her a
story. This is a soothing interval for Violet and her mother.

Mother: *(Reading)* And as I sat there without making a sound, so
             they wouldn't get scared and run away (the animals) . . . I
             held my breath. He came so near, I could have touched
             him . . . but I didn't move and I didn't speak and he came
             up and he licked my cheek! Look.
             (Mother and child look at the picture.)
Violet: Deer don't do that.
Mother: Oh yes, he did. Like Zeppy (Anni Bergman's dog), huh?
AB: You like it when Zeppy does that.
Mother: *(Continues reading.)*
             And what did she say?
Violet: Oh.

Mother: . . . as happy as could be—all of them. All of them were playing with me. Even the chipmunk came up (end of story).

Is that a good story?

Violet: Yes.

Mother: Should we take it home?

Violet: Yes.

Film is stopped—Informal discussion

DR. MAHLER: The next film sequence shows the therapist, the mother, and the child sitting at a table. It deals with Violet's psychotic projective identifications, in which cars are equated with people. Mother recalls for Violet a memorable car-breakdown event. The mother and therapist work together trying to alleviate Violet's overwhelming fears and psychotic guilt feelings which are the result of Violet's belief in the magic power of her thoughts and wishes. Even though the spoken words are difficult to understand, Violet's psychotic defense of animating the inanimate world will become evident. *"The broken down Datsun car is dead.* He is dead, mom. He is not alive anymore," she says. This tripartite scene ends with the mother in identification with the therapist interpreting to Violet that the breakdown of the cars was not due to anything Violet thought, anything that Violet said, or anything that Violet did—it just happened.

Film resumes

> (Mrs. Bergman, mother, and Violet are at a table, continuing the tripartite session.)

Mother: Remember the night we came back from our vacation and we were in the Datsun car . . .

AB comments: After play, Violet's mother expresses her understanding of what is troubling Violet. Cars and crowded highways play an exaggerated role for Violet.

Mother:	And the car wouldn't go anymore and it stopped. Daddy went back as fast as he could, remember that? And mommy got outside and waved cars away. Yolanda took you and Andre away from the car. And a nice man stopped another car and said: You can get in my car until help comes. It was a very cold night. And then—
Violet:	How cold? How many degrees?
Mother:	About 38 degrees.
Violet:	No.
Mother:	It was colder than that?
Violet:	No, hotter.
Mother:	Hotter? What do you think it was?
Violet:	It might be—it might be 67 degrees.
Mother:	No, it wasn't 67 degrees.
Violet:	Yes, it is.
Mother:	It was a cool night because we all had on light coats and we were all—all a little bit cold and I was worried about you.
AB:	And you were tired after a long trip and then the car wouldn't go—the car broke down—in the middle of the highway. And mommy had to—
Violet:	Not the middle of the highway, the *side* of the highway.
Mother:	We were all upset and frightened. That was the end of the Datsun car.
AB:	The end of the Datsun car. Mommy and daddy must have thought: That car breaks down just when we need it so badly to take us home from the highway.
Violet:	We need it.
AB:	*...to take us home from the airport. And it's no more good that Datsun car! We have to get rid of it and get a new car, mommy and daddy said.*
Mother:	But we didn't cause a traffic jam on the highway, did we? People just went around us. Traffic didn't back up for long. And then we got the new car, the Saab car.
Violet:	*(Making noise with the stethoscope.)* He' dead.
AB:	He's dead, did you say?
Mother:	Is that the Saab car?
AB:	He's dead? Who is dead?

Mother:	The Datsun?
Violet:	Yes, He's dead.
AB:	Dead?
Mother:	Won't go anymore.
Violet:	*He is dead, mom. He's* not alive anymore.
Mother:	No, it never really was alive because cars aren't alive. They have a lot of things—motors that make them move, make them go. And something was wrong with the motor and it wouldn't go anymore.
AB:	Anni's car broke down too. The nice little MG that I think you did like.
Violet:	Hey, hey. *(Violet has stethoscope during this.)*
Mother:	And then, the next thing that happened is that mommy and daddy's car, the Saab car, broke down.
AB:	Just yesterday—right? Yesterday morning. Daddy got into the Saab car in the morning and then what kind of noises did the Saab car make?
Violet:	*(Makes noise.)* That kind of noise.
AB:	And daddy got in and said: Oh, that Saab car, that car won't start, and he got so angry. *(Violet smiles as if pleased about the Saab car stalling.)*
Mother:	And it was kind of scary because that's exactly what Violet had been wishing would happen.
AB:	All the time Violet had been wishing that the Saab car would break down because she didn't like it and there—it really did. And that made you very scared, didn't it?
Violet:	Yes.
AB:	That made you very scared that *you* did it?
Violet:	Yes.

AB comments: Violet didn't like the replacement for the broken-down car and when the new car did not start she felt herself responsible.

AB:	Mommy knows you didn't do it, daddy knows, Anni knows. Daddy wasn't angry with you, you know. Daddy was very angry yesterday, you told me, and sometimes

when people are angry you always think they are angry with you. And so maybe you thought yesterday that daddy was really angry with you.

Violet: No, I don't. I used to. I don't like daddy to get angry with me.

Mother: That's scary, isn't it?

Violet: That's very bad.

Mother: It even scares me when he gets angry with me. I get scared too. But it wasn't anything you thought that made it break down; it wasn't anything you did or anything you said that made it break down. It just happened.

Film is stopped—Informal discussion

DR. MAHLER: Violet's mother at this point expressed how the parents felt about Violet when she was one year old: how they consulted different professionals, how their anxieties and their perplexities prompted them to seek help at Masters. She described their near hopelessness when Violet was about two years of age. Now, when Violet is ten years old however, the parents feel differently. Mother feels it is "worthwhile to stay around this area longer"—in other words, to stay with treatment.

And *then*, when you see the very last section of the film showing Violet as an adolescent, you will be able to judge for yourself how worthwhile it was to continue Violet's treatment with Mrs. Bergman.

Film resumes with sound track

The *mother comments:* When we first came here Violet was two and one-half and the situation was rather critical. We had just had her tested which indicated she had a very high intelligence. One doctor had said that she was brain-injured, and the pediatrician had promised a very dire future for us.

So we were all quite depressed and quite disturbed and upset. And I think that it took maybe two or three years before there were any major changes. The child was so—so far removed from anything close to real life that it was impossible for her ever—ever to approach humanity. And I don't feel that anymore. She was not really a person then; she was a thing. And she is no longer a thing. She may be a very difficult person—and a very trying one—and there are times when I just wish to be away from her for a long, long, long time.

There was a time when I didn't think our family with Violet had much future at all. I no longer feel this way. I don't know what it is, and I don't know what we will do, or how long we will be in this area because of her—but I do feel that it is worth staying around for—and trying.

Second reel

AB comments: Violet is now fifteen and one-half years old—only one year behind her regular class.

AB:	Would you like to read some of that (her diary)? Or we could also just talk. Whatever you'd like.
Violet:	It doesn't matter to me.
AB:	Why don't you read? Read a little bit. Maybe that will get you started. Pick something you like.
Violet:	I wrote five chapters so far.
AB:	What?
Violet:	I have five chapters.
AB:	Well, you can't read it all. So choose something that you like very much, and read that.
Violet:	The fact is I don't really care for anything yet.
AB:	. . . and that will get you started talking.
Violet:	Oh well, I guess I'll read.
AB:	OK.
Violet:	"We are almost there now," said my father to me and mom. I did not turn my head to his voice. I walked between mom and dad silently. I felt resentful inside. Just one more block and we'd be there—the front door. We were always going to Anni Bergman's house. I had to see her because I was stricken with mental illness. I was practically insane!

My parents hated me—or in my eyes they did. I was a pain in the neck. I looked down at the dirty cement sidewalk covered with crushed chewing gum and dog crap. Disgusting! You had to watch where you step. Well, we got there in five minutes. Daddy lifted me up to ring the doorbell button. Masters was a four-story, red brick building. Anni worked there. Anni greeted us warmly as usual—but unfortunately today was one of my bad days. I was ashamed of my mental illness and of Anni—and especially of myself, period. I loved her but I would never admit that to myself, never! I hated her encouragement and lectures about my illness. I didn't like to be pitied! I did not! I brushed my short blond hair from my face impatiently and removed my mental mind out of reality, out of my body into a strange world of my own. I saw myself instead at a beach, not unlike Coney Island. In fact, it was Coney Island. I was playing in the cool, bluish green waves with other kids my own age and I actually talked to them. I was perfect! I had long hair, soft and silky, and it was wavy all the way down to my waist. I also had a rubber seahorse raft which was inflated with air. It was a cool blue with green fins and face. It was perfect, too; better than anything in my reality. And I was also wearing a red and white, polka-dotted, two-piece swimsuit. I was sexy, man! Anni rudely entered upon my train of thought and said: Come, Violet, let's go to the playroom. And here I was once more with my short hair, which I hated, and my mental illness. But one day, I thought, I would have long hair and I'd be perfect.

AB: Let's see, yesterday we talked about so many things.

Violet: Yes, like how I changed—another year of Blueberry Cove—right?

AB: Right.

Violet: How to start? That's a good one (question).

AB: How to start is always hard.

Violet: It's sure worse than writing a book. If I may say so.

AB: You mean to start a conversation like this is even worse than writing a book?

Violet:	Right! At least we are not showing it (the film) to everybody on Broadway.
AB:	On Broadway?
Violet:	On Times Square.
AB:	No. What kind of curtains do you want?
Violet:	Patchwork. I was going to make my own curtains. What I really wanted was roll-up shades.
AB:	Roll-up shades? Well, I thought that your mom said that you had to get shades, no? And you finally ended up getting curtains?
Violet:	That's right. Shades and curtains. I wish she would let me choose my own furniture. It's my room.
AB:	That's right. You like to choose things.
Violet:	That's why I'm so mad at my parents lately. And now I'm mad at them because they got this stupid folding door. I almost broke it today. Almost broke one of those little thingies right off the door.
AB:	How did that happen?
Violet:	I don't know. I just didn't shut it right. So damned delicate. God! As soon as I get the time, I'm going to patch up a whole thing of curtains, clothes—a bedspread, and a quilt. I'm going to make it of all my fabrics, because I must get rid of all my scraps. I have so much scrap, I can't get any more fabric until it's done.
AB:	I see. So you're going to make your own curtains and—
Violet:	I'm going to make my curtains. Like the one over there. Only more colorful, the colors will be stronger, they won't be so faded. And I'm going to make a quilt. It won't be anything special—really fantastic—but it'll be nice.
AB:	And you'll like it.
Violet:	And probably my own rug. And that should tell my mother no matter what she does she cannot get in my way. I am so set in my own way.
AB:	And she and you have a hard time agreeing on things.
Violet:	That's right. I'm not going to ask her for any clothes this spring. I'm not. I'm going to buy everything myself! I mean it. I just don't think I need any more clothes until

next summer. I have a lot of clothes which I never wear anyway. Because I never get a chance to wear them.

It will be hard as hell for me, but I'll have to get used to it. Because, after all, when I'm grown up I won't have to buy so much clothes.

AB: What should we talk about now?

Violet: About music.

AB: About music—And about your parents who play music so much. And they have so many friends who are musicians. And they play music.

Violet: That's right and almost none of my friends are musicians.

AB: When they play music you were just saying how you felt left out.

Violet: Not *my* friends!

AB: No, no—when your parents play music.

Violet: I feel bored. They have friends over—I wished I had friends over. I feel like getting even with them.

AB: But you said when they play music they don't pay attention to you.

Violet: Not my friends. Theirs.

AB: No, when your parents' (friends)—

Violet: They're very nice with friends but then when they're alone they get grumpy again. That's the thing. And you know, like today—my father's sick and I acted up and I didn't mean to, I was innocent.

Violet: *(Thoughtfully)* Most kids love their mother one way or another, don't they? . . . Also, she listens to my telephone conversations!

AB: Which telephone conversations?

Violet: To my friends, especially Rebecca, that's the one she really likes to listen. And to Chip—that's one she really gets a kick out of it. And then Chip—in her opinion, I really play the tragic actress.

AB: I see.

Violet: You know, that's really bullshit. It's just that I particularly don't care for music when my parents mess around with it too much. That's the time I still don't feel very independent.

I want to chance to be myself, to find out who I am really—
without their interfering.
(Violet meanwhile assembles the flute.)

End of film—Open discussion from the floor

DR. MAHLER: We are lucky to have Mrs. Bergman, Violet's therapist, in our midst and I shall ask her to answer questions that I am
sure the audience must have in mind about details of this remarkable
work. For example, I do not have any data how gradual manifestion
of the child's language function came about. As we noted in the film,
Violet's language-sign-understanding greatly antedated her using
verbal means of communication.

ANNI BERGMAN: Long before she talked, actually all along, I
always did think that she understood what I said to her. Reading was
a different matter. She did read a little bit, even very early (age five)
when she printed subway signs like "Seventh Avenue Express," but
real reading only came later, after she talked.

The beginning of speech was a gradual, very slow process. It
began around the age of eight when she spent many hours a week
with a young nursery school teacher, in addition to the long therapy
hours; the purpose was to relieve the mother further and also to make
it possible for Violet to have experiences in the outside world
through contact with an understanding, nonanxious young adult—
someone to act as a bridge to the outside world.

This young teacher was the first in a long series of therapeutic
companions. Only this year, 1975, for the first time did Violet say that
she no longer needs a "grown-up friend."

Now to go back to the beginning of speech. The first words all
had to do with the body: she touched mother's ears and said "ears"—
other early words were "belly button" and "lollipop." I remember
the first time she said "mommy." Her mother said "mommy" back to
her. The mother felt, at that point, as if her child had always said
"mommy" to her. But then, as you heard in the film depicting Violet
at ten years of age, she addressed her mother as Jean Anne and also
her father by his first name. She hated the words "mommy" and
"daddy" until very recently.

DR. MAHLER: May I say that even in her early years, when I still knew Violet very intimately, I felt that she understood words, that she understood even very complicated sentences. As with much less disturbed children and even normal children, there was a very, very long gap between the understanding of words and the uttering of the same words. It is very interesting that this child who really could communicate and express her feelings through music (she had been a veritable musical prodigy) later on lost the overgiftedness and even moderate amount of libido for communicating through music after she had acquired language.

Mrs. Bergman is asked to say a word about the father

ANNI BERGMAN: The father is also a musician who has had to work very, very hard to keep the family going. When they first came they had very little money—he was really a struggling musician. He's doing much better now. Violet's relationship to him is much closer now than it was earlier in her life. She complains that she doesn't see much of him because he works so hard. When she was small, sometimes he could be available when the mother was not; but there were other times, especially when she grew up, when he was very, very sarcastic with her and that troubled her very much. There was really a long time when he just couldn't believe that she would be all right and he was very disturbed by this. But right now I think their relationship is better. He's a rather distant person anyway, who tends to withdraw quite a bit himself; but he is a very talented musician.

DR. MAHLER: May I just say a few words? Mrs. Bergman has emphasized to me that the child has reached the oedipal phase. I don't know how many of you have read Manuel Furer's excellent paper (1964) in which he describes the very great delay in psychosexual development of psychotic children. Mrs. Bergman explained to me how much this particular child has been delayed in her psychosexual development. I don't know at what time or at what age the usual psychosexual phases were reached. We do know they were reached much, much later than one would expect.

ANNI BERGMAN: At the moment she's thinking about boy friends and she's thinking about getting married; she thinks about making love, when she will do it, and who will be the first boy. She makes a great point of how she will wait until she finds someone she really, really likes and who really, really likes her. And she repeatedly says she will wait until she finds somebody special so that even if they get mad at each other they can still appreciate each other. And she adds: like my parents, they've been very lucky that way.

DR. PAO: Mrs. Bergman, I admire your work a great deal. There is a lot of parallelism between our work and your work. One question I'd like to raise is this: sometimes we get very discouraged and we need some kind of—as Dr. Mahler called it—a refueling from our supervisors. How did you deal with the temporary despair that sometimes you must have had?

ANNI BERGMAN: I also needed and got some kind of refueling. What was tremendously important was the staff of Masters Children's Center and especially the work with our supervisors, Dr. Mahler and Dr. Furer. Without all that help and support it certainly wouldn't have been possible. And then, beyond that, I don't know what takes you through. Sometimes I wonder how I kept going, especially during the years when she wasn't talking at all and I had to spend hour after hour with her without any verbal communication. But I guess there was just something about her that prevented me from giving up! She was very talented and something made you feel that she was moving. She had a strong appeal.

Chapter 15

ON SADNESS AND GRIEF IN INFANCY AND CHILDHOOD: LOSS AND RESTORATION OF THE SYMBIOTIC LOVE OBJECT

[1961]

There is a conspicuous gap in our understanding of the connecting links between those conditions which Spitz (1946) has described as "anaclitic depression" and other psychotic pictures in early infancy. While anaclitic depressions occur in the second half of the first year of life, the other psychotic conditions may, or may not, have their prestages in the first year of life; however, they definitely develop during the separation-individuation phase of normal development, that is, from five to thirteen months of age.

According to Spitz, anaclitic depression is the equivalent of "primal parathymia," which was described by Abraham (1924) as the infantile prototype of a later depressive psychosis. Spitz considers the syndrome of anaclitic depression a psychosis, although, due to the immaturity of the psychic apparatus, the signs and symptoms differ from those manifested in the psychoses of later life. He feels that by the second half of the first year of life, the ego is sufficiently well organized to control motility and express negative and positive affects. An extreme disturbance in these ego functions could therefore be considered to be psychotic. The chief signs of anaclitic depression in the infants Spitz observed were a dejected expression and posture, and a distaste for motility.

We are all agreed that the cardinal etiological agent in this syndrome, as in other forms of infantile psychosis, is the object loss suffered by these infants. In this connection, Spitz explains that after six months of age, an infant can seek out an adult—that infants who have suffered object loss will attempt to regain the lost object world, as do adults. In infancy, this involves finding a substitute object. The infants in the particular institution Spitz studied had little opportunity to find a substitute object because few could in reality be found.

There is another important etiological factor involved here, and one which we cannot afford to minimize: these anaclitically depressed infants were deprived of maternal care during the second half of the first year of life. *I conceive of this as the symbiotic phase of development, and consider a need-satisfying mother-infant relationship during this period a prerequisite for normal growth.* In previous papers (SPI:6, 7, 9, 10) I delineated my concepts of developmental phases—those of normal autism and normal symbiosis, and of separation-individuation—which form the core of my formulation of infantile psychosis.

In that twilight stage of early life which Freud designated as primary narcissism, the infant shows few signs of being able to perceive anything beyond his own body. He seems to live in a world of inner stimuli. The first weeks of extrauterine life are characterized by what Ferenczi (1913) called the stage of hallucinatory wish fulfillment. Whereas the enteroceptive system functions from birth, the perceptual conscious system, the sensorium, is not yet cathected. This lack of peripheral sensory cathexis only gradually gives way to perception, particularly to distance perception of the outside world. This earliest extrauterine phase, which may be considered a normal autistic phase of the mother-infant unity, gives way to the symbiotic phase proper (from the second month of life on). During his wakeful, hungry periods, the three- to four-month-old baby seems to perceive, temporarily at least, the Gestalt of that small part of external reality which is represented by the mother's breast, face, and hands—that is, what is perceived as her ministrations.

I wish to emphasize the fact that normal symbiosis implies a complex interaction between the baby and the mother. The Gestalt of the mother's ministrations is a component of the Gestalt of the symbiotic partner, with its highly libidinized affective quality. This stage of development is characterized by the specific smiling response which the symbiotic object elicits, and the discriminatory anxiety and fear of strangers which the infant exhibits at or around eight months of age (Spitz 1950b). The importance of these responses cannot be overestimated. I would also point out that whereas the development from normal autism to normal symbiosis occurs within the matrix of the oral gratification-frustration sequences of the normal nursing situation, it is dependent upon, and synonymous with, need satisfaction only in a very broad sense. This development involves much more than the satisfaction of oral and other vegetative needs. The primitive ego seems to possess an amazing ability to absorb and synthesize complex object images without adverse effect, and on occasion even with benefit. Thus, the Gestalt of the nurse, who may be relegated to the function of providing immediate need satisfaction, is synthesized with the Gestalt of the mother, who may be available only as an additional or transient external ego. However, it is truly impressive that although the mother may be less involved in the actual care of the infant, her image seems to attract so much cathexis that it often, though not always, becomes the cardinal object representation. This crucial phenomenon is rarely mentioned in the literature, and to my knowledge has never been investigated in a systematic study. Freud's paper on Leonardo (1910a) and Helene Deutsch's "A Two-Year-Old's First Love Comes to Grief" (1919) are thought-provoking classics in this direction.

Although the representations of the symbiotic object are extremely complex during this crucial phase of development, and although the Gestalt of the need-satisfying object and her ministrations are highly specific, there seems to be dim awareness only of the boundaries of the self, as distinct from the boundaries of the "symbiotic object." During the symbiotic phase the infant behaves and functions as though he and his mother were an omnipotent system (a dual unity) within one common boundary (a symbiotic membrane, as it were).

Toward the latter part of the symbiotic stage, we generally assume, primary narcissism declines and gradually gives way to secondary narcissism. The infant takes his own body, as well as the mother, as the object of his secondary narcissism. The concept of narcissism, however, remains rather obscure in both psychoanalytic theory and usage unless we place sufficient emphasis on the vicissitudes of the aggressive drive.

During the course of normal development, protective systems safeguard the infant's body from the oral-sadistic pressures which begin to constitute a potential threat to his body integrity from the fourth month on (Hoffer 1950a). The pain barrier is one such device. In addition, Hoffer (1950b) particularly emphasized that adequate libidinization of the body, within the mother-infant relationship, is important for the development of the body image.

Only when the body becomes the object of the infant's secondary narcissism, via the mother's loving care, does the external object become eligible for identification. To quote Hoffer (1950a), from the age of three or four months on, "primary narcissism has already been modified, but the world of objects has not necessarily yet taken on definite shape." Identification enables the infant to separate from the mother gradually, and to leave her outside the hitherto "omnipotent common orbit," by cathecting the "self-boundaries" (p. 159).

Normal symbiosis paves the way for the separation-individuation phase, which overlaps with and replaces the symbiotic phase. As a result of the maturational spurt during the second year of life, the normal toddler achieves relatively advanced physical autonomy. At this time, the autonomous ego function of locomotion may become the most conspicuous paradigm of discrepancy between the rate of maturation and the rate of personality development.[1] Locomotion enables the child to separate physically—to move away—from the mother, although he may be emotionally quite unprepared to do so. The two-year-old becomes aware of his separateness in many other ways as well. He enjoys his independence, and perseveres with great tenacity in his attempts at mastery. In this way, large quantities of libido and aggression are utilized by the ego. On the other hand, some children react to this newly acquired autonomy adversely and with increased clinging to the mother. The realization that they

1. Hartmann, Kris, and Loewenstein (1946) have introduced the helpful distinction between the concepts of development and maturation.

function separately may elicit intense anxiety in vulnerable toddlers, who then try desperately to deny their separateness and to struggle against reengulfment by increased opposition to the adults in their environment. At the Masters Children's Center we are currently investigating the various reactions of separation-individuation.[2] This research project involves the intensive study of the interaction between the infants from four-five to thirty-six months of age and their mothers. It is being conducted in a natural and informal indoor-playground setting. We are gathering participant and non-participant observational material of normal development, with particular emphasis on the specific steps in the various processes of disengagement from the symbiotic object, which we know so little about. In a second research project, we are investigating symbiotic psychotic toddlers. This study is being conducted within the framework of a therapeutic setting, in which the children and their mothers are simultaneously present (*SPI*: 13).[3]

The toddler is able to experiment with, practice, and enjoy the autonomous functions of his ego only if personality development and maturation proceed at a comparable rate. Mastery of these functions gives the child secondary narcissistic pleasure, as Hendrick (1942) has pointed out. Moreover, such experiences eventually help the child to acquire a sense of individual identity.

It must be quite obvious at this point, theoretically at least, that the toddler is not able to cope with the demands of the separation-individuation phase of development unless the preceding symbiotic phase has been satisfactory.

The most severe traumatization during the symbiotic phase is that suffered by anaclitically depressed infants who had actually been separated from the central love object during this phase. They had suffered object loss in reality—and substitute mothers had not been available. Yet, when the mother was restored to the baby, and when this occurred within a reasonable period of time, before his ego had

2. This research project had been sponsored by the Field Foundation and was later supported by the Psychoanalytic Research and Development Fund, Inc., and by the Taconic Foundation.

3. "The Natural History of Symbiotic Child Psychosis," sponsored by a grant from the National Institutes of Mental Health of the United States Public Health Service.

suffered irreversible damage, the infant recovered. It is interesting to speculate which mechanisms account for this striking recovery potential in these anaclitically depressed infants.

We are similarly puzzled, though for quite different reasons, by another fact: the anamnesis of children with autistic and symbiotic psychosis do not indicate, or only very rarely, that separation, of any significant duration, from the mother actually occurred. In the majority of these cases, there was no real loss of the symbiotic object, beyond those brief separations which most normal infants experience in the course of the first two or three years of life. I refer to such ubiquitous traumata as transient separation from the mother due to the birth of a sibling, or due to hospitalization of either mother or child. When such events occur during the second half of the first year of life and later, during the crucial separation-individuation phase, there is no doubt that the toddler suffers considerably. However, most toddlers and most babies are able to accept substitute love objects if these are at all available during the mother's absence. They seem to be able to develop and sustain the mental image of the original symbiotic object. This enables them to enjoy need satisfaction from a substitute temporarily and then to restore the original image after reunion.

Two groups of babies come to mind which bring this seeming contradiction in our prognostic formulations into even sharper focus. The infants I am thinking of were subjected to unusually frequent substitution of need-satisfying (symbiotic) objects. Concurrently, they had to cope with the permanent loss of the original love object—the mother. I refer to the infants described by Anna Freud and Sophie Dann (1951) and the group studied by William Goldfarb (1945). The children described by Anna Freud and Sophie Dann had been in concentration camps. Their mothers had been brutally taken from them. Nor were they able to establish a stable symbiotic relationship with the succession of substitute mothers who were abruptly taken from them also. The babies in William Goldfarb's studies, referred to by Bowlby (1951), had been placed in foster homes, and moved from one home to another with great frequency. Yet, amidst the most trying circumstances, these infants were able to extract, as it were, substitutions for the actual loss of mothering.

Although they may have paid the price for this object loss with neurotic disorders, character distortions, or psychopathic difficulties later in life, they *never* severed their ties with reality. We must assume that their rudimentary egos were able to sustain some kind of memory trace of earlier need satisfaction from an external human source, that some vestige of confident expectation remained operative, that they could integrate whatever meager substitute maternal care was available, and that they were able to utilize to the utmost the autoerotic resources of their own bodies and probably also of transitional objects (Winnicott 1953). In other words, they were able to create a nondehumanized narcissistic orbit for themselves.

Edith Jacobson's work (1954) regarding the ego's capacity to create mental representations of the self and the object world, which complements the concepts of Anna Freud (1952c) and Heinz Hartmann (1952) of ego development as dependent on the libidinal object, is particularly pertinent here.

In what follows I shall attempt to apply Jacobson's concept of mental representation to those cases of so-called atypical development where the psychosis was not due to *actual* separation from the symbiotic object. The pivotal disturbance in early infantile autism— or *primary autism*, as I would prefer to call it (Mahler, Furer, and Settlage 1959)—lies in the child's inability to perceive the Gestalt of the mother, and concomitantly the Gestalt of her vital functioning on his behalf. There seems to be no perceptual differentiation between an inside world as opposed to an outside world; the child seems to have no awareness of his self, as distinct from the inanimate environment.

The symbiotic psychotic syndrome (*SPI*:7) represents fixation at, or regression to, the *second undifferentiated stage* of the mother-child unity, which is characterized by delusional, omnipotent symbiotic fusion with the need-satisfying object.

In the cases described in the psychoanalytic literature as atypical, psychotic, primarily depressed, schizophrenic, etc., authors have duly and emphatically explored the minute details of the traumata inflicted by fate, or by the nature of the mother's personality, upon the mother-infant dual unity in the early life of those infants.

1. In one group of such cases there were repeated separations from

the mother. It was either immediately evident, or was reconstructed by the parents in retrospect, that these infants would not accept substitutes for the original maternal care, although such substitutes were available.

2. In a second group there was overwhelming proprioceptive stimulation and painful illness, coupled with a hampering of affectomotor tension release. The disturbance in these cases did not come to the fore before the peak of the separation-individuation phase. When it did become manifest, the environment was confronted with the fact that the infant had suffered a severe break with reality.

3. There is a third group of children whose anamneses contained both factual and exaggerated retrospective accounts, provided by parents who were motivated by a deep sense of guilt and a desire for atonement, of multiple traumatizations, which were inflicted on the primitive ego by a cruel disregard of the child's needs and signals.

4. In another group of cases there was an abnormal bodily closeness between mother and child, a primitive, exclusive appersonation, inflicted on the child during the first eighteen months of life by the mother, which then might have been abruptly ended by some fateful event. Concomitantly with this exclusive, mutually parasitic symbiosis, there was an utter disregard of the infant's need for individuation—indeed, any differentiated needs other than purely vegetative ones were disregarded. The sequelae of these conditions included a blurring or extinguishing of the perceptual awareness of the gratification-frustration sequences. As might be expected, the symbiotic relationship in such cases was stifling, the emotional relationship empty and joyless, providing little opportunity for promoting mutuality and object constancy.

5. The most conspicuous factor in the fifth and final category of these atypical cases is the grossly unpredictable quality of maternal attitudes. There is evidence of crude overstimulation and all kinds of seductions of the baby, alternating with abrupt withdrawal and abandonment, leaving the infant to his own devices.[4]

In reviewing the cases in the literature, and those histories with

---

4. In my clinical work as well as in our research project, we have seen an increasing number of cases which would fall into the last two categories.

which I am personally familiar, I found many examples in which the mother's relationship with the child was undoubtedly gravely deficient. I would emphasize, however, that I also found many which indicated that there was a reasonable emotional response on the part of the mother, and where, furthermore, the infant seemed to have shown signs of pleasurable anticipation of need satisfaction by the living object, at least during the first twelve to eighteen months of his life. I am thinking of that group of cases of early infantile psychosis in which, temporarily at least, marked symbiotic interaction between baby and mother did obtain. We are further puzzled by the fact that although in the majority of cases we find abundant traumatization of the mother-child unity, there are many cases in which neither the timing, nor the severity, nor the multiplicity of these insults would account for the severe fragmentation and regression of the ego of these infants.

The foregoing description of the various categories of anamneses does of course permit us to draw certain conclusions about the personality of the mothers of these children. Undoubtedly, there is a large percentage of infantile personalities among them; there is a sprinkling of detached schizoid personalities; there are many who have acted out symbiotic-parasitic claims upon the infant, over-stimulating and then abruptly abandoning him. Many of the mothers had suffered from a measure of postpartum depression. But on the whole, we are impressed with the number of mothers who would have been accepted for membership in Winnicott's large group of ordinary devoted mothers. Many experienced workers in the field— e.g., Bender, Despert, Anna Maenchen, and Annemarie Weil—have reached the same conclusion regarding these so-called "schizophrenogenic" mothers.

We thus become increasingly aware of the enigma which confronts us. On the one hand, in the face of serious insults to the mother-infant symbiotic relationship, most infants progress without severing their ties with reality. On the other hand, these atypical children, whose traumatization was no more severe, either in quality or quantity, have broken with reality, regressed, and fallen back to their own devices—that is to say, regressed to the autistic state.

Obviously, some unknown factor, or combination of factors, is at work. I believe that the cardinal precipitating event in these cases of infantile psychosis is the breakdown of that highly subtle "circular process" to which Emmy Sylvester (1947, 1953) has called attention: the mutually reciprocal relationship which enables mother and infant to send out, and receive, each other's signals, a compatible predictable interreaction, as it were.

If the infant's signals do not reach the mother because he is unable to send them, or if the infant's signals are not heeded because the mother does not have the capacity to react to them, the mother-infant circular interreaction pattern takes on a dangerously discordant rhythm. Gratification-frustration sequences are unpredictable, and utter disorientation as to inner tension versus gratification from an outside source obtains. Under such circumstances, the infant cannot develop a capacity for confident expectation (Benedek 1938), for basic trust (Erikson 1950), which would enable him, from the third or fourth month on, to keep disruptive impulses toward immediate tension discharge in abeyance—a first prerequisite for the formation of ego structure.

Another vicissitude of the earliest mother-infant dual unity stage (which represents the normal autistic stage in the infant's development) may derive from the fact that the infant is handled as a purely vegetative being and consequently is unable to develop signals to indicate his needs. His hunger is saturated and stifled before he can become aware of tension from within. Furthermore, the gratification of oral and other purely physiological needs is dissociated from the more subtle and complex satisfaction of those human needs which David M. Levy (1937) had called affect hunger. I mean by this that there is no integration of the memory traces of oral and other purely physiological gratifications with their affective concomitants, that is, the complex Gestalt of human maternal ministrations. In short, there is no incentive for the infant to anticipate tension release from an outside need-satisfying agent, and no reliable beacon to orient him toward such a pattern.

Whereas the primarily autistic child has never been able to develop the complex mental image of the symbiotic maternal partner, there are other infants, particularly those with an inherently great sensitivity (Bergman and Escalona 1949) and very low tolerance for frustration, who seem to develop the complex representation of the symbiotic object and seem to proceed to the symbiotic phase. However, they seem to be able to achieve homeostasis only by permanently drawing the need-satisfying object into the inner milieu in Hoffer's sense. Hence, there is fixation to the omnipotent symbiotic dual unity without the quality of fluidity which pertains to its normal form and which should pave the way to separation-individuation. In such cases, mental representation of the symbiotic object is quite rigidly and permanently fixated to the primitive representation of the self. When in the course of maturational growth the ego is confronted with the incontrovertible *fact of separateness*, the fused symbiotic representations of self and object do not allow for progress toward individuation. We then see the catastrophic rage-panic reactions, which I have described as typical of the symbiotic psychotic syndrome. However, no organism can tolerate chronic panic. Hence, there occurs regression to secondary autism and other primary symbiotic and secondary autistic mechanisms in various combinations. The sequelae of object loss were described by many authors, among them by Rochlin (1953a, 1959), Mahler and Elkisch (SPI:11), Elkisch and Mahler (SPI:12), and Mahler (SPI:10).

In a rather advanced conceptualization, Spitz equated, or at least compared, anaclitic depression in infancy with melancholia in adulthood. Spitz suggests that whereas in melancholia the aggression of the superego is turned against the ego, in anaclitic depression the superego is still the external love object, whose sadism is turned against the infant.

We know that systematized affective disorders are unknown in childhood. It has been conclusively established that the immature personality structure of the infant or older child is not capable of producing a state of depression such as that seen in the adult (Zetzel 1953, 1960). *But grief as a basic ego reaction does prevail.* This implies that as soon as the ego emerges from the undifferentiated phase, the mimetic, gestural, and physiological signs of grief do appear, albeit in rudimentary form. The child's grief is remarkably short-lived because his ego cannot sustain itself without taking prompt defensive actions against object loss. It cannot survive in an objectless state for any length of time (SPI:10). Mechanisms other than bereavement, such as substitution, denial, and repression, soon take over in various combinations. Children recover from transient reactions of mourning, accordingly, with lesser or greater scar formation.

Edward Bibring (1953) pointed out that both anxiety and depression are basic ego reactions. Bibring's definition of depression as the emotional expression of a state of helplessness is generally applicable, I believe, and contributes to our understanding of the ego's fluidity and vulnerability during the phase when the dim self-image and symbiotic object representation are differentiated. Bibring emphasized that frequent frustrations of the child's needs may at first mobilize anxiety and anger. However, if frustration continues, despite the "signals" produced by the infant, his initial anger will be replaced by feelings of exhaustion, helplessness, and depression. The emphasis in this hypothesis is not on oral frustration and subsequent oral fixation but on the infant's or young child's shocklike experience of, and fixation to, feelings of helplessness. Freud (1926) made the following statement concerning grief:

> [The infant] is not yet able to distinguish temporary absence from permanent loss; when he fails to see his mother . . . , he behaves as though he would never see her again, and it requires repeated consoling experiences before he learns that such disappearance on his mother's part is usually followed by her reappearance. The mother promotes this knowledge . . . by playing with him the familiar game of covering her face and then to his joy revealing it again. Thus he is enabled, as it were, to experience longing without despair. . . . Subsequent thereto, repeated situations in which gratification was experienced have created out of the mother the object who is the recipient, when a need arises, of an intense cathexis, a cathexis which we may call *"longingful"* [pp. 118-119].

We may define grief as the reaction specific to object loss, and anxiety as the reaction specific to the danger which this loss entails. This connection, this kinship, between the affective state of longing and the modulated, ego-filtered emotions of grief and depression was emphasized by David Rapaport (1959) in his paper given in memory of Edward Bibring. This subjective affective reaction, reminiscent of depression, seems in children to consist of a vague realization of helplessness, of the ego's apprehension lest the libidinal object fail to come to its rescue in the face of mounting inner tension. But I would emphasize that the ego must be structured enough to permit enough respite to mobilize sufficient vestiges of confident expectation and hence must allow for the secondary process to delay discharge. Only if these conditions obtain is it possible to experience the subjective affect of longing, which, to my mind, is a precursor of the ego-filtered affect of sadness and grief.

I shall illustrate the dynamics of this process by briefly citing some of the findings we have so far amassed in our therapeutic action research with symbiotic psychotic toddlers. This therapeutic research aims at facilitating the child's capacity to restore the need-satisfying symbiotic object, to create a representation of the good object, as it were. We have been particularly interested in observing the general feeling tone of the child's affective manifestations and moods during this process. It is a well-known fact that the affective responses of the psychotic child who has regressed to a comfortably restricted autistic world of his own will be minimal unless this autistic, omnipotent, dedifferentiated world is upset. Thus, when both therapy and the unfamiliar environment of the Center impinge upon his autistic withdrawal, his affective reactions may range widely from wandering off and searching,[5] to incessant, hyperactive, irritable restlessness and fretting, to abysmal panic reactions, fits of rage, temper tantrums, head banging, self-biting, and other grossly autoaggressive acts, until he reaches a state of exhaustion or extreme apathy. Then, as the child begins to retrieve the symbiotic object and to cathect its representation with libido, we observe more ego-filtered moods and emotions. These manifestations mark the first stage of giving up and replacing autistic defenses; they also mark the ego's emergence as a functional structure of the personality.

These processes could be observed in several children. Amy, at the age of three and a half, was aimlessly preoccupied with such stereo-typed activities as pouring water or sand all over. She was unable to focus and instead seemed to look through people. She urinated and

5. Compare Imre Hermann's work (1936).

defecated whenever she was so prompted by an urge for bodily discharge; and she darted about, snatching at objects. The slightest change in the environment evoked loud shrieks or prolonged whining. Amy reacted to frustrations, however minor, with desperate temper tantrums and excessive hyperactivity.

In the course of our therapeutic action research, Amy became noticeably attached to her therapist using the latter in a most primitive way as an extension to her ego, as a need-satisfying tool. Concomitant with this development, Amy retained her stools and held other tensions in abeyance as well. At this point the child who previously had alternated between reckless hyperactivity and exhausted lethargy occasionally began to display by her mien and gestures sadness and even grief.

By restoring the human object, therapy had helped Amy to form some representations of a symbiotic object. Yet, precisely in this phase of therapy Amy cried inconsolably at the sound of such trigger words as crib, blanket, lying down, going to sleep. Though her sleep itself was not disturbed, it seemed to us that Amy at this point showed a mechanism resembling those which transiently occur in the normal sleep disturbances of two-year-old normal toddlers.

In a panel on Sleep Disturbances in Children (see Friend 1956), Anna Maenchen considered "the *unspecified maturational reluctance* to retreat from all the activity and autonomy of waking life" in early childhood. Marianne Kris mentioned Dr. Frankl's experience as a newspaper consultant in London. Dr. Frankl had "most requests for help with sleep disturbances in a two-year-old group." The intimate connection between the loss of object relationship and considerations of regression is important in these transient sleep disturbances. It is interesting that we, as well as other investigators of psychoses in children, have had the experience that predominantly autistic children did not suffer from sleep disturbances, while those who were predominantly symbiotic sooner or later did develop sleep impairments. Maenchen feels that the child "once withdrawn into its autistic shell is no longer afraid until he comes out of the withdrawal." Conversely, the appearance of sleep disturbances, according to her, could be an indication that progress in ego development is being resumed. In Amy's case, I think her anxiety reaction and fretting when words reminding her of the state of ego regression in sleep were mentioned indicated a growing awareness of human object relationship. When Amy began to evolve the image or concept of a symbiotic object, she became aware of the danger which losing the symbiosis with this object in sleep entailed.

When Michael, another three-and-a-half-year-old psychotic child, came to our attention, he had achieved a much higher level of integration than Amy. When he arrived with his "ordinary, devoted mother" at the Center he wore at times the frozen expression which is so characteristic of primarily or secondarily autistic children. He responded to his mother and usually was in contact with her—albeit in a rather primary-process fashion. He later established a similarly patterned relationship with his therapist, provided his demands were correctly guessed and promptly fulfilled. His little face lit up imme-diately, however, when someone suggested the game of telephoning his daddy. He assumed a longing, wistful expression while on the toy telephone he carried on his imaginary conversation with his father. Michael also engaged in a passionate contact with a male doctor in our research group, snuggled up to him, and looked crestfallen and sad whenever the doctor left the room. Michael's peculiar symbiotic relationship with his father gave way only very gradually—via a re-experiencing of the symbiotic relationship with the therapist, and subsequently with his mother, by externalizing split-up representa-tions of self and object, and by concentrating libido on the represen-tation of the good mother and projecting his aggression onto the image of the bad mother. Only after the delusional, pathological symbiotic tie with his father was loosened could Michael experience, for the first time, the communion he had missed in his relationship with his mother. During this phase, which began after Michael allowed himself to spit at people, his therapeutic sessions involved endless babbling, cooing, and gurgling with his mother. Inciden-tally, his mother said to us: "Michael seems to be having the same experiences with me now that his two older brothers had with me when they were babes in arms."

Within the framework of our research, the emotional manifesta-tions of psychotic children have been observed to range widely, from unmitigated, extreme affective and affectomotor phenomena, which are characterized by the predominance of unneutralized aggression and tension-discharge processes, to the more ego-filtered, amalgamated emotional accompaniments of the secondary process which Edith Jacobson (1957b) has described as moods.

In therapy, we have also observed that restoration of the libidinal object renders these toddlers susceptible to sadness and grief. In fact, once their autistic armor has been pierced, they become particularly vulnerable to emotional frustration, helplessness, and despair.

David Rapaport (1959) has pointed out, as Bibring (1953) implied, that grief is a genetically late, "tamed" reactivation of feelings of helplessness. In our present frame of reference this concept must be amplified by additional genetic considerations. Grief is dependent upon that measure of human object cathexis which prevails from the second half of the first year on; it is dependent upon the cathexis of the living Gestalt of the need-satisfying mother.

In the conventional therapeutic setting, the goal has been to permit the child to relive in a corrective way the missed and distorted developmental stages. However, all to frequently, this goal is undermined by the fact that it requires superhuman effort and endurance on the part of the mother.

As early as 1952, I realized the inadequacy of treating the psychotic child who had regressed and organized his defenses for adaptation and survival within his secondarily created autistic shell, without full participation of the original symbiotic object, the mother. At that time I wrote:

> If the [primarily or secondarily] autistic [child] is forced too rapidly into social contact, . . . he is often thrown into a catatonic state and then [into a] . . . fulminant psychotic process. . . . if such catastrophic reactions cannot be avoided, it seems that such autistic infants are better off if allowed to remain in their autistic shell, even though in "a daze of restricted orientation" they may drift into a very limited degree of reality adjustment only. Diagnosis of their "original condition," of course, then usually escapes recognition; they are thrown into the category of the feebleminded [SPI:6].

A most dramatic episode occurred in little Lotta's life, who was brought for treatment at the age of three years four months as a mute autistic child. At four and a half years of age, after she had established a symbiotic relationship with me in the second year of analytic treatment, the family moved to a distant suburb. As a result, her treatment was interrupted and her inanimate environment was radically changed. I subsequently received a call from her desperate mother, and visited them. Lotta epitomized the most heart-rending and tragic picture of utter bereavement. She was unable to focus on me; instead she behaved as if she wished to ward off the very perception of my presence by agitated creeping and sliding on her buttocks on the garden grounds, by rocking and throwing garden earth onto her disheveled little head with both hands; by whining pitifully, but without tears and without any sign of appeal to the humans around her. All the signals which she had learned in therapy, and which had enabled me to fulfill Lotta's needs, were lost. This signal language, syncretic in nature, but well libidinized, had involved confidence and pleasurable anticipation. Now Lotta warded off any approach from either her mother or me. Needless to say, it was most difficult and needed great effort to reestablish contact with Lotta when she was brought back for treatment.

Lotta's ego suffered a similar, but much more permanent, and, in fact, irreversible psychic damage when, at the age of about six, she was placed in an institution which housed autistic and organically brain-damaged children. Ironically, she was placed there after she had made a spurt of development in therapy and attained an extensive, though automatonlike vocabulary. This vocabulary had been taught to her by her mother, who had also been able to teach her to perform automatized mental operations which were quite remarkable in their complexity, including the ability to read. Unfortunately, Lotta reached a plateau in this automatic learning, and her mother, preoccupied with a new pregnancy, was unable to meet Lotta's needs which were manifested in the form of a very distorted and very delicate reaching out. Both parents decided it was just "no use."

Lotta's mother wrote to me about her visit to the institution. The description of Lotta in that letter sounded like the description of an adult in a state of acute melancholia. Lotta did not speak, merely pleaded desperately with her eyes. Her movements were slow and listless; she walked with a shuffling gait. The mother also reported that she refused to eat. Lotta was subsequently taken home, and nursed back to life, so to speak—an utterly automatized and delibidinized life. Her mother was able to train her successfully enough so that Lotta was accepted and enrolled in the public school of the community.

Lotta was brought to my office to visit when she was nine. Her responses were automatic; there was no recognition of me as a person. She remembered syncretically the most minute details of the playroom, and enumerated, in primary-process fashion, all the objects around her. There was an amazing execution of commands which her mother had obviously given her beforehand. For example, whenever I tried to say something personal to her, she would ward off an aggressive impulse from within by loudly reciting, in the voice of a town crier: "Always be polite"; "You should love all the children"; "Go to the blackboard"; "I can do long divisions, I can spell"; "The elevator will take you down"; "You will go home"; "You will sleep home." She used these internalized but unintegrated commands to tame her anxiety and basic mistrust.

Precisely such experiences as those with Lotta and similar ones prompted Dr. Furer and myself to design a therapeutic approach in which the mother can be fully engaged in the treatment process and thus helped to lend herself to her child for reexperiencing the missed and distorted developmental phases. Within this newly developed tripartite therapeutic design, the therapist serves as the catalyst, the transfer agent, and the buffer between the child and mother. Such an approach should forestall the irreversible and catastrophic reaction to the disintegration of a recently established therapeutically imposed symbiosis as we witnessed in Lotta's case.

In a recent paper, David Beres (1960) stated succinctly: "only with the development of the capacity to create mental representations of the absent object, does the child progress from the syncretic, sensory-motor, affective, immediate response to the delayed, abstract, conceptualized response that is characteristically human." This intrapsychic image, this mental representation of the temporarily absent symbiotic object, seems to serve as an indispensable catalyst in that it enables all the potentially autonomous capacities of the primitive ego to become functional. I consider it the spark which ignites the ego's capacity for human affect, for human social and emotional development.

In psychotic children, the breakdown of the ego's basic functions—of all or many of them—can be attributed to either one of the following conditions: (1) the ego's inability to create the relatively complex intrapsychic image of the human symbiotic object; or (2) the loss of a precarious mental representation of the symbiotic object which, because it is excessively linked to need satisfaction on a symbiotic-parasitic level, cannot grow toward object constancy, and which therefore cannot cope with the demands of the separation-individuation phase. We are all familiar with the chronic sequelae of these psychic events. *What we seldom see, and what is rarely described in the literature, is the period of grief and mourning which I believe inevitably precedes and ushers in the complete psychotic break with reality, that is to say, the secondary autistic withdrawal.* In this paper, I have also tried to show that sadness and grief are the first signs of progressive development and seem to be obligatory accompaniments of the child's emergence from the deanimated autistic world through restoration of the libidinal object.

SOURCE NOTES

Chapter 1

Pseudoimbecility: A Magic Cap of Invisibility (1942). REPRINTED FROM *Psychoanalytic Quarterly* 11(2):149-164.

Chapter 2

Les "Enfants Terribles" (1949). Paper read at the Meeting of the New York Psychoanalytic Society, December 1947. REPRINTED FROM *Searchlights on Delinquency,* ed. K. R. Eissler, pp. 77-89. New York: International Universities Press.

Chapter 3

A Psychoanalytic Evaluation of Tic in Psychopathology of Children: Symptomatic Tic and Tic Syndrome (1949). REPRINTED FROM *Psychoanalytic Study of the Child* 3/4:279-310.

Chapter 4

Tics and Impulsions in Children: A Study of Motility (1944). Paper read before the New York Psychoanalytic Society, October 1943. REPRINTED FROM *Psychoanalytic Quarterly* 13(4):430-444.

Chapter 5

Outcome of the Tic Syndrome (1946). In collaboration with Jean A. Luke. REPRINTED FROM *Journal of Nervous and Mental Disease* 103:433-445.

This paper is based upon "Clinical and Follow-up Study of the Tic Syndrome in Children" (1945). *American Journal of Orthopsychiatry* 15:631-647.

Both papers are the results of a research project which was partly financed through the National Committee for Mental Hygiene, from funds granted by the Committee on Research in Dementia Praecox founded by the Supreme Council, 33° Scottish Rite, Northern Masonic Jurisdiction, U.S.A.

Chapter 6

On Symbiotic Child Psychosis: Genetic, Dynamic, and Restitutive Aspects (1955). In collaboration with Bertram J. Gosliner, M.D. Paper read before the New York Psychoanalytic Society, February 1955; later read before the Philadelphia Psychoanalytic Society and at the Austen Riggs Center, Stockbridge, Mass. REPRINTED FROM *Psychoanalytic Study of the Child* 10:195-212.

Chapter 7

On Child Psychosis and Schizophrenia: Autistic and Symbiotic Infantile Psychoses (1952). This is a revised version of a paper given at the 17th International Psychoanalytical Congress, August 1951, Amsterdam. REPRINTED FROM *Psychoanalytic Study of the Child* 7:286-305.

Chapter 8

On Early Infantile Psychosis: The Symbiotic and Autistic Syndromes (1965). This paper is partly based on research conducted at the Masters Children's Center, New York, sponsored by grant M-3353 of the National Institute of Mental Health, USPHS, Bethesda, Md.; Drs. Mahler and Furer, co-principal investigators.

This paper was read to the Department of Psychiatry of New York University School of Medicine, February 1964; to a joint meeting of the Department of Psychiatry, Hadassah University Hospital, and the Albert and Mary Lasker Child Psychiatry Department of Hadassah Medical Organization, March 1964, Jerusalem; and, by invitation at the monthly Basic Sciences Conferences series at McGill University Department of Psychiatry, February 1965, Montreal; and to the Chicago Psychoanalytic Society, February 1965.

REPRINTED FROM *Journal of the American Academy of Child Psychiatry* 4(4):554-568.

Chapter 9

Autism and Symbiosis: Two Extreme Disturbances of Identity (1958). Paper prepared for the Twentieth Congress of the International Psycho-Analytical Association, July-August 1957, Paris. REPRINTED FROM *International Journal of Psycho-Analysis* 39:77-83.

Chapter 10

Perceptual Dedifferentiation and Psychotic Object Relationships (1960). Paper read at the Twenty-first Congress of the International Psycho-Analytical Association, July 1959, Copenhagen. REPRINTED FROM *International Journal of Psychoanalysis* 41:548-553.

Chapter 11

Some Observations on Disturbances of the Ego in a Case of Infantile Psychosis (1953). In collaboration with Paula Elkisch, Ph.D. REPRINTED FROM *Psychoanalytic Study of the Child* 8:252-261.

Chapter 12

On Infantile Precursors of the "Influencing Machine" (Tausk) (1959). Paula Elkisch, Ph.D. in collaboration with Margaret S. Mahler, M.D. First version read at the Meeting of the American Psychoanalytic Association, December 1958. REPRINTED FROM *Psychoanalytic Study of the Child* 14:219-235.

Chapter 13

Observations On Research Regarding The "Symbiotic Syndrome" of Infantile Psychosis (1960). In collaboration with Manuel Furer, M.D. This paper is based on research conducted at the Masters Children's Center, New York, sponsored by grant M-3353 of the National Institute of Mental Health, USPHS, Bethesda, Md.; Drs. Mahler and Furer, co-principal investigators.

This paper was presented at the Pan American Medical Congress, Section on Child Psychiatry, May 1960, Mexico City. REPRINTED FROM *Psychoanalytic Quarterly* 29:317-327.

Chapter 14

Longitudinal Study of the Treatment of a Psychotic Child with the Tripartite Design (1976). Illustrated with Film. REPRINTED FROM *Journal of the Philadelphia Association for Psychoanalysis* 3:21-42.

Chapter 15

On Sadness and Grief in Infancy and Childhood: Loss and Restoration of the Symbiotic Love Object (1961). This paper is based mainly upon research supported by the National Institutes of Mental Health, USPHS, Grant M-3353; Drs. Mahler and Furer, co-principal investigators.

This paper was presented at the Tenth Anniversary Symposium, the Child Psychiatry Unit, Massachusetts Mental Health Center, Harvard Medical School. REPRINTED FROM *Psychoanalytic Study of the Child* 16:332-351.

NAME INDEX

SUBJECT INDEX

abstraction, defect in faculty of, 203

adaptive role of ego, 131, 159

affect, language of, 4

"affect hunger" (Levy), 156, 270

affective memory, 193–195

affective motor function, 76, 82

affective outbursts in infancy, 4–5

affectomotor storm-rage reactions, 157

aggression
  in autistic psychosis, 138, 145
  body ego development and, 133
  deflected from body, 113, 206
  disguised by pseudoimbecility, 7
  in *enfant terrible* behavior, 18–21
  narcissism and, 264
  neutralization of, disturbance

in, 117
  oral, 113
  repression and, 42
  primitive, vicissitudes of, 113
  in symbiotic psychosis, 125, 126, 139, 147, 176, 239
  in tiqueurs, 49, 52–54, 56–58, 62, 83

aggressive fantasies, 176

aggressivization of body ego, 218

anaclitic depression, 261–262, 265, 271

anal fixation
  in pseudoimbecility, 11
  in tic syndrome, 53–56, 59

analysts, children of, 18–19

anatomical difference between the sexes
  anxiety caused by questions about, 45